Contents

Illustration credits	viii
List of contributors	ix
Foreword: confronting epistemes	xvi
Acknowledgements	xxvii

Introduction: cross-cultural practice – why experiment now? 1
Catherin Bull and Claire Parin

PART 1
Reconceptualizing the city 14

Introduction: new ways to read difference 15
Claire Parin

1 Finding the identity of place through local landscapes: *Mooban* and *Kampong* 25
Sani Limthongsakul

2 Erasure, layering, transformation, absorption: the convergence of formal traditions 29
Sidh Sintusingha

3 Between 'asianization' and 'new cosmopolitanism': housing in twenty-first-century Singapore 34
Xavier Guillot

4 Dissolved identity and disintegrated globalization 39
Steven Whitford

5 The communal project and the reinforcement of values 46
Emmanuel Amougou Mballa

6 Urban development and context: the traditional
   landscape and globalization in Marrakech   49
   Jean-Noël Tournier

7 The urban edge: Bangkok *soi* as mediators of the
   global and local   57
   Koen De Wandeler

8 Eco-planning for development in northern Thailand   65
   Thada Sutthitham

9 Local identity in Bangkok's business districts   71
   Ornsiri Panin

PART 2
Experiments in practice   76

   Introduction: the dynamics of the urban design project 77
   Guy Tapie and Darko Radović

10 Transparency in sustainable development:
   Nhong Han Basin, Thailand   89
   Eggarin Anukulyudhathon

11 Restructuring the medina in Tunis: El Hafsia   94
   Wassim Ben Mahmoud

12 Garden urbanism in China and New Zealand   99
   Matthew Bradbury

13 Revitalizing the Montenegrin village: Gornja Lastva   103
   *Laurence Feveile, Marija Nikolic and
   Nicolas Petrovitch Njegosh*

14 Strategies to support urban identity: are there
   European models?   108
   Carlos Gotlieb

15 Mediating global and local: the Montreal experience   112
   Daniel Latouche

16 New practices in urban development   115
   Jean-Claude Margueritte

17	Sustainable tourism for local identity: the hill-tribe villages of northern Thailand *Wandee Pinijvarasin and Pasinee Sunakorn*	119
18	Making the city: the Bordeaux experience *Michel Bergeron and Patrice Godier*	124

PART 3
Learning cross-cultural practice — 128

	Introduction: reflecting on cross-cultural interactions *Catherin Bull and Davisi Boontharm*	129
19	Casts, roles and scripts of otherness *Darko Radović*	135
20	Analysis, concept and the value of words *Davisi Boontharm*	150
21	Work and/or play? *Piyalada D. Thaveeprungsriporn*	163
22	Why use English? *Singh Intrachooto*	168
23	Sustainability learnt from difference *Glenn Thomas*	174
24	Experiencing cross-cultural practice *Catherin Bull*	187
25	Workshops as culture *Guy Tapie*	204
	Conclusion: urban design for a cross-cultural future *Catherin Bull, Darko Radović and Claire Parin*	208
	Index	234

Illustration credits

Carlos Gotlieb © 14.1, 14.2, 14.3, 14.4, 14.5
Cuttaleeya Noparatnaraporn © 9.4, 9.5, 9.6, 9.7, 9.8
Davisi Boontharm © 19.3, 20.1, 20.2, 20.3
Darko Radović © 19.1, 19.2
Eggarin Anukulyudhathon © 10.1, 10.2, 10.3
Fiona Currie © 8.1, 9.1, 24.1, 24.2, 24.3, 24.4, 24.5, 24.6
Glenn Thomas © 23.1, 23.2, 23.3, 23.4
Grichka Martinetti © 13.2
Jean-Noël Tournier © 6.1, 6.2, 6.3
Julien Mingui © 13.3
Koen De Wandeler © 7.1, 7.2
Laurence Feveile © 13.1
M. L. Vudipong Davivong © 1.1, 1.3
Matthew Bradbury © 12.1, 12.2, 12.3
Michel Bergeron and Patrice Godier © 18.1, 18.2, 18.3
Ministry of Defense, Thailand © 8.2, 8.3, 8.4, 8.5, 8.6
Omsiri Panin © 9.2, 9.3
Place Ville Marie © 15.1, 15.2
Sidh Sintusingha © 2.1, 2.1, 2.3, 7.3, 7.4, 7.5, 7.6
Steven Whitford © 4.1, 4.2
Thitiwoot Chaisawataree © 1.2
Wandee Pinijvarasin © 17.1, 17.2, 17.3, 17.4
Wassim Ben Mahmoud © 11.4, 11.5, 11.6
Xavier Guillot © 3.1, 3.2, 3.3, 3.4

Contributors

Eggarin Anukulyudhathon is currently Dean of the Faculty of Architecture at Kasetsart University, Bangkok. For over 20 years he has been engaged in research and professional practice in the fields of environmental and urban planning. From 1999 to 2005, he was a member of the national committee for the Environmental Impact Assessment Control. He is the president of the Thai Urbanism Society of Thailand Committee of Urban Community and Environmental Control under the Office of Natural Resource and Environmental Planning Policy. A guest lecturer at a number of universities and organizations in Thailand, his research interests encompass Urban and Environmental Impact Assessment, Urban and Community Sustainable Development, Eco-Sustainable Development and Urban and Rural Community Design.

Michel Bergeron is an engineer at the Ecole Spéciale des Travaux Publics, du Bâtiment et de l'Industrie (ESTP), an engineering college at university level for professionals in the construction industry. He is also Deputy Director of Urban Development and Housing for the Urban Community of Bordeaux.

Davisi Boontharm an architect and urbanist, is an Assistant Professor in the Department of Architecture at the National University of Singapore. She has taught and researched in architecture and urban design in France and Thailand. In 2005 she published *Bangkok: forme du commerce et evolution urbaine*, developing her research interest in commercial space as an urban resource for a sustainable future. In 2006 she published *City Home* (shophouse design and renewal.

Matthew Bradbury, a practising landscape architect and architect, was a Fulbright Fellow 2003–2004, and is now Senior Lecturer in the Landscape Architecture programme at the School of Architecture and Landscape Architecture, UNITEC, New Zealand. In that role he has researched a new garden city model through the development of a design methodology that combines landscape analysis and garden technique (http://gardencities.net/). He has also written extensively about the history of post-war modernist landscape architecture, including *A History of the Garden in New Zealand* (Viking).

Catherin Bull holds the Elisabeth Murdoch Chair of Landscape Architecture at the University of Melbourne. Her doctorate is from The Graduate School of Design at Harvard where she researched infrastructure provision and sustainable tourism. Her award-winning book *New Conversations with an Old Landscape. Landscape Architecture in Contemporary Australia* introduced the profession in Australia to an international audience. Her research interests include the challenges of planning and design for open space in the twenty-first-century city. An advocate for better quality planning and design in contemporary cities, she chairs and serves on many design and review panels, advising government and industry on open space and urban design matters.

Laurence Feveile, architect, town planner and landscape designer, teaches at the School of Architecture, Paris-Val de Seine and at the University of Paris X-Nanterre. Her doctoral dissertation in town planning and development resulted in the publication *Panauti, a City in Nepal* in collaboration with Vincent Barré, Patrick Berger, architects, and Gerard Toffin, anthropologist at the CNRS.

Patrice Godier is a sociologist and teacher–researcher at the Higher National School of Architecture and Landscape of Bordeaux, and a member of the research team PAVE (which stands for Profession, Architecture, Ville [city] and Environment).

Carlos Gotlieb has been a professor at the Higher National School of Architecture and Landscape of Bordeaux since 2000, at the same time practising as an architect–urban planner consulting with local communities. His main projects in France to date are a local development plan of the city of Dax; the master plan of the urban restructuring for Ivry-sur Seine; and the master plan and project design of urban spaces for the city of Cergy. He has published articles in the French revues *Diagonal, Urbanisme*, and *L'architecture d'aujourd'hui*.

Xavier Guillot received his PhD from the French Institute for Urbanism (University of Paris VIII). He is currently teaching at the National School of Architecture of Saint Etienne and is a research associate at the CNRS laboratory Théories des Mutations Urbaines (University of Paris VIII). His main research interests are in urbanization, the study of globalization processes, and cultural changes in relation to local identities and heritage. He has published articles on these issues in the context of Japan, South East Asia and the Middle East.

Singh Intrachooto is an architect, Assistant Professor of Building Technology and Head of the Department of Building Innovation and Technology at the Faculty of Architecture at Kasetsart University, Bangkok and has a PhD in Design Technology from MIT. He also teaches at the School of Architecture and Urban Planning, University of Washington, and lectures in Japan, Hong Kong and the United States while maintaining his design practice in Thailand. Interests include material developments from manufacturing and agricultural by-products as well as waste management in building construction, operation and maintenance. Of particular interest is his focus on bridging academia and industry to stimulate innovation within the design and architecture industry.

Ross King is a Professorial Fellow in the Faculty of Architecture, Building and Planning at the University of Melbourne. His present interest is in the roles of urban planning, urban design and architecture in achieving sustainable cities in East and South-east Asia. Current research is on Kuala Lumpur (a monograph on that city and the role of the new administrative capital of Putrajaya), and Bangkok ('the Bangkok of everyday life'). A longer-term project is a text on sustaining Asian cities.

Daniel Latouche is a political economist. Since 1988, he has been a Professor at the INRS-UCS, Montreal where his particular interests lie in economy and urban governorship. His recent work concerns the role of information technologies, the place of artists in the creative city and urban development in African cities. His chapter developed from work on a project on urban development in the 'universe of globalization', financed by the Canadian Council of Research in Social Sciences.

Sani Limthongsakul is Assistant Professor of Landscape Architecture and serves as Head of Landscape Architecture Division, Faculty of Architecture at Kasetsart University, Bangkok. Her areas of interest are in ecological planning, rural and vernacular landscape studies and site planning.

Wassim Ben Mahmoud is an architect and urban planner who has studied both in Paris and at MIT in the United States. Initially he worked with the Association de Sauvegarde de Médina of Tunis (ASM), within the municipality of Tunis, becoming familiar with preservation issues in the area, especially strategies to highlight the ancient city and its urban and architectural and cultural heritage. Within his architectural agency he has realized many projects (public buildings, housing, tourism projects, etc.) in Tunisia and several Arabic countries. He has always endeavoured to produce a contemporary architecture which respects the past, and which draws its inspiration from that of lasting value in cultural heritage. Wassim Ben Mahmoud is a winner of the Aga Khan award for Islamic architecture.

Jean-Claude Margueritte is a town planner, and currently Director of the Technical Services and Town Planning of Lormont in France. He also teaches at the Institute of Development, Town Planning and Tourism at the University of Bordeaux III. His interests lie particularly in the issues related to the regeneration of territories affected by the town planning of the 1960s in France. He is also engaged in a process of reflection and 'research – action' relating to the tram within the framework of the Grand Projet de Ville Intercommunal de Hauts de Garonne [large-scale intercommunal city project within the département of Garonne].

Emmanuel Amougou Mballa is a sociologist and lecturer–researcher at the Higher National School of Architecture and Landscape of Bordeaux. He is a member of the Research Team of the CNRS [science research council], based in Bordeaux. He completed his doctoral dissertation on the architectural renovation of the old historical centres in France in 1992, at the University of Social Sciences in Strasbourg. Since then, his research activities focus mainly on forms of social domination, one expression of which is the question of cultural heritage in modern societies. He has published articles on the dilemmas of cultural heritage.

Nicolas Petrovitch Njegosh is an architect and president of the Biennial of Cetinie, International Meetings of Contemporary Art. He is a descendant of King Nicolas, exiled from Montenegro in 1918.

Marija Nikolić works as an architect and town planner in the administrative services of the town of Tivat, near the village of Gornja Lastva. She is an active member of the village's cultural organization NAPREDAK.

Ornsiri Panin is Professor Emeritus at the Faculty of Architecture, Kasetsart University, Bangkok and was awarded an honorary doctorate of Architecture and doctorate of Philosophy in Vernacular Architecture from Kasetsart University. A research scholarship from the Thailand Research Fund funded the research reported here, and she has been nominated as an outstanding researcher of Thailand by the Thailand Research Council. Her research interests include the conservation of built vernacular heritage, cultural ecology and conceptual design based on vernacular values.

Claire Parin is an architect and urbanist whose research, teaching and practice concentrates on the way the form of the historic and emerging city responds to change and contributes to sustainable urban form. She is Assistant Professor at the Higher National School of Architecture and Landscape of Bordeaux, and visiting professor at Kasetsart University in Bangkok, Thailand.

She was educated in France and the United States and is a recipient of the Legion d'Honour for her contribution to urban planning and design in France.

Wandee Pinijvarasin is currently head of the Architecture Division of the Faculty of Architecture, Kasetsart University, Bangkok. In 2004, she completed her PhD in the Faculty of Architecture, Building and Planning, of the University of Melbourne, where her thesis was considered the most outstanding for the previous year. Her research interests are the physical and socio-cultural evolution of Thai vernacular dwellings; aesthetics and cultural sustainability in architecture; ecological design; representing and constructing conceptual design and notions of architectural conservation in youth.

Darko Radović received his doctorate in Architecture and Urbanism from the University of Belgrade, Yugoslavia. He has taught, researched and practised architecture and urbanism in Europe, Australia and Asia. Currently he is with the Faculty of Architecture, Building and Planning at the University of Melbourne and the University of Tokyo's Centre for Sustainable Urban Regeneration. His research focuses on situations where architecture and urban design overlap; where traditional 'architectural' and 'urban' scales blur; where the social starts to acquire physical form. His investigation of the concepts of urbanity and sustainable development focuses on culturally and environmentally diverse contexts that exemplify and expose difference and offer encounters with 'the other'.

Sidh Sintusingha practised as an architect in Thailand and landscape architect in Australia for several years before commencing his PhD at the University of Melbourne. He completed his PhD thesis 'Steps towards a sustainable Bangkok: reorganizing and retrofitting to mitigate sprawl' in 2004 and joined the university as a lecturer in landscape architecture in 2005. His research interests, where he also seeks convergences, are in the areas of urban landscape planning and design, urban sustainability and urban sprawl particularly in cities in developing countries.

Pasinee Sunakorn is the previous Dean of the Faculty of Architecture, Kasetsart University (2001–2005). She completed her Master of Architectural design at the Pratt Institute, USA. Her work encompasses sustainable architecture, and environmentally responsive design and building materials.

Thada Sutthitham is an Associate Professor from Khon Kaen University, in the north-east of Thailand. This is the largest region of the country, occupying one-third of Thailand and has the greatest number of cultural settlements; hence it is where her research and conservation and development plans have been conducted. She is also recognized in the field of Thai architectural conservation, one of her works receiving the UNESCO Award of Merit for Asia-Pacific Heritage Conservation in 2002.

Guy Tapie is a sociologist whose research and teaching focuses on the relationship between social phenomena and urban change, particularly in relation to the urban project. He is Assistant Professor at the Higher National School of Architecture and Landscape at Bordeaux and was educated in France. He is a visiting professor at Kasetsart University, Bangkok.

Piyalada D Thaveeprungsriporn is an Assistant Professor of Architecture at the Faculty of Architecture, Chulalongkorn University, Thailand. Her previous publications, such as 'Ruan Thai: an aesthetic of femininity', largely focus on a reinterpretation of the traditional Thai house of central Thailand. Her current teaching and research areas include architectural design, architectural aesthetics, contemporary architectural theory and the cultural dimensions of architecture.

Glenn Thomas recently retired as Associate Professor of Landscape Architecture in the School of Design at Queensland University of Technology, where he taught for more than 21 years. He holds dual qualifications in architecture and landscape architecture. His teaching was characterized by effective engagement between his students and diverse communities throughout Queensland and Northern New South Wales in Real World Learning, and the integration of field studies into the landscape architecture curriculum. He is a Fellow of the Australian Institute of Landscape Architects and received a University Award for Outstanding Academic Achievement in the Area of Teaching.

Jean-Noel Tournier originally trained in France as an agricultural engineer, and now practises there as a landscape architect–town planner. He also lectures at the Higher National School of Architecture and Landscape at Bordeaux, and researches urban and environmental change in Morocco.

Koen De Wandeler obtained a Masters in Architecture from the St. Lucas Department of Architecture in Ghent (Belgium) and a PhD in Anthropology from the School of Oriental and African Studies (London). As a researcher with the Asian Institute of Technology he became acquainted with urban issues in Asia. He later fine-tuned this knowledge through free-lance training and consultancies in Belgium, Cambodia, India, Kenya, Laos, Morocco and Vietnam. He currently is a lecturer in the Architecture programme at his Alma Mater in Belgium and co-initiator of an Urban Management Programme at the School of Architecture and Design (KMUTT) in Thailand.

Steve Whitford graduated from RMIT in 1979 and worked with Cocks and Carmichael Architects, becoming a director in 1982; the firm changed its name in 1988 to Cocks Carmichael Whitford. During this time the practice received awards for architectural and urban design excellence from both the State Chapter and the National Council of the RAIA. In 1996 he joined the Faculty of Architecture, Building and Planning at the University of Melbourne after completing a Masters of Urban Design, and is currently a PhD candidate there. He has been a visiting professor at the School of Architecture and Landscape Architecture in Bordeaux, France, at the Shenyang Architecture and Civil Engineering University, and at Tsinghua University, Beijing, China.

Foreword
Confronting epistemes[1]

Although cross-national commerce, professional practice and education have been permanent features of human history, they have taken decidedly different forms in the present, so-called postcolonial age. In the sphere of education, for example, as a strategy of empire, colonialism brought the idea of obligation to educate the subject peoples. Decolonization freed the colonizers of that burden, and today educational 'assistance' takes a new, paternalistic form either implicitly or explicitly, as 'foreign aid'. Commerce and professional practice similarly mutate.

The investors and the consultants can continue their exploitations as if colonization never ended. Indeed for them it never did, though they must pretend otherwise, but the educators profess 'ethics', and are more circumspect in their exploitations. The noble goals of foreign assistance, however, mask darker agendas of academe – variously as by-products of the intellectual enterprise of studying 'strange and exotic peoples' (so we study the indigenes as we educate them), or strategically as part of a new form of colonization (we help in order to draw their students into our own spheres), or to foster a new sense of dependence (so that they will subsequently employ us to solve their 'problems' which, in the main, we have helped create). We work intentionally to secure our own advancement, whether economically or in terms of intellectual capital.

Two variants of this essentially exploitative enterprise pose questions here: what is the effect when the neo-colonizing desire is from more than one metropolitan culture (say, on contemporary Vietnam and its hybrid infiltrations – France, Russia, then most recently the anglophone world)? And what of the neo-colonizing infiltrations when they are outside the ostensible colonial sphere (infiltrating Thailand rather than India or Malaysia or Indonesia)?

This Foreword is mainly a reflection on Thailand having to negotiate an identity when under both the francophone and the anglophone thrall. However, it could equally be, with modifications, about Indonesia under the Dutch recall and the Australian intrusion, or about present multi-assailed Vietnam, or Morocco simultaneously receiving French and Spanish 'assistance' and pan-Arab infiltrations. Similarly, though the main focus here is on the educational sphere, the argument is equally applicable to international consultancy, or business 'co-operation' or humanitarian aid. Informing the following explorations is the suspicion that different world experiences will underlie different ways of viewing reality. The idea of enquiry that is manifested in all education and scholarship – and inevitably informs the worldviews of planners, architects, economists and investors – stands upon an epistemology: that is, on an understanding of what constitutes a question, what constitutes an answer and what constitutes a method for getting from one to the other. There may be fundamentally different epistemologies weaving through a Thai logic, a French logic, and an English or Australian logic.

The question of logics

While Mikhail Bakhtin was not French but Russian, he stands as a seminal figure in the emergence of that tradition of critical thinking that is commonly labelled 'French post-structuralism'. For Bakhtin (1981), dialogicality informs every utterance and every text, including the 'text' of urban space. Thus arises 'dialogue', the interaction of the 'double logics' of speaker and listener (Clark and Holquist 1984; King 1996).

Much of the material in the contributions to this volume derives from a three-year collaboration between three schools of design, respectively in Bangkok, Melbourne and Bordeaux.[2] The distinguishing characteristic of the enterprise is that three logics intersect, and the idea of 'trialogue' might be coined for it. To the positivist–materialist, instrumentalist logic of British (and by descent Australian) traditions, and the speculative logic of the French – both in part formed and transformed in the colonizing experience – there is then added an episteme from an entirely different worldview, in part Buddhist and syncretist, problematizing (Western) principles of non-contradiction, and constantly questioning a materialist reality. That, however, is only part of the story, as the gaze of the following authors is from a far more diverse range of worldviews than merely those three, and so the trialogues will variously confront Arab, Chinese, Malay and other worldviews and their constituent logics.

This assertion of epistemological differences is, of course, speculation (and worse, it runs the risk of essentializing!). It is, however, a field for empirical investigation. Hence the current volume. What follows is essentially a series of accounts of cross-cultural confrontations on the question of what constitutes a 'better' urban space. Different worldviews would inevitably ensure that 'better' will be contested – my sense of 'better' may not be yours! Differences in worldview will also underlie colliding ideas about the morality of means for getting to that elusive 'better' urban space. The fundamental assertion of this book is that these clashes of ideas, ideals, epistemes and logics, if brought into discourse and thereby reflected upon, can bring about the questioning of one's own values, assumptions and logic.

Marina Warner (2002) has written of the underlying energies and processes whereby one representation or idea generates another. The argument is that, on the evidence of history, the transformations that mark great creativity and the leaps to new modes of thought and life are most likely to occur in the collisions between cultures, in transitional places and at the confluence of traditions and civilizations. Thus we get metamorphosis or life as change. So the highest aim in bringing together the multiple, disparate confrontations and frictions of the following chapters is to display just these sorts of collisions of cultures and the consequent possibilities of metamorphosis – towards a better urban space.

If there are these differences in logic that distinguish 'cultures' – differences in epistemes or 'systems of thought' as Foucault would term them – we surely have to seek them, at least in part, in their genealogy.[3] And it is to that we turn.

The question of epistemes and their genealogy

In a typically provocative stab at the origins of that vast intellectual enterprise that constituted European Orientalism, post-colonial theorist Edward Said contrasted the eighteenth-century French and English gazes towards 'the Orient':

> Consider … the differences between an English speaker and a French speaker. For the former the Orient was India of course, an actual British possession; to pass through the Near Orient was therefore to pass en route to a major colony. Already, then, the room available for imaginative play was limited by the realities of administration, territorial legality, and executive power.… In contrast the French pilgrim was imbued with a sense of acute loss in the Orient. He came there to a place where France, unlike Britain, had no sovereign presence. The Mediterranean echoed to the sounds of French defeats, from the Crusades to Napoleon.
>
> (Said 1979: 169)

So, argues Said, the Orient was defined for the British by a material imagination that, in turn, underlay the rise of British philosophical empiricism. For the French there could only be an imagination rooted in memories, speculations – 'suggestive ruins, forgotten secrets, hidden correspondences, and an almost virtuosic style of being' (Said 1979: 170). The links here were to an altogether more speculative, introspective (French) literature. While British triumphalist empiricism may have now run its constricting course, the flights of Renan, Baudelaire and Flaubert can be seen to have foreshadowed – even given birth to – the brilliance of twentieth-century French thought from Bachelard to existentialism to post-structuralism.

Australians might like to think of themselves as open to French speculative thought – Foucault, Bourdieu, Derrida – but their intellectual traditions have for a century and a half been set by British professors of philosophy, history and literature. The gaze from Melbourne to Bangkok is cast in an instrumentalist, empiricist materialism. From Bordeaux it is more likely to be through the prism of post-structuralism and deconstructionist thought.

The attention to the East fails to be reciprocated; the East did not similarly engage the West, and present language fails to address the view obtained of France or Australia through the lens of Bangkok.

The question of a Thai episteme

Whatever else the above suggests, it would definitively assert that there is no privileged viewpoint from which the West is to observe the genealogy of a Siamese 'system of thought'.[4] What follows may be a somewhat eclectic, even hybridized account, but it is still overwhelmingly from that instrumentalist–materialist Anglo perspective. A French post-structuralist account would be different.

In a recent set of papers, Peter Jackson (2004a, 2004b) has traced the evolution of Siamese forms of power from what he terms a pre-modern 'theatre state' – a culture of 'face' and 'reputation', preoccupied with appearances and surface ritual – to the nineteenth-century evolution of the 'performative state'.

> Non-colonized Siam did not need to wage a war of independence to expel foreign colonizers. Nevertheless, to preserve national autonomy a new form of local power was called into being, and the regime of images emerges from this strategic mobilization of local power in the service of preserving Siamese independence.
>
> (Jackson 2004b: 219)

The need to create this 'regime of images' of a 'civilized' Siam – to delegitimize any external colonizing intent, typically from the British and the French – nevertheless stood in some disjuncture with the private sphere: 'A defining feature of the Thai regime of images is a rigid demarcation between what is publicly unspeakable, especially in the presence of a non-Thai audience, and what is "common knowledge" in private, local discourses' (Jackson 2004b: 220).

Jackson traces this disjuncture back to a pre-modern northern Thai episteme characterized by intolerance to ambiguity in surface ritual, but a structural ambiguity of local myths (Jackson 2004a:

188). The myths obliterate and fuse logical categories that are carefully built up in the rites: rites are cognitively disjunctive, myths are conjunctive.[5] He further cites a diverse literature that recognizes the extension of this determinative power of the 'surface' over the 'essence' into a present Siamese system of thought, identifying what is effectively a reversal of the order of Western epistemologies. For example there is Rosalind Morris's description of this 'many-sided phenomenon' as the Thai 'order of appearances', 'the love of the disciplined surface' and 'an overinvestment in appearances' (Morris 2000).

While Morris's work has a regional focus, there are two further points of wider significance to be drawn from it. One is her observation on the function of appearances (signs, masks) in the (Protestant/capitalist) West, vis-à-vis Thailand: whereas the former has demanded 'a relationship of transparency between inner truth and outward appearances, between value and its sign, … the cultural logics that were historically dominant in Thailand permitted appearances and truths to be radically disjunct', (Morris 2002: 53). Nothing could be further from the unmasking, 'deconstructive' preoccupations of the French critical tradition than this, nor more distant (though differently so) from positivist–empiricist Anglo traditions. The second point is that although this radically different epistemology may have had its origin in the folk realm, its present manifestation is neither pre-modern, nor contradictory and unstable, nor simply transitional to some Western idea of modernity, but modern – albeit alternatively modern.

Nor, however, is this or any other mode of thought unchanging: there is now a rapidly expanding, non-official Thai bourgeoisie (Anderson 1998: 182–184), and increasing questioning of the surface of King, Nation and Religion;[6] and since the 1997 financial crisis, even aspects of private (family) venality have begun to be publicly questioned. Although the surface starts to fracture, the private sphere of the social production of space remains private – beneath the surface – and there is effectively no architectural or urban design discourse.

The question of the global and the local

A characteristic of the present time is that worldviews must come to terms with the increasing exaggeration of both the global and the local. Frederic Jameson (1991) has written of 'the post-modern hyperspace', that stretching of space and time to accommodate the multinational space of late capitalism. It is a space of vastly accelerated flows – of capital, information, people, ideas and desires. The hyperspace comprises international networks of capital, communications (the Internet, the cellular phone, CNN, BBC World) and travel, undifferentiated airports, hotels, office parks, shopping malls and their franchised outlets for globalist products, billboards and logos.

The hyperspace enables cities to compete for what Saskia Sassen (1999) calls the 'new users' of the city: the footloose, international tourists, business travellers, entrepreneurs, innovators and investors who can take their consumption, interests, creativity or investments wherever they choose. The transnational practitioners and transnational academics represented in this volume – and hopefully in its readership – are among these new users. However, the mobility of the new users requires each city to differentiate itself from the rest. For Bangkok to compete with Hong Kong, Singapore, Shanghai, etc, it must distinguish itself from those rival cities by emphasizing its difference from them. So there is a turn to heritage, or tradition – the power of the local. This is then exaggerated, and thereby transformed. Thus we get hyper-traditions, the exaggeration of old practices and images and, when deemed necessary, even the invention of new 'traditions' (historically the British Raj style in India and Malaya, or present-day 'Bali style'). Hyper-traditions are a condition of possibility of the post-modern hyperspace.

In more quarantined, local design practice, hyper-tradition has tended to fall into caricature – in upturned 'Chinese' roofs on the bland glass boxes of Beijing, in Singapore's Disneyfied Chinatown, in stepped 'traditional' gabled roofs on shops or university campus blocks in Thailand, in Balinese split gates on all manner of buildings in Bali or, more anomalously, in Jakarta, etc. In transnational design practice as in transnational design education, in contrast, there is the perceived compulsion to 'find' the local, and to 'reinterpret' it. There are searches for 'the real', or perhaps 'authenticity'. Early examples of the playing out of this delusion might include Lutyens in New Delhi, Le Corbusier in Chandigarh or Kahn in Dacca. More recently, Denton Corker Marshall challenged Chinese classical traditions in Beijing; Skidmore Owings & Merrill have reinterpreted Chinese preoccupations with classical forms, traditions of numerology, the 1930s art deco of Shanghai and the rush to new technology; Malay forms have been transformed by Cesar Pelli, Kisho Kurokawa and others; and the list could go on. Certainly these are intrusions, and to be seen by many as arrogance and, worse, as intellectual neo-colonization. Yet they also enter the discourse on the dialectic of 'Identity and Difference' (Jameson 2005): these interpretations of the local will, at best, be hotly debated across the incommensurable epistemes and their languages. So if Malays object to the interpretations of their identity by a Pelli or a Kurakawa (or for that matter by Chinese-Malaysian Ken Yeang), then the obligation falls on them to provide their own, 'more truthful' representation of their traditions, beliefs and worldview. Thus the discourse is prised open.

The strength of the contributions to this volume is that it is not just the single alien intrusion that is encountered by the Thais or Moroccans or Montenegrins, but multiple bringers of assistance (neo-colonizers). Also, in the main, what is being prised open is not mere architectural representation or interpretations of landscape, but the design of the spaces of everyday life – what we popularly term 'urban design'.

Thailand presents a special problem in this context. There is no formal practice of urban design, while architectural and landscape design are, in the main, reserved for Thai designers, and effectively quarantined from that global discourse that can compel the reconsideration of the local. Nor is there any vigorous local discourse on the place of architecture and landscape in the definition and likely future trajectory of identity and the national urban space. The episteme of surfaces described above extends into behaviour, ethics and public morality. As Phillips (1965) argues, such a characteristic is embedded in people's attitudes towards achieving 'social success in life' and in cultural values of 'social cosmetics', such as appearing 'caring and considerate' (the Thai concept of *kreng chai*), 'politeness', 'kindness and helpfulness' (Komin 1985: 179–180). More problematically, however, the culture also mandates 'politeness' in complimenting the actions of others – regardless of how crass, exploitative, oppressive or environmentally destructive they might be. Further, to criticize a fellow architect, landscape architect or investor is, by implication, to criticize the noble institution of 'the family', for we must always assume that the atrocities are committed with the higher good of the perpetrator's family in focus. The discursive vigour that one encounters in China, Malaysia, Indonesia and many other societies is here dampened by 'politeness'.

If the epistemic barriers can somehow be breached, we might reasonably expect a discourse on an architecture and landscape that can negotiate the links between a water-world and a terrestrial realm, return reflectively to the epistemic concern with being 'caring and considerate' and with politeness and kindness, and above all reflect upon that realm of surfaces and, in design, reveal them as surfaces – but now self-consciously and constructively (Noparatnaraporn and King 2007). The Thais deserve something decidedly better than what they currently get from their designers, investors and politicians.

The question of agendas

Two, three or even more groups, each internally diverse, each arguably enmeshed in distinctive systems of thought (epistemes), typically intersect with each other over what each assumes to be a common interest: namely, what might constitute a better space of everyday life. So arises *trialogue* (to again bend the Bakhtinian understanding). In the wider context of this volume, it is even *multilogue*. To repeat, the discourse is prised open. There is more to it than that, however, and indeed we need to return to the insights of Mikhail Bakhtin. The term 'utterance' is invoked by Bakhtin, as 'the real unit of speech communication'; it is always 'situated' – it has a context away from which it cannot be understood. So context and contingency are inescapable. Utterance is also inexorably linked to 'voice', 'the speaking personality, the speaking consciousness' (Holquist and Emerson 1981: 434).

The voice modulates all communication, both written and spoken; it reflects the person's perspective, conceptual horizon, intention and worldview – their 'agenda' (Clark and Holquist 1984). This contingency cross-cuts any confrontation of epistemes either in dialogue or, with the possibility of far greater complexity (fragmentation of both modes of thought and intentions), in trialogue/multilogue.

The complexity of communication magnifies further, in what Walter Benjamin identified as 'the task of the translator'. What cannot be said (represented) cannot be communicated; an episteme can only be reflected upon in a language, and no language bears a one-for-one correspondence with any other. What is intended in translation, Benjamin insisted, is not the simple transmission of information: 'any translation which intends to perform a transmitting function cannot transmit anything but information – hence, something inessential. This is the hallmark of bad translations' (Benjamin 1992: 70).

A translation, rather, is to strike that effect upon the new language 'which produces in it the echo of the original,' enriching the new. The translator stands outside 'the language forest ... aiming at that single spot where the echo is able to give, in its own language, the reverberation of the work in the alien one', (Benjamin 1992: 77). So what is to reverberate? The original mode of representation is the answer – that is, the mode of intention rather than some intended object – the voice on which the motivating agenda is still detectable. But Benjamin's most extraordinary suggestion on the effect of translation is one of fundamental transformation – even metamorphosis in that sense intended by Marina Warner above:

> For just as the tenor and the significance of the great works of literature undergo a complete transformation over the centuries, the mother tongue of the translator is transformed as well.... Translation is so far removed from being the sterile equation of two dead languages that of all literary forms it is the one charged with the special mission of watching over the maturing process of the original language and the birth pangs of its own.
>
> (Benjamin 1992: 74)

If the effect of translation is to see the birth of new language, and if modes of thought are interdependent with the languages in which thought is expressed, then the consequence of new language must similarly be the metamorphosis of worldviews and epistemes themselves. We can go further than this however, for what are being translated across these incompatible languages are ideas of the most fundamental significance, to do with the spaces of everyday life itself – with better such spaces. A claim from Jacques Derrida echoes that above from Walter Benjamin:

> Every sign, linguistic or non-linguistic, spoken or written (in the current sense of this opposition), in a small or large unit, can be cited, put between quotation marks; in so doing it can break with every given context, engendering an infinity of new contexts in a manner which is absolutely illimitable.
>
> (Derrida 1977: 185)

It is here that we find the great potential of the collisions of diverse histories, ways of knowing (epistemes), languages and linguistic traditions, agendas and different ideas of urban space and time. Our objectives are no less than to reinvent our own spaces of everyday life rather than to 'change' alien colleagues to our own too-often unchallenged positions – to understand the genealogy and the cultural contingency of our worlds, but also those 'absolutely illimitable' possibilities of metamorphosis that can burst forth from the reflexive collisions of epistemes and languages.

If metamorphosis is indeed to be sought in those fissures and interstices between cultures, epistemes and languages, as Marina Warner asserts, then one must turn – with some anticipation – to the sorts of collisions to which the following contributions will allude. A final warning, however: do not expect the explosions of creativity, new worlds and a better space of everyday life to be laid out neatly, clearly and there for the taking from these pages. Rather, the ideas, ideals and logic of the reader are also to enter into the equation, to be set against the conflicts and abrasions paraded in the arguments that follow and, in turn, against the reflections, contrasting viewpoints and further explorations contained in the introductions and conclusions from the book's authors.

Ross King

Notes

1 The following in part derives from reflections and concerns expressed in a diversity of meetings by Pierre Culand, Pasinee Sunakorn and Ross King in planning a tri-part, tri-cultural programme of research and learning involving three schools of the built environment in Bangkok, Melbourne and Bordeaux (BMB). While the language of the reporting has determined that the reporter will be Ross King, all three are the proper authors of its ideas.
2 The Bangkok–Melbourne–Bordeaux (BMB) programme and the chapters directly and indirectly linked to it are described in the various introductory essays following.
3 As Foucault would insist! See for example Foucault (1977); and for com-

mentary, Gutting (2005: 43–53). It seems reasonable to assert that something of a Foucauldian genealogical intent runs through the present essay and indeed through the project it aims to preface, and traces of it are similarly to be sought in the chapters of the present volume.
4 For reasons that will become obvious from the following, there is an absence of a Thai tradition of such critical introspection. An outstanding exception is Winichakul (1994).
5 Here Jackson is citing the structuralist analyses of Richard Davis (1974).
6 While reverence for the present King remains undiminished, the institutions are increasingly scrutinized. For a review, see for example Reynolds (2006).

Bibliography

Anderson, B. (1998) *The Spectre of Comparisons: Nationalism, Southeast Asia and the World*, London: Verso.
Bakhtin, M.M. (1981) *The Dialogic Imagination: Four Essays by M.M. Bakhtin*; ed. M. Holquist, trans. C. Emerson and M. Holquist, Austin, TX: University of Texas Press.
Benjamin, W. (1923) 'The task of the translator: an introduction to the translation of Baudelaire's Tableaux Parisiens', in H. Arendt (ed.) (1992) *Illuminations*, trans. H. Zohn, London: Fontana.
Clark, K. and Holquist, M. (1984) *Mikhail Bakhtin*, Cambridge, MA: Harvard University Press.
Davis, R. (1974) 'Tolerance and intolerance of ambiguity in Northern Thai myth and ritual', *Ethnology* 13(1): 1–24.
Derrida, J. (1977) 'Signature event context', *Glyph*, Vol. 1.
Foucault, M. (1977) *Discipline and Punish: the Birth of the Prison*, trans. A. Sheridan, London: Allen Lane.
Gutting, G. (2005) *Foucault: A Very Short Introduction*, Oxford: Oxford University Press.
Holquist, M. and Emerson, C. (1981) 'Glossary', in M. Holquist (ed.) *The Dialogic Imagination: Four Essays by M.M. Bakhtin*, trans. C. Emerson and M. Holquist, Austin, TX: University of Texas Press.
Jackson, P.A. (2004a) 'The Thai regime of images', *SOJOURN: Journal of Social Issues in Southeast Asia*, 19(2): 181–218.
—— (2004b) 'The performative state: semi-coloniality and the tyranny of images in modern Thailand', *SOJOURN: Journal of Social Issues in Southeast Asia*, 19(2): 219–253.
Jameson, F. (1991) *Postmodernism, or the Cultural Logic of Late Capitalism*, Durham, NC: Duke University Press.
—— (2005) *Archaeologies of the Future: the Desire Called Utopia and Other Science Fictions*, London and New York: Verso.
King, R.J. (1996) *Emancipating Space: Geography, Architecture and Urban Design*, New York and London: Guilford Press.
Komin, S. (1985) 'The world view through Thai value systems', in A. Pongsapich (ed.) *Traditional and Changing Thai World View*, Bangkok and Singapore: Chulalongkorn University Social Research Institute.
Morris, R. (2000) *In the Place of Origins: Modernity and it Mediums in Northern Thailand*, Durham and London: Duke University Press.
—— (2002) 'Failures of domestication: speculations on globality, economy, and the sex of excess in Thailand', *Differences: A Journal of Feminist Cultural Studies*, 13(1): 45–76.

Noparatnaraporn, C. and King, R. (2007) 'Memory or nostalgia: the imagining of everyday Bangkok', *SOJOURN: Journal of Social Issues in Southeast Asia* 22(1): 57–82.

Phillips, H. (1965) *Thai Peasant Personality*, Berkeley: University of California Press.

Reynolds, C.J. (2006) *Seditious Histories: Contesting Thai and Southeast Asian Pasts*, Seattle: University of Washington Press.

Said, E.W. (1979) *Orientalism*, New York: Vintage Books; with new Afterword, (1995) London: Penguin.

Sassen, S. (1999) 'Hong Kong–Shanghai: networking as global cities', in 'Instant China: notes on an urban transformation', *2G Revista Internacional de Arquitectura*, 10–11: 108.

Warner, M (2002) *Fantastic Metamorphoses, Other Worlds: Ways of Telling the Self*, New York: Oxford University Press.

Winichakul, T. (1994) *Siam Mapped: A History of the Geo-body of a Nation*, Honolulu: University of Hawaii Press.

Acknowledgements

There are many people and organizations to acknowledge and thank, not only for their contribution to the preparation of this book but to the experimental process that led to its preparation – an experimental process that traversed many places and involved so many people. All are distinguished by a genuine commitment to the development of knowledge, particularly about urban design. Quite simply, they want our cities and environments to work better and see the sharing of knowledge as one way of achieving that goal.

First the instigating and participating institutions are the Faculty of Architecture, Building and Planning at the University of Melbourne; the Faculty of Architecture at Kasetsart University, Bangkok and L'Ecole d'Architecture et de Paysage de Bordeaux and their Deans, Professor Ross King, Professor Pasinee Sunakorn and Pierre Culand, Director of ENSAP.Bx. They hosted workshops and symposia with the organizational assistance of Michele Michele, Vice-Director for International Affairs and Ineka Amesz. Ms Amesz also co-ordinated the French contributions to this book.

Our thanks go to the French Ministry of International Affairs and the French Ministry of Education who supported faculty exchanges and the French Embassy in Thailand, particularly Pierre Colombier, Conseiller Culturel and Jacques Morcos, Attaché de Cooperation Universitaire. In Bordeaux, the Conseil Régional d'Aquitaine and the Ville de Bordeaux assisted with the workshops and symposia, as did Michel Bergeron, Françoise Blanc, Catherine Chimits and Thierry Jeanmonod. In Melbourne in addition to the university, the City of Melbourne, especially Rob Adams, their principal urban designer, The Docklands Authority (now VicUrban) and Mark Allen, the City of Port Philip, and David Brand and Jim Holdsworth deserve special thanks. In Bangkok we especially acknowledge the contribution of Dr Sumet Jumsai, the Bangkok Metropolitan Authority, the District of Bangkhuntian; Dr Sornprach Thanisawanyangkura, the Vice President of International Affairs and all others at Kasetsart University.

The editorial team at Taylor & Francis must be thanked, starting with Caroline Mallinder who showed interest in and support for the project from the start and Kate McDevitt, Eleanor Rivers and Jane Wilde, for carrying the project through to completion.

Finally, very special thanks must go to Kate Gamble who, as Research Assistant at the University of Melbourne, compiled, managed and contributed to the editing of the many contributions through to publication – a complex and demanding task that she handled with grace and patience.

Introduction
Cross-cultural practice – why experiment now?

Catherin Bull and Claire Parin

This book addresses a growing issue for urban designers and those who contemplate *the urban* – how to act responsibly in a global market place and in a period of unprecedented urban change? Practitioners are increasingly international in their work, traversing regional and national boundaries on a regular basis to give advice to clients and work with many other professionals in the process. The members of many disciplines who contribute to urban design globally, including planners, architects, landscape architects, project managers and engineers, now expect to work internationally. Their education is expected to prepare them for international practice by adding an international dimension to the way they learn what urban design is.

While so much professional practice is now 'global', ultimately its manifestations are local. It must accommodate local values, conditions and expectations, as well as those of commissioning clients in government and commerce, who benchmark themselves against international standards and forms of development and may expect these to override the local particularities. Practitioners, whether international or local, are engaged in this process and are often expected to deliver urban design and planning advice rapidly despite the complexity that the cross-cultural dimension adds to their work. In a globalizing world, spatial and temporal compression provide the context, and challenge these professionals to think more about practice beyond the boundaries of their own cultures, be they geographic or disciplinary.

As designers' own cities and settlements now tend to be characterized by economic and ethnic diversity arising from unprecedented migration, such intercultural concerns are of relevance to them not only when they practise in other countries but increasingly when they practise in their home domains. Expectations and behaviors are diverse, manifesting as what could be called the 'rhythm' of interaction in each urban domain – with its own particularities, according to the cultural characteristics of the place. While some countries have longstanding traditions of social assimilation and others have even been founded on ideals of multiculturalism, in all countries the idea of what is local is under renegotiation, reflecting pressures for change brought by global forces and local reactions. Just what do terms such as 'cultural continuity' and 'historic value' actually mean in a shifting social terrain characterized by an increasing array of players? And how should these players be involved in the negotiation and realization of projects in their urban domains?

Specifically, how should urban design professionals think about and act in the many complex and varied situations that are increasingly the everyday condition of their working lives? How should they prepare for more meaningful professional encounters and responsible practice in an increasingly cross-cultural working domain – both at home and abroad?

Recognizing the complexity of the contemporary condition[1] and its impacts on professional activity and outcomes in urban design, the authors and editors of this volume propose that one way to advance practice is to confront that complexity, enquire into its nature and generate more debate about the way practice can and should proceed. Using the term applied by Donald Schon (1983), they are 'reflective practitioners' in an expanded realm of action and reflection.[2]

This volume presents and discusses what the authors and editors consider an experiment in reflective urban design practice for the twenty-first century.[3] By choice, that experiment did not seek universal processes or solutions. Rather, it engaged directly and openly with many ways of thinking and forms of practice, encouraging a more expansive vision of what urban design now is, who it is for and where it is practised, and embracing a wider range of models for action in a globalizing world. As reflective practitioners the authors and editors learn, and ask their readers to learn, recognizing that in the contemporary working world of cultural complexity we are all, to varying degrees, learners.

Fundamental to their experimental approach is the recognition that a multiplicity of voices can and should contribute to any cross-cultural debate about how urban design practice operates now. As urban practitioners in government, commercial practice and universities, contributors reflect on the contemporary city (reported and discussed in Part 1, 'Reconceptualizing the city'); on contemporary professional activity (Part 2, 'Experiments in practice'); and, on the very process of learning better cross-cultural practice (Part 3, 'Learning cross-cultural practice'). These reflections and debates are presented as a form of 'greater dialogue', to use the term coined by Charles Jencks (1993: 75). In his original use of the term and in later references to it (Jencks cited in Dear 2000: 154), Jencks associated it with the type of communication across cultures that would, ideally, create an understanding between the increasing array of ethnic groups he saw in his particular 'heteropolis', Los Angeles, after the riots there. That communication called for an acceptance of many different voices in the process of making a city.

Our experiment takes up this approach, applying it to a global experiment in urban design thinking and practice. As part of that experiment, urban designers and planners, in and from many parts of the world, were invited to participate in a particular dialogue about the future, without suppression, to create a new form of cross-cultural interaction. Rather than standardized treatises, the results produced in this book are the words of those who, despite their differences, share the discipline. They are urban designers who work in and across many cultures and working environments, and who can reflect on that experience. Their voices, of necessity given the variety, are different. Their circumstances differ, their modes of practice differ and their ways of communicating differ. The focus of their dialogue has some similarities, however. It is the complex set of interactions that now provides the context for urban design and planning, a context where, despite the strength of standardizing forces, dealing with difference is the *modus operandi*, requiring new ways of thinking and acting in practice.

This book, therefore, offers two interwoven texts. One is the play of voices that explain and reflect on the case studies worldwide. The other is the discussion and interpretation of those cases by the authors and editors using the theoretical framework developed as part of their experimental project.

The authors and contributors recognize that in order to advance practice, analysis and reflection on urban projects as they actually occur at a local level in many localities will assist them as practitioners and thinkers to understand the postmodern city and act effectively in it. In this complex working environment, where the fabrication of the city can no longer be reduced to a system of predictable or standard causalities (Jameson 1994), urban design and planning must be continually learnt and relearnt. Learning is achieved through exposure to an expanded domain of knowledge about the differences inherent in traditional cultures, about the impact of standardizing forces of global culture, about lived experience and about better models of urban practice. Such knowledge increases the capacity of those in practice to understand both universal phenomena and the specifics of the local, and to operate more effectively in both domains.

The urban project, for example, is revealed as a shared mechanism through which urban transformation is achieved by urban designers and planners, often far beyond its specific territory and even its period of negotiation and delivery. Urban projects are used as catalysts for change – at the large scale as strategies and at the site- or precinct-specific scale as tactics – to transmit cultural information as discourse, by the institutions of government and commerce (Certeau 1984), by the diverse members of local communities and by the designers themselves. Their discourse, as an expression of culture, asks to be interpreted and analysed and that process is undertaken here, translated especially to encourage debate among a cross-cultural readership with different ways of knowing, as well as different ways of acting.

Specifically, the authors and editors ask themselves and their readers to consider how the ubiquitous contemporary conditions of cultural complexity and difference are manifest in their direct experience as urban professionals, in the realm of the urban project. They are answered by a selection of essays and case studies – some short, some long depending on topic and working approach – that draw together the thinking and experience of a group of contributors from many parts of the world who reflect on the nature of practice in a great variety of urban territories of many scale, at home and abroad. In all these situations some form of cultural, or cross-cultural interaction exists. Such interactions, typically, are between those with differing expectations of what urban design should achieve as physical and social outcomes and the processes by which those outcomes are made to happen. Places and projects are interrogated in terms of their cultural context, their development histories, their contemporary operating reality, their form, the processes that make them and, especially, the meaning of all these for future practice.

The contributors offer insights into a complex contemporary world where urban designers and planners endeavour to understand and work with the processes of urban change.[4] Such change, it can be observed through the cases, is driven by universal phenomena such as urbanization and suburbanization, tourism and commercialization and market positioning, including the hosting of global events. Many contributors discuss how these more recent and ubiquitous processes respond, through the urban design project, to cultural roots embedded deep in the past of a particular place and the tensions that result in interactions between the two. Such discussions are often framed as debates about relative values and the complex way those values are expressed in the formal products and delivery processes that typify urban design now – whether global or local. Whose values prevail, how and why?

For all contributors, it would seem, the cities and settlements of the future are envisioned as places of complex co-existence – of many cultures, many forms and many technologies – where multiple expressions of past and present, global and local compete and are represented. In such a future, the relative position of each will manifest the way in which many interested parties, decision makers and stakeholders (local or otherwise) are involved in the process of change, a necessity that contributors see as adding significantly to the complexity of their work. While they support the variety, difference and complexity inherent in such co-existence, they promote the development of many new ways of thinking and practice, rooted in many cultural traditions and, indeed, global culture itself. Rather than a universal model, they propose multiple forms of practice that combine international and local sensibilities and methods to promote that difference.

Whether, generically, the urban domain is the heteropolis that Jencks envisaged in the early 1990s, or is a territory of even greater diversity and complexity, is yet to be seen. What is suggested by these discussions is that the techniques used by urban designers to explore, challenge and manifest cultural change and difference in the form of urban projects are evolving. Urban professionals work widely, learning from and practising in the smallest village through to the largest cities, wherever change is underway. They manifest an emerging era of networked interactions (Buell 1994: 337) between cultures and practices.

Contributors were selected not only because of the originality of their approach or their passionate commitment to confronting complexity and finding new solutions in practice. Nor were they selected because their experience in urban design or planning practice combines the global and local or is multi-disciplinary. These are characteristics that the contributors share with many of their colleagues and their audience of readers. What distinguishes their work is a commitment to reflection on and communication of their experiences – to strengthen the capacity of urban designers and planners everywhere to confront complexity and to practise better.

For most, complexity is the result of the convergence (or the crossing) of cultures, of disciplines, of physical conditions and of technologies and the expectation that as responsible practitioners, urban designers and planners can and should, somehow, address these all. Many of the discussions and examples that comprise the book explore how these complexities can be viewed, how they should inform other professional activity and how they should influence standard approaches (or pre-existing models) to practice. They propose new thinking and alternative modes of professional behaviour.

In their introductions to the three parts of this volume and their overall conclusions, the editors explore and draw conclusions on the meanings of these contributions for urban design practice in the future. They resist the tendency inherent in much of the literature on contemporary urban development to see the decline in quality of cities, towns, suburbs and settlements as inevitable. In such propositions, commercializing global forces and modernism in its less sensitive guises combine forces to result in the homogenization of urban character and the erasure of local particularities, conspiring with unprecedented urbanization to create a uniform post-urban domain the world over.[5] Such an approach is supported by universal application of a single conceptual model of practice based on functionalism unconditioned by pre-existing conditions.

Many contributors analyse the impacts of such an approach in the light of their experience, challenging it by proposing other methods of urban design more suited to the specifics of their own situations. Theirs is a cultural, even we would say, cross-cultural, response in the sense that it comprehends the impacts and imperatives of global culture, but posits a culturally specific response. In this way, contributors demonstrate their approach to cross-cultural urban design practice in the way they think, act, learn and teach their discipline now. Their work illustrates that, in the urban domain, simplistic assumptions about homogenization cannot be supported, as borne out by observations in other domains (King 1990: 11).

As has been broadly discussed already, the material presented here was developed from an experimental project in cross-cultural and cross-disciplinary urban design and planning that spanned three years. That experiment aimed, at an operational level, to create a 'laboratory' across space (three countries and cultures, and many regions) that would be the locus of research activity about cross-cultural practice by the co-ordinating team over that period. This laboratory was envisaged as a working space where the instigators and researchers experimented, using urban design techniques, symposia, workshops and analysis, around the topic of the contemporary city, settlement and the urban project. They provoked, facilitated and observed many debates about challenging situations of relevance to cross-cultural urban design. Hundreds of contributors were invited into and became part of the experiment – practitioners in government and commercial practice, academics, researchers and teachers, those in government and those learning urban design. Participants were deliberately chosen from diverse cultures and places, even diverse professions, and that diversity was fundamental to the premise of the project. Their difference was encouraged, so as to stimulate debate and the exploration of similarities and differences in their experience as urban professionals.

Over the three-year period and the many interactions that occurred in this global, or international, laboratory, it became clear that even with this form of 'greater dialogue' between working and ethnic cultures in a supportive setting, ambiguity in communication is ubiquitous. That ambiguity takes different forms, depending on the type of encounter, as parties negotiate a path to productive cross-cultural working relationships – between professional groupings (architecture, landscape architecture, planning and urban design); between practitioners, clients and users (or stakeholders); and between ethnicities. The interactive settings employed were those normally used in urban design projects: symposia or meetings for information exchange and philosophical debate, plus workshops to explore opportunities and issues and expose and challenge predetermined positions. There were also opportunities for reflection and shared observations among researchers. At the symposia certain communicative styles, techniques and preoccupations were revealed; in workshops, others. The techniques that advance or inhibit debate, interaction and communication in all forums and at all stages of the urban design process were observed and contribute towards the experimental findings and conclusions. The contributions included in this volume were selected to expose as great a range of geographical and cross-cultural urban situations as possible, reflecting the overall goal of maximizing the cultural dynamics within the experimental and reflective frame.

All contributors are active urban design professionals, variously oriented according to their working environments. All are committed to the evolution of the city and their discipline. Some of the examples presented and discussed are framed by current philosophical and theoretical discourse, particularly orientalism and post-colonial theory, and postmodernism, and the variety of understandings of and approaches to *the Other*. This collection reflects the collaborative structure and ethic of that experiment – to recognize complexity and difference (the Other) by enabling multiple voices to be heard and understanding the possibilities of giving expression to 'Otherness'. This resulted in the poly-vocal character of the project and as a result, this volume. It incorporates many voices, many places, many modes and many scales of activity from the smallest example of the urban, the village, to the largest urban regions. The issues it raises for practice and education cross four continents, suggesting solutions and setting the agenda for future steps – how to encounter, how to accept, how to comprehend, and how to act in complex urban design and planning situations characterized by many kinds of difference.

Significantly for this volume, the 'greater dialogue' envisaged by those who were the instigators of the experiment, accepts these many voices and the different ways they speak. Those from practice, who focus more on action, vary from those in the academy, who focus more on thinking; the voices from other cultures vary from those of our own; and, given the importance of their many ways of thinking, acting and learning, all are welcomed into the debate about what urban design practice is now. Some contributions are written by those for whom English is their second language; some have been written in English as the mother tongue. Yet others have been translated. Some ways of thinking and practising based in other cultures may even surprise the reader because of the very difference of their approach, but all contributions show a commitment to exploring and understanding the potential role of design, particularly as part of the urban project in the contemporary city and settlement, the kinds of technical and cultural issues designers now confront and the processes they must now adopt to be effective and achieve their goals. Some phenomena appear universal, some specific to particular places, but all show how urban design thinking and skills can contribute.

Following this introduction, Part 1, 'Re-conceptualizing the city?' responds to the question: 'How should we think about the city and urban design and planning in an era characterized by complexity and difference?' by presenting and discussing nine illustrative examples that, in various ways, demonstrate how urban designers and planners are developing new ways of imagining not only what our cities can or should be, but just as importantly, what they actually are now. Rather than accepting traditional views, these theorists suggest that in order to fulfil our professional roles and imagine and create alternative futures, we need new ways of seeing what is already occurring and how to use these in our work. They are also concerned to map the many interacting processes of change in practice – spatial, social and organizational – as a contribution to their disciplines.

Three themes explore: ways to see and interpret the character of local space and its changes; the position and contribution of designers to the process of change; and possible design methods or tools to restore equilibrium in the urban domain. As suggested in the introduction, notions of the local are rooted in the subjective experience of a place and its history. By contrast, many global phenomena and their impacts can be measured objectively. While not diminishing its inherent value, the subjectivity of the local experience complicates its reading by local inhabitants. This reading can actually be assisted by the cross-cultural interpretations of specialists who bring a degree of useful objectivity to the task. This objectivity is illustrated by Limthongsakul (Chapter 1), who carries out a comparative reading of the spatial arrangements of Muslim villages across two neighbouring countries.

Other illustrative examples show how the presumption that global modes and forms of development necessarily override local values in the re-formation of places can, on close reading, be challenged. The way that local cultures embrace and adapt 'global' forms such as the suburban estate and residential tower block (in Singapore), or how 'global' forms such as tourist or residential compounds conserve local heritage and artefacts in the face of urbanization (Thailand) is described. The opportunistic development patterns along the *sois*, or lanes, and super-blocks on the urban edge of Bangkok (de Wandeler in Chapter 7) also demonstrate a fusion of land development cultures, both contemporary and traditional, at the level of the everyday and local. Such observations suggest that the dynamics of cultural interaction between local and global ways of making the city are worthy of further interrogation. Also exploring how urban design projects unavoidably manifest extant values about culture, whether contemporary and international, or local and historic, Whitford and Amougou Mballa (Chapters 4 and 5) call for a more explicit recognition of this in future professional activity and a recasting of thinking about practice and learning to that end.

The idea of sustainability is, of course, also explored, demonstrating its reach across cultures and places with some surprising findings. Recent developments appear to cut across long-established, sustainable modes of settlement in North Africa and Asia. Tournier's (Chapter 6) analysis demonstrates what sustainable urbanization might actually mean in a water-hungry desert environment and Sutthitham (Chapter 8) postulates an approach for the settlement of the Asian subtropics. Both are rooted in the cultures of each place, explicitly incorporating the traditional social and cultural, as well as economic and environmental, values, reminding the reader of the importance of this dimension to urban design practice. They also promote an iterative dialogue between global and local values as development and change progress.

All contributors to this first section explore new conceptual territories, proposing that more needs to be known about the meaning of traditional ideas of place at a local level in our settlements; how change actually occurs now when driven by global phenomena; and how to engage local peoples and local and international practitioners in exploring these so that we better understand the process and dynamics of change. Their work supports the proposition that while many local cultures are under threat from the impact of some global ideas and practices, in reality they rely on others for their very existence (Buell 1994: 34).

Part 2, 'Experiments in practice', develops the central proposition that there is already vast and valuable international experience of action and practice in cross-cultural urban design to draw on and engage, and that such experience provides clues to future approaches – if it is gathered, presented and analysed (Robertson cited in Buell 1994: 8). The contributing practitioners present reflective summaries as illustrative examples of their professional experience and analyses of many projects and places. The international reach and variety of their work and their origins are of importance here, demonstrating the extent of the debate about how global expectations meet local place in the world of urban planning and design practice. Issues are contextualized in locations spanning sites in Asia, North America, Africa and Australasia. They focus not on simplistic notions of old world, new world and developing world, but on a global network of places linked by professionals who study in one place, live in another, practise in yet another and communicate with co-professionals from all of these. Their lives manifest the complex, decentralized web of interactions that characterize contemporary life (Buell 1994: 337).

Their observations of experience in practice range from the strategic, at a territorial or metropolitan level, through to the specific urban project locally realized. Each is explored for the way it demonstrates global, regional or national forces – such as strategic positioning, tourism in its many forms and guises and the role of patronage by international, regional and national agencies such as Unesco, the European Union and in Thailand the Royal Project – in creating international and regional exemplars of good practice. In this context, the transformation of practice is observed as well as the transformation of place. Contributors reflect on the increasingly complex set of interactions and interest groups (local inhabitants, politicians, agencies and other professionals) that must be orchestrated to achieve outcomes on the ground and move beyond what is typical in many contemporary cities: the distancing of communities from the power structures that decide about their urban environments (Jencks cited in Dear 2000: 145).

The transformation of place remains central to these discussions, however, and its meaning is explored by all contributors. Most reflect on the new vocabularies of urban design now needed, exploring new forms of urbanism, as practised in the heart of the established city (Montreal, Genoa, Barcelona, Tunis or Bordeaux) and just as important, given the universal trends towards suburbanization, the urban periphery – or beyond that again in the expanding domain of the urbanizing or suburbanizing village (Guangzhou, Montenegro and Thailand). The authors trace the interplay between the strategic at the scale of the urban system and the tactical at the level of the site, principally within the frame of sustaining local cultural values, identity and function in the face of potentially dramatic negative change and loss.

A recurring theme is apparent: that multiple scales of practice and variety of interests are to be accommodated to achieve the overarching goal of sustaining local qualities and cultural and natural functions. Transformation, rather than erasure, of places and communities appears the dominant model among these examples. There are simply more types of urban design work in a greater variety of places, and at a greater variety of scales, made more intricate and complex because of the integrative approaches taken to form, and inclusive approaches to process. More players need to be accommodated and interests to be balanced to practise urban design 'well' both in government and the commercial domain by moderating and reversing negative impacts on environments. Contributors promote new forms of practice in recognition of these changes and the potential of urban projects, whether residential districts, transport systems, urban renewal or revitalization, to rewrite what urbanism means for the contemporary and future city (Bordeaux, Barcelona, Tunis and Guangzhou). Such rewriting appears to be central to their endeavours and shows how, through their projects, practitioners are in their own ways, reconceptualizing the city, as are the traditional thinkers in the academy.

In Part 3 'Learning cross-cultural practice' the contributors, in more detailed chapters as befits their working domain as teachers and researchers in the academy, identify a key question oriented particularly towards modes of working and interaction – how do we learn more effective cross-cultural practice? They pose more specific questions around this theme, including the role of language, the use of narrative and semiotic games and other interactive techniques. As designers, they continue to argue for the workshop, specifically the cross-cultural (and sometimes cross-disciplinary) workshop in the field, as an ideal site for experimental and reflective practice.[6] Now characterized by cross-cultural exploration as well as the more traditional modes of problem solving, the international design studio provides a laboratory for experimentation, and these cases show how that occurs.

Educators from the various disciplines practicing urban design analyse the experience of their students, themselves and their peers in situations of cultural and disciplinary complexity, exploring how design practice operates now, and suggesting, on reflection, how it might operate better. Specifically in relation to cross-cultural interaction in practice, they discuss: the power of three teams working together on problems rather than the more traditional two (Radović in Chapter 19); the role of words in advancing from analysis to design concept (Boontharm in Chapter 20); the challenges and benefits that arise from a common working language (Singh and Bull in Chapters 22 and 24); ways to generate local ownership of new ideas (Thomas in Chapter 23); the role of time in the workshop process (Bull in Chapter 24); how play can inform cross-cultural work (Thaveeprungsriporn in Chapter 21); the stimulation inherent in difference, and the invisibility implicit in the ubiquitous (Bull in Chapter 24); and the basis and meaning of methodological difference (Tapie in Chapter 25). These lessons usefully apply to all domains of cross-cultural practice, to the academy and to the worlds of government and commercial practice.

Finally in their conclusions, the authors and editors reflect on what they see as the inevitably complex, cross-cultural future of urban design and planning. They reassess their positions and presumptions in light of the many new ways of thinking, acting and of learning that are experienced, analysed and discussed here. Through the experiences and thinking that are shared in the book, in situations of cultural and disciplinary complexity and difference, they have refined their thinking and suggest new ways to conceptualize what is often touted as the divide between 'global' and 'local'.

The authors reiterate that the contemporary condition of cultural and geographic complexity and difference presents the most important challenge for urban designers and planners now and in the future. They have therefore confronted that challenge, presenting new ways of thinking about that cross-cultural complexity in urban and urbanizing domains, of acting (or practising) in those domains and of learning about both. Through the various combinations of global phenomena and local practice that they describe and discuss, the contributors demonstrate how local areas lose or sustain their difference in the face of standardizing global forces for change and how urban design can aid or abet that process. They discuss places of co-existence, and cross-cultural complexity – in minds, in practice and in physical reality. The editors and authors propose that these examples demonstrate how the energy and stimulation inherent in the international practice of urban design and planning (through the experience of difference) can be harnessed to achieve more responsible outcomes for future practice. They also suggest the possibility of a new place of informed and creative co-existence for both global and local design practices. A number of contributions challenge the presumption that the global always dominates global–local exchanges and illustrate how in a number of domains, and with or without the conscious assistance of designers and planners,[7] a complex fusion of the two actually occurs. Simplistic presumptions about the inevitability of standard approaches and outcomes are also challenged by their real experience in practice.

Through the writings collected together here, the authors and editors conclude that urban designers and planners who work across cultures and professional domains should have various characteristics, behaviours and capacities, and therefore need, consciously, to develop these. They should be informed practitioners, educated in the complexities of the contemporary world – both global and local. They should see urban design and planning practice, now and in the future, as cultural practice. In such practice, understanding and creatively orchestrating social interactions is as professionally important as understanding and creatively reconfiguring space. Specifically, in the cross-cultural domain that now typifies the working domain, urban design practice should be seen as cross-cultural.

Urban designers and planners should, the contributors argue, recognize and harness the energy inherent in international practice, embrace the complexity and difference it presents, and find diverse models of practice to assist them. They need specific tools (such as workshops and semiotic games) to assist them to work co-operatively – across diverse cultures, across diverse geographies, across diverse spatial scales and across disciplines. More volumes of this kind are required to create and advance that much touted 'greater dialogue' and inform practice across the globe about what 'local' and 'global' mean in urban terms across its many territories. Finally, the authors propose that, ultimately, the goal of urban designers and planners should be to use their expanded knowledge and experience to help the richness, complexity and difference in our cities, settlements and urban regions not only to survive but to co-exist and prosper in a dynamic partnership between global and local.

Notes

1 In *National Culture and the New Global System*, Frederick Buell discusses the volatility, uncertainty and constant change that characterize contemporary global culture and the need to understand and represent experience of that condition (Buell 1994: 8).
2 We suggest an expansion of Donald Schon's (1983) original conception of the 'reflective practitioner' to a working domain of global proportions.
3 That experiment was BMB (Bangkok–Melbourne–Bordeaux), an international teaching and research project conducted by the Faculty of Archi-

tecture at Kasetsart University, Bangkok; the Faculty of Architecture, Building and Planning at the University of Melbourne and École d'Architecture et Paysage, Bordeaux over the three years from 2003 to 2005. Various experiences from that project (drawn from its workshops and symposia) are presented as chapters of this book and provide the framework for further contributions, reflections and discussions.
4 Buell (1994) and Roland Robertson (1992: 109) observe a lack of analysis and interpretation of the very process of globalization, something we attempt to redress here in the urban domain, where they assert there is an over focus on the national.
5 The threat of homogenization was, famously, articulated by Herbert Schiller who argued that 'cultural homogenization that has been underway for years threatens to overtake the globe' (Schiller 1969: 12).
6 Armstrong (1999: 5) discusses the role of the studio as part of larger research programmes to theorize creativity and pioneer new approaches to teaching that can expand to new forms of practice.
7 While Frampton (1983) discusses the role of designers as creators of sites of resistance through the practice of critical regionalism, it would seem from these illustrations that appropriation can occur in many ways and for many purposes. Some presumed examples of positive or negative appropriation are revealed as actually being the opposite (see Chapters 2 and 3 by Sintusingha and Guillot in this volume). The local may willingly and energetically embrace and adapt the international. In other chapters, the role of international organizations such as Unesco is presented as assisting in building local capacity to engage more equally in global partnerships.

Bibliography

Armstrong, H. (1999) 'Design studios as research: an emerging paradigm for landscape architecture', *Landscape Review*, 5(2): 5–23.
Buell, F. (1994) *National Culture and the New Global System*, Baltimore: The Johns Hopkins Press.
Certeau, M. de (1984) *The Practice of Everyday Life*, trans. S. Randall (1988), Berkeley, Los Angeles and London: University of California Press.
Dear, M. (2000) *The Postmodern Urban Condition*, Oxford and Malden: Blackwells Publishers.
Frampton, K. (1983) 'Towards a critical regionalism: six points for an architecture of resistance', reprinted in H. Foster (ed.) (1998) *The Anti-aesthetic: Essays on Postmodern Culture*, New York: The New Press.
Jameson, F. (1994) *The Seeds of Time*, New York: Columbia University Press.
Jencks, C. (1993) *Heteropolis: Los Angeles, the Riots and the Strange Beauty of Hetero-Architecture*, Berlin: Academy Editions and Ernst, London and Sohn KG.
King, A.D. (1990) *Global Cities: Post-Imperialism and the Internationalization of London*, New York: Routledge.
Robertson, R. (1992) *Globalization: Social Theory and Global Culture*, London: Sage Publications.
Schiller, H. (1969) *Mass Communications and American Empire*, Boulder: Westview Press.
Schon, D.A. (1983) *The Reflective Practitioner: How Professionals Think in Action*, New York: Basic Books; new ed. (1995) Aldershot, UK: Arena.

Part 1
Reconceptualizing the city

Introduction
New ways to read difference

Claire Parin

The concept of 'local identity' and the issues with which it presents urban planners and designers in the face of globalizing trends towards standardization and homogenization are central to the debates about the future city included here. At the same time, the concept of local identity is subject to diverse definitions and interpretations. Can it usefully be generalized to guide future practice? And if so, how? What indeed does local identity mean, and how is it manifest?

What the exchanges presented reveal is that while objective criteria about what local identity is here, or there, cannot be generalized across urban territories and domains, not, the processes that manifest as a particular culture, space and place can, with analysis, be better understood. Analysis of the processes by which culture manifests as space and place can usefully inform practice, but many presumptions about how global forces appear superficially to standardize and homogenize and may not be based on fact. Understanding how local culture works, how it produces space and values it, and why, yields some surprising outcomes.

Local identity: a subjective value?

The very idea of the local identity of a place seems to be essentially subjective, intrinsically linked to whoever describes it, and unable to be dissociated from the cultural context from which it emerges. Such a subjective, even sentimental position is somewhat paradoxical given the objective orientation that legitimates much contemporary discourse. Such a position recalls the ambiguity noted by Alois Riegl (1903) at the beginning of the twentieth century concerning the concept of 'ancientness' – a quality that has proved particularly effective in promoting the preservation and conservation of material elements of cultural heritage able to be identified by specialists as worthy of preservation.

Indeed in *Der moderne denkmalkultus*, Riegl argued that contrary to the notions of historical and artistic value that lay within the realms of proven knowledge, the value of ancientness was associated with the need of individuals to be attached to forms and objects that acted as material witnesses to the past, especially in a world of accelerated change, a world where the concept of time is becoming increasingly abstract.

Similarly, today, in the postmodern era where the mobility of people and the communication of information seem destined to develop without limits, it appears that in whatever cultural context, there is even more demand for material reference points that provide continuity with past times. This suggests that the question of retaining local identity in a globalizing world is central to the design of local space and place. It seems however, to be a question that is beyond answering effectively within the practical and symbolic value systems that usually apply in the production of contemporary urban projects.

To the urban professionals who contribute here, however, the design and delivery of local or everyday space, needs to meet increasingly complex functions, and abstract demands. Such projects, for example, are meant to communicate significance in the global domain and to contribute to an ensemble of sites that are landmarks, identifying territory. Technical expertise must be supplemented by expertise in expressing identity using many different scales, from the local to the global.

The contributors not only discuss their experiences in understanding how local identity in urban form is created, lost or eroded, they also discuss similar processes relating to local ecological systems under threat from development driven by the global economy. Local culture, built systems and landscapes, all appear to be undergoing systematic exploitation by development activities, specifically tourism, whose impacts are especially pervasive, perhaps because it is an industry whose very survival, paradoxically, appears to rely on the confluence between local identity and global accessibility. Such concerns are, however, coupled with an emerging recognition and acceptance that territories and cultures should be, to some degree, protected from intrusions. Inevitably they will change and evolve into completely new forms that articulate the evolving relationship between ubiquitous global forces, and local capacities to express the particularities of their culture in the process of transformation.

This evolution signals the importance of reflection on, and debates about, experiences of process among urban professionals – the process of project delivery; the process of conserving or developing urban precincts, places and territories; and the dynamic between global and local forces through time, manifest as space and place. Encouraging reflection and reflective practice in Donald Schon's (1983) terms, on the dynamics and interdependences inherent in contemporary practice, internationally and across cultural domains, seems essential if urban designers are to mediate between the competing demands they confront on a daily basis in their work.

While a common definition of local identity cannot be drawn

from these exchanges, nor a common methodology for its protection or construction, lessons can be learnt. The very idea of local identity – its importance in the process of transformation – needs to be explored. Sharing the experience of many professionals internationally, as these cases do, paves the way for reconceptualizing urban design, and enabling it to better confront this predicament.

Learning to read difference

What is revealed by these reflections is the variety of methods used to read the culture and form of the various territories, and to represent their distinctiveness in the face of trends towards methodological as well as formal standardization. The three cases reported by French and Thai contributors propose as many methods. While all places were responding to what could be considered standard processes of urbanization, the methods of response varied according to the particular dynamics of culture, form and development process.

Sani Limthongsakul, in Chapter 1 'Finding the identity of place through local landscapes: *Mooban* and *Kampong*', investigates vernacular space in the context of the rural village before modern development. Using methods derived from the anthropology of space, she identifies the spatial system that regulates land use, landscape and built form at the scale of that territory in order to make plain the values that are the basis of its identity as a place. She explores the relationship between underlying land form, spatial arrangement and use that is contingent on the complex cultural and religious demands that operate there. The village economy and its social relations contribute to the conservation of its social and environmental equilibrium. The analysis reveals the overlap of different layers of socio-spatial organization and their interdependence, making this landscape particularly sensitive to intrusion by other ways of life and urban forms. Equally however, her work exposes the availability of an underlying social structure of real robustness.

Sidh Sintusingha, in Chapter 2, 'Erasure, layering, transformation, absorption. The convergence of formal traditions', explores how new values become integrated in the Thai landscape across territories where urbanization is well established. He highlights the shifts in meaning that accompany the evolution of landscape, the architectural and urban forms as they are transformed under the influence of external (global) and local forces. The concept of the 'cultural landscape' becomes the medium through which to explore the complexities of the evolution of space at sites where standard forms of urban development (the urban park and the resort enclave) are appropriated and reinterpreted as new forms of local space. In these examples they become layered with elements of local meaning, resulting in complex hybrids that combine both local and global forms, and reveal much about how transformation is actually occurring.

The third contribution selected is that of Xavier Guillot, Chapter 3, 'Between "asianization" and "new compolitanism". Housing in twenty-first-century Singapore'. Like Sintusingha, Guillot analyses the continuing process of localization of global concepts – in this case the imported concept of the residential estate, first in the form of the suburban villa and latterly in the form of the condominium. The condominium becomes the particular medium of change in an environment already at an advanced stage of urbanization. The discussion shows the significance of the design of the residential estates in communicating local identity and supporting modes of local living.

Although these analyses deal with contexts that are already in the process of urbanization to varying degrees, and the contributions hail from such different domains, the motivations for and ways of reading both the spaces and the processes of transformation have many points in common.

First, within the frameworks of their analyses, the contributors attach importance to the relationship between built and landscape form in the urban domain. They also place importance on the kinds of activities that these domains support, suggesting these as authentic expressions of local culture, even when they manifest local responses to global trends (tourism for example). They call upon broader concepts of landscape as the means to establish the link between place as it is perceived by its inhabitants, and space as an objective reality. Landscape becomes the means to establish the characteristics that are most particular to the milieu.

Second, common to the different methodological approaches is their focus on territorial scales that attract their interest. The authors consider these as epitomizing certain types of social practices (Limthongsakul), ways of producing or transforming space (Guillot), or expressing the dynamic equilibrium between collective practices, representation and spatial production (Sintusingha). All aim at defining local space in both its physical and cultural dimensions, using methods of analysis based on shared knowledge at a global level (universal concepts of time according to Claude Levi-Strauss), historical representations of spatial production according to Frampton (1983). Such analyses across space illuminate the process of change insofar as they allow, at each territorial scale and in each location, knowledge about the characteristic way spaces change in contemporary times, and the role of local actors in that process.

Defined like this, such analyses suggest two ways of conceptualizing the processes of transformation and acculturation now underway, that manifest as change to urban environments. The first relates to the way urban fabric is renewed or remade and the level of resistance to change inherent in spatial structures, forms and local society. The second relates to the way that existing urban forms, models or ways of thinking at the scale of the local milieu can be adapted and assimilate 'the new' or different. Such observations suggest new lines of enquiry and research that will question the way local specificities should be approached, and what actually constitutes difference. Indeed they suggest that beyond observation of what exists here or there, the real issue is the resilience or robustness of environments in the face of globalizing influences and the way that various places and cultures layer, transform and adapt standard forms to their own needs.

The places of the global–local confrontation

The enquiries reveal that new forms of local identity are emerging, based on a complex alchemy resulting from the reaction between the culture of each locale, and the challenges with which contemporary urbanization presents it. While readings of local traditions suggest that many local places are under threat of disappearance, elements of the local urban landscape and architecture are, rather, in the process of evolution. Such evolutionary processes, however, do not appear predictable as yet, from the local viewpoint or on a comparative basis, despite the contributors, from their removed viewpoints, pointing to some emerging patterns. Such patterns seem dynamic, resulting from the way the forces of attraction and repulsion play out locally.

A number of contributors interrogate what they see as typical places where such confrontations take place and can be observed, including Sintusingha and Guillot as already observed. Others include Chapter 9 by Ornsiri Panin, 'Local identity in Bangkok's business districts', which explores this phenomenon, showing how commercial districts in Bangkok are threatened by the introduction of new shopping centres of the suburban type. She shows how these traditional places of exchange are unique environments which can be adapted to modern commerce and how, if they were, would also continue the complex system of relations between the local district and its urban context.

Also in Bangkok, in Chapter 7 Koen de Wandeler reflects on the environment of super-blocks served by the system of *soi* [dead-end lanes] in 'The urban edge. Bangkok *soi* as mediators of the global and local'. He shows how urban (or suburban) enclaves of intensive and to some degree, spontaneous, developments on the urban frontier constitute a framework that supports progressive acculturation into the contemporary city by both original inhabitants and successive waves of immigrants.

Both of these cases explore sites of friction or confrontation between different temporalities and typologies. In these examples, urban typologies are sufficiently robust and flexible to enable the development of new practices. The first shows how the stratified organization of space in the district of Bo-Bae reduces flows and connections at the broader urban scale. The second shows how the particular urban fabric has allowed several changes across generations, according to the rhythm of the time.

In both, existing (and unique) spatial systems have demonstrated the capacity to adapt and integrate new forms and functions despite their apparent vulnerability to fluctuations in the real estate market and demand. Such changes have been driven by local inhabitants aspiring to new standards of technology and living, rather than by 'outsiders' per se.

In both cases, local environments were resisting or adapting to a similar system of undifferentiated consumption that favours the standardization of spatial typologies and threatens to dislocate local cultures and territories. In each, increasingly, included and excluded populations are discernable. Management of the process of spatial adaptation to urban change at the local level seems at the heart of the discussions, especially the role of urban professionals in that process. Urban professionals are challenged to recognize that many changes to urban form are cultural in their origins, manifesting complex dynamics between the locale and the global context. They are also challenged to adapt themselves in the face of such recognition.

Redefining the role of urban professionals

If contributors agree that global impacts can lead to over-reliance on standardized technologies and models of form that ignore local particularities, they also agree that such a process is not inescapable.

While they see the need for a significant shift in the way space and time are understood in the urban domain, they see exceptional and unprecedented opportunities for professional practitioners to deal with the dynamics of global/local exchanges as manifest in the urban domain. Such opportunities are based on practitioners' capacities for innovative interventions, but must be underpinned by knowledge of the dynamics of development processes locally and globally. Their observations suggest that another form of cultural globalization may actually be afoot, rooted in the complexity, resilience and adaptability, not just of local form but of local practices. They see practice everywhere as overly dependent, overly reliant on a few dominant ways of thinking, and call for these to be revised.

Steven Whitford in Chapter 4, 'Dissolved identity and disintegrated globalization', reflects on urban design and architecture in the context of contemporary change. He argues that the days when projects affirmed absolute architectural or urban truths are gone. In an environment where evolution is less predictable than it has been, there is simply no place for the obliging reproduction of conventional imagery. Rather, by considering the space (or place) as a text in perpetual development (or indeed in the terms more broadly used here – evolution), at the urban as well as architectural scale, he proposes two major issues that professionals need to confront.

The first arises from the increasing panoply of data and criteria to be taken into account today in the production of space. This availability of data suggests the need for more preliminary phases of design to gain agreement about urban programs, and to raise questions about the meaning of progressive interventions. To do this, an inductive and broad-ranging approach should, he argues, replace the existing deductive and thematic approach.

The second issue needing to be confronted he sees as arising from the tendency for designers to rely on the pre-existing and standardized models, to be inspired by an a priori formal vocabulary wherever they are asked to intervene. In order to escape the idea of such predetermined spatial resolutions Whitford suggests that the design approach should confront and even invite potentially contradictory forces and logics, and aim to invent places that are receptive to multiple appropriations. As part of this, he also suggests a rejection of traditional spatial hierarchies.

The need to affirm the autonomous character of the idea of space is also promoted by Emmanuel Amougou Mballa in Chapter 5, 'The communal project and the reinforcement of values'. Amougou Mballa shows the involuntary aspects of intellectual activity that surround existing approaches to development in urban and architectural projects. He stresses the need to rethink and re-evaluate such approaches by questioning the value systems that underpin them and the way that the choices designers make about material form – particularly what should be retained or replaced in existing environments – express those value systems. Just what, he asks, is the value of the local? He also describes project designers and urban professionals as, unavoidably, agents engaged in the transformation of culture because they transform culturally significant places. He demands that they clarify how they contribute to this process in their design approach.

These two discussions highlight urban design as a unique and original way to imbue the transformation of space with meaning by projecting action into such space as well as creating form. At a fundamental level they see urban designers as creators of place. They encourage continued theoretical reflection on design thinking as it relates to the urban project, not only as the formal vector of universal truths as it was promoted by the modern movement. Rather they see such reflection and the resulting action as significant processes of reasoning, reading and interpreting the dynamic interplay between many and varied local cultures and places, and their global context.

Implementing strategies at a territorial scale

Debates about the relationship between global influences and the survival or not of local identity leads to consideration of the project process as part of the larger process of globally driven transformation. This in turn leads contributors to situate spatial interventions within the framing discourse of sustainability and the management of environmental resources generally.

Several contributors emphasize the need to understand cultures at a territorial or project scale, in parallel with the conception of development strategies. In order to identify the factors which disrupt local equilibrium, they show how particular economic functions and social organizations have underpinned, through history, the different elements that characterize the physical environments they observe. Some claim that all the cultural practices that have led to the development of local resources are fundamental to the production of these spaces. Recognition of these, they would say, underpins the success of any project. The concept of identity is, in their view, associated indirectly, or even directly, with the support of local capacity, and unavoidably implicates local communities and populations in the development process.

A discussion of this position is put by Jean-Noël Tournier in Chapter 6, 'Urban development and context: the traditional landscape and globalization in Marrakech'. This case discusses the crucial issue of water management in the urban area of Marrakech by carrying out a retrospective analysis of the modes of social and economic development that have until recently guaranteed the balanced management of natural resources, including water supply. This historical analysis supports a diagnosis of the present situation, making it possible to understand the irreversible process of degradation of the environment caused by urbanization. Tournier underlines how these phenomena, however important, have not been taken into account, either in the recent strategic plans that identify and value cultural heritage (particularly the built fabric), nor by tourism development policies.

Thada Sutthitham, in Chapter 8, 'Eco-planning for development in northern Thailand', develops a methodology for urban projects based on a reading of the formation of territory through time. Hers is a method based on knowledge of social practices, and, just as importantly, systems of belief. She pays particular attention to the way appropriate objective knowledge (of physical processes) integrates with beliefs to mobilize the process of territorial diagnosis and proposals for intervention. Sutthitham also advocates that such knowledge forms the basis of communication that encourages the community to be involved in the modified development processes.

These two contributors suggest new ways of approaching development based on knowledge of cultural and physical dynamics, and show the complexity of methods and processes that now need to be mobilized in order to realize such an ambition. Indeed their approaches integrate very diverse fields of knowledge, relating the social sciences to the physical sciences and the creative field of design. They suggest a continuous toing and froing in the development process, adjusting programme priorities to take account of practical (and local) experience. They also suggest that continuous political and technical management are needed to ensure consistency between different scales of thinking as the design and realization phases of the urban project proceed.

To conclude, it is emphasized that these reflections illustrate a common desire – to stand back and to take stock by reflecting on the many experiences discussed here, and their meaning for urban practice everywhere, now, and in the future. The confluence of different approaches and methodologies within the conceptual domain of 'local identity' and urban transformation makes it possible to observe how the global–local confrontation is occurring, and can be mediated through the urban project and under the influence of design professionals.

Beyond this broader goal, such knowledge can be used immediately within the framework of urban project processes in many situations. It suggests the desirability of carrying out comparative research at the global level into the way contemporary practices modify local space in different cultural contexts and their capacity (or incapacity) to generate new models for more effective practice in the future. Indeed, such analyses would provide a solid theoretical base, somewhat paradoxically, for tackling the questions relating to the survival of local identity in space and place in the face of globalization.

Bibliography

Frampton, K. (1983) 'Towards a critical regionalism: six points for an architecture of resistance', reprinted in H. Foster (ed.) (1998) *The Anti-Aesthetic: Essays on Postmodern Culture*, New York: The New Press.
Levi-Strauss, C. (1962) *La pensée sauvage*, Paris: Librairie Plon.
Riegl, A. (1903) *Der moderne Denkmalkultus, sein Wesen, seine Enstehung*, trans. K.W. Forster and D. Ghirardo, 'The modern cult of monuments: its character and origin', *Oppositions* 25: 21–51.
Schon, D.A. (1983) *The Reflective Practitioner: How Professionals Think in Action*, New York: Basic Books, new ed. (1995) Aldershot: Arena.

Chapter 1
Finding the identity of place through local landscapes
Mooban and *Kampong*

Sani Limthongsakul

Introduction

Vernacular landscapes possess unique qualities and a character that results from the intervention of local inhabitants in their natural environments. Such interventions create specific and particular types of built environments and forms of agricultural landscapes (Saleh 1995). A way of apprehending and interpreting the vernacular spatial practice of the local landscapes of Muslim communities in the four southern border provinces of Thailand and the state of Perak and Penang on the northern Malay peninsula is discussed in this case study. By sharing the same geographical area and socio-cultural background where the Islamic religion predominates, the local landscapes of Thai-Muslim and local Malay communities at the village level possess similar characteristics. The word village, *mooban* in Thai and *kampong* in Malay, means the rural village settlements composed of small housing clusters, and sustained by subsistence activities like paddy-growing, fishing, rubber-tapping and other agricultural practices (Gibbs 1987, Radenahmad 1985, Rattanajorrana 1994, Shamsul 1996, Niljang 1985, Yuan 1987). The anthropology of space is used here to inform the observation of vernacular spatial patterns, investigating settlement patterns, village land-use, housing compounds, landscape features and social space.

Settlement patterns

With the same geographical character of lowlands alternating with hilly terrain and high mountains, most settlements explored in this discussion are found along the flat terrain adjacent to rivers, shorelines, foothills and transportation corridors such as highways, roads and railways. The settlement pattern in the studied region can be categorized into three main types: clustered pattern, ribbon pattern and dispersed pattern (Gibbs 1987, Rattanajorrana 1994, Niljang 1985, Wilson 1967, Yuan 1987). Such linear settlements were formed along roads, rivers and railways while clustered settlements

1.1
The social spaces within a housing compound in a southern village.

1.2
An example of the vernacular housing style of southern Thailand.

1.3
A housing compound in a village in southern Thailand.

were found on the intersection of road corridors and in the form of homesteads among the rice fields. The dispersed settlements usually occurred where the soil is rich and water could be easily obtained for the agricultural activities.

Village land-use

The majority of villagers in the Thai-Muslim and local Malay communities sustain themselves by growing rice, tapping rubber, fishing and other agricultural practices (Niljang 1985, Wilson 1967, Yuan 1987). Village land-use can be categorized into the following areas: residential, public facilities, religious areas for worship and commercial. Each area is connected by a meandering network of pathways (Wilson 1967).

The mosque is the communities' central area and usually surrounded by *pornor* [religious teacher's houses], *kubo* [the cemetery close to the mosque], markets with shops and stores, governmental service buildings, clinics and residential units. Around this central area of the village there is public open space for flexible use, including both religious and social purposes.

The housing compound

Both local Thai-Muslims and local Malays believe that spirits reside in nature and natural elements such as big trees, rivers and mountains (Na-Talang 2001, Gibbs 1987, Yuan 1987). Typically, a minimum of trees is removed and houses are inserted under a mixed canopy of trees of different heights that are located somewhat haphazardly. The open space around each house is cleared and well kept, the house yard accommodating multiple uses such as the drying of clothes and rubber sheets, rice threshing, the raising of domestic animals, chatting outdoors and resting, and children's play and special feasting. The spaces between houses are left open and unfenced to accommodate group activities between families and among family members, making it difficult to distinguish between public and private space within a given cluster.

Landscape elements

Around each cleared yard, tropical fruit trees are planted randomly among herbaceous shrubs and groundcovers to the outer fringes of the house compound. There is no apparent order, no clear boundaries nor form to the garden, except that the ground adjacent to the house is left clear and open for activities. Flowering pot plants signify the front yard of the house and are placed near the stair to each entry porch.

Other structures typically found within the house yard include wells, chicken coops, paddy houses, jars, rainwater tank and shelters for sundry purposes. Fences used in the house compound are made from local materials such as bamboo canes and timber. Hedgerows of edible and indigenous plants and groups of trees are also popular for fencing purposes.

Social spaces

At the village level, the centre of the village, where the mosque, schools, markets, governmental service buildings, shops and stores are located, functions as a social gathering space for the villagers. The customary law of Islam requires the separation of men and women in all formal social interactions, thus there is segregation between men and women when they use public space.

At the level of the household compounds, however, open spaces emerge from the apparently haphazard arrangement of dwellings and allow for spontaneous use and spaces for social and cultural activity. These include children's play areas, feasting grounds for weddings and house-warming ceremonies and other social interactions within the housing cluster.

Conclusion

The local landscape of the study area has been influenced by and evolved as a result of both natural and cultural factors. The clustered settlement pattern with its interconnected open spaces that flow from one area to another reflects the close ties among the Muslim community as well as its agrarian roots. Manifesting the community's respect of and belief in the spirit of nature, therefore, there is minimum disturbance when clearing land to build houses and make habitable space. The result is unique in its character, with the housing clusters that are loosely but carefully arranged and blend into the surroundings under the shade of large trees.

The surrounding agricultural landscape contributes to the sense of identity of place for the Thai-Muslim communities in the four southern border provinces of Thailand and the local Muslim community in the state of Perak and Penang on the Malay peninsula. Values, beliefs and cultures of the agrarian society combine with the Islamic religion to influence the local lifestyle. Recently however, modern ways of living have led to changes in these lifestyles as the agricultural community is transformed into an urban community, inevitably affecting the characteristics of the local landscape. The relative insularity of the Islamic culture, however, which requires rigid adherence to practice by Muslim communities and individuals may, by inhibiting change, result in a more gradual rate. It might be assumed that the identity of these places will exist as long as the local inhabitants continue their agricultural practices and that these dominate as contemporary lifestyles evolve.

Bibliography

Chaoompruek, R. (1985) 'Thai-Muslim social character', *The Symposium on Villages and Domestic Architecture of the Thai Muslim Culture in the Southern Border Provinces of Thailand. Proceedings*, Pattani: Centre of Southern Study, Prince of Songkla University, 7–9 January: 41–59.

Galeh, A. (1985) 'Thai-Muslims' way of life in four southern borders provinces of Thailand', *The Symposium on Villages and Domestic Architecture of the Thai Muslim Culture in the Southern Border Provinces of Thailand. Proceedings*, Pattani: Centre of Southern Study, Prince of Songkla University, 7–9 January: 60–69.

Gibbs, P. (1987) *Building a Malay House*, Singapore: Oxford University Press.

Na-Talang, E. (2001) *Local Wisdom in Southern area of Thailand (Poom-Pan-Ya-Tak-Sin)*, Bangkok: Amarin Printing and Publishing.

Niljang, S. (1985) 'Thai-Muslim settlement (selected case studies)', *The Symposium on Villages and Domestic Architecture of the Thai Muslim Culture in the Southern Border Provinces of Thailand. Proceedings*, Pattani: Centre of Southern Study, Prince of Songkla University, 7–9 January: 25–40.

Radenahmad, J. (1985) 'Thai-Muslim settlement', *The Symposium on Villages and Domestic Architecture of the Thai Muslim Culture in the Southern Border Provinces of Thailand. Proceedings*, Pattani: Centre of Southern Study, Prince of Songkla University, 7–9 January: 17–24.

Rattanajorrana, K. (1994) *Thai-Muslim House in the Southern most of Thailand*, Bangkok: Amarin Printing and Publishing.

Saleh, E. (1995) 'Al-Alkhalaf vernacular landscape: the planning and management of land in an insular context, Asir region, southwestern Saudi Arabia', *Landscape and Urban Planning*, 34: 79–95.

Shamsul A.B. (1996) 'Promise versus performance: formal organizations in rural Malaysia', in Hoadley, M.C. and Christer, G. (eds). (1996) *The Village Concept in the Transformation of Rural Southeast Asia*, Richmond, UK: Nordic Institute of Asian Studies (Curzon Press).

Wilson, P. (1967) *A Malay Village and Malaysia*, New Haven: Hraf Press.

Yuan, Lim Jee (1987) *The Malay House*, Malaysia: Institute Masyarakat and Phoenix Press.

Chapter 2
Erasure, layering, transformation, absorption
The convergence of formal traditions

Sidh Sintusingha

This is a discussion of the modes of persistence of traditional cultural products in the designed landscapes of Thailand, framed through the discourses of 'critical regionalism' (Frampton 1983) and 'cultural landscapes' (O'Hare 1997). These are local phenomena that markedly 'rebrand' the Siamese elite (Peleggi 2002). Their traditional role is transformed from being the transmitter of imported civilization and modernity in response to the colonial threat from the mid-nineteenth to early twentieth century to becoming upholders of ideal indigenous values in face of the more recent influence of globalization and the global phenomenon of fabricating difference for the exclusive consumption of tourists.[1] It is a two-pronged resistance to globalization, forged by unlikely allies with seemingly contradictory agendas. The first is the local elite who seek legitimacy through the reassertion of the value of traditional forms and their associated symbolic capital and meaning in the imported urban forms of the park. The second is the foreign tourists who seek exotic cultural landscapes in resort enclaves.

The idea of critical regionalism proposes resistance to the homogenizing forces of product manufacturing and construction techniques – the commodification that accompanies the concept of the universal megalopolis (Nesbitt 1996: 468–469). According to Nesbitt, Frampton (1983) primarily seeks architecture with the 'capacity to condense the artistic potential of the region while interpreting cultural influences coming from the outside'. He recommends that any critique of universal modernization should well up from local enclaves, 'cultural fissures' or pockets of resistance. Architecture, he says, can and should support the expression of political identity and in the process, clarify place identity.

Distinctive cultural landscapes – defined as the characteristic patterns in the physical environment that are modified, classified and interpreted by humans – are attractive to tourists, and are subsequently changed by tourism, physically and perceptually (O'Hare 1997: 34–35). O'Hare posits tourism as the consumption of cultural landscapes – with tourists 'looking for differences'[2] primarily from their places of origin. Tourism is similar to other forms of consumption and consumerism, particularly the activity that economists and land-use planners call 'comparison shopping' since in a global market, tourism destinations are competing with other similar 'products' (O'Hare 1997: 43).

In terms of Frampton's critical regionalism discourse, two examples of the 'enclave' typology are employed against and oppose, the 'ceaseless inundation of a placeless, alienating consumerism' of the megalopolis development (Frampton 1983: 481–482). As meanings in Thai cultural landscapes, however, consistent with Aasen's investigation of Thai architecture, are rarely 'fixed, singular, or a matter of public agreement, even in a society as reputedly conservative and traditional as Siam's' (Aasen 1998: 1), Thai cultural landscapes are 'cultural hybrids, even anomalies, which are transplanted and displaced, sometimes both spatially and temporally' (Aasen 1998: 3). In view of local practice, then, the two examples of park and resort enclave also appear to continue the age-old Thai/Siamese traditions of cultural layering, transformation and absorption. Benjasiri Park[3] draws its relevance from the tripartite concept of the nation state, of Buddhism and of royalty – the very pillars of the Thai nation as symbolized by the three colours on the national flag (another foreign-appropriated, locally transformed product) – reasserting and signifying itself on urbanized Bangkok.

By contrast, the Regent Chiang Mai,[4] the offspring of capitalist global tourism can be seen as a stage set for antique fragments located in the reconstructed vernacular landscape. Its conceptualization and assembly, however – the bold, eclectic, not to mention highly individualistic, critical combination of the global resort typology and traditional forms – also result in something very traditional although without direct local precedent, consistent with Thai syncretistic practices. As Frampton suggests, regionalism isn't so often a collective effort as 'it is the output of talented individuals working with commitment towards some sort of rooted expression' (Frampton 1983: 477).

2.1
The main entry space to Benjasiri Park, from Sukhumvit Road, framed by Thai forms. Note the circular bas-relief statue of HM the Queen in the right background.

The word 'resistance' may be too simplistic, as the utilization of traditional form can be viewed as on a continuum with global influences. The urban park and the gated resort are global typologies transplanted and thinly veneered by local facades. The rigour of resistance can be discerned in the transformation and translation processes – whether in the synthesis between global typologies and traditional forms or in the layering of symbolic meanings familiar to locals yet exotic to foreigners. On the other hand, these two enclaves are not merely reproductions of traditional forms for tourist and mass consumption, but, arguably the extension, reinvention, and recontextualization of those forms – not just in response to the influx of global forms but also to differentiate from the messy, chaotic 'vernacular' (sub)urbanization outside. They are the self-proclaimed sanctuaries of authenticity amid the inauthentic jumble and incoherence of the suburbia of developing cities.

The irony is that while such enclaves can be seen as monuments sustaining Thai forms and meanings, they in turn sustain and are sustained by the cycles of consumption and processes of globalization that are now universal. In the city, industrialization and urban sprawl resulting in pollution and erasure of the rural cultural landscapes have led to the insertion of green spaces or parks, which in turn provide a convenient avenue for the expression of royal patronage and Buddhist values. They become reassuring beacons of 'Thai-ness' in the urban landscape, once the function of temples' *bhots* and *chedis*, long obscured by concrete shophouses, tall buildings and malls. In turn, gated resort enclaves contribute to the transformation and displacement of rural lifestyles, yet they reproduce those erased forms (such as the rice paddies at the Regent) for profitable tourist consumption.

With increasing consumption, more traditional forms are produced that often emulate successful cultural landscape products, such as Benjasiri and the Regent, which attempt to outbid each other in a game where the stakes are to achieve the greatest 'authenticity'. The latest to up the ante was the controversial Mandarin Oriental Dhara Dhevi in Chiang Mai, which, apart from incorporating rice paddies as part of the hotel landscape (following the

2.2
Rice paddies being 'farmed' by performers form the central landscape feature at the Regent Chiang Mai.

2.3
Replica of Wat Lai Hin temple in the embellished landscape of the Mandarin Oriental Dhara Dhevi resort, Chiang Mai.

precedent of the Regent) built a replica of an old temple *vihan*[5] at Wat Lai Hin in the resort compound despite the protests from Buddhist groups, academics and Tambon Lai Hin villagers. The latter considered the resort 'insulting to Buddhism and local wisdom' and also feared that 'fewer tourists would visit the real Wat Lai Hin' (Sattha 2004). The replica, 'authentically' packaged and marketed within the bounded enclave, competes with the original, long 'contaminated' by modernization/globalization.[6] It is in this dynamic of tensions and contestations within the total Thai cultural landscape between the enclave and beyond, the bounded nation state and the global that traditional cultural products are well and thriving – sustaining and extending those forms although not necessary their associated meanings.

Notes

1 Bull (1992: 16–20) suggests that the creation of sanctuaries of escapism from the sameness of the everyday is a typical response to globalization.
2 On this O'Hare cites Michael Hough (1990).
3 The park was built to commemorate HM the Queen's 60th birthday on 12 August, 1992 (the 5th *rhob* or cycle of 12 years). This arguably continues the 'tradition' of building public parks started by King Vajiravudh (Rama VI), who built Lumphini Park, Thailand's first public park, in 1925 as a gift to the people. On a site nearby, a new urban park, Benjakitti (to eventually cover 430 *rai*), was opened in 2004 to commemorate HM the Queen's 6th *rhob*.
4 The Regent Chiang Mai (since 2004, taken over by the Four Seasons Hotels and Resorts group), located at Mae Rim District, was opened in April 1995 and is Chiang Mai's first five-star resort.
5 Or *vihara*: 'Originally the dwelling place of Buddhist monks. In Thailand, it refers to a hall in the temple compound where religious services are held. It may or may not house a Buddha image' (Chuturachinda *et al.* 2000: 135).
6 Goad (2000: 37), investigating hotels in Bali, observed that: 'Several of the ten hotels in this book go close to that boundary where the reproduction is more seductive than the original.'

Bibliography

Anon. (1992) *Uthayan Benjasiri* (Benjasiri Park), Bangkok: Public Relations Committee of HM The Queen's 60 Years' Anniversary Urban Park Project.

Aasen, C.T. (1998) *Architecture of Siam: a Cultural History Interpretation*, Kuala Lumpur and New York: Oxford University Press.

Bull, C.J. (1992) 'Tourism in Australia part 1', *Landscape Australia*, 1: 16–20.

Chaturachinda, G.S., Krishnamurty, S. and Tabtiang, P.W. (2001) *Dictionary of South and Southeast Asian Art*, Chiangmai: Silkwork Books.

Frampton, K. (1983) 'Prospects for a critical regionalism', in K. Nesbitt (ed.) (1996) *Theorizing a New Agenda for Architecture: an Anthology of Architectural Theory 1965–1995*, New York: Princeton Architectural Press.

Goad, P. (2000) *Architecture Bali: Architectures of Welcome*, Balmain: Pesaro Publishing.

Hough, M. (1990) *Out of Place: Restoring Identity to the Regional Landscape*, New Haven, CT: Yale University Press.

Nesbitt, K. (ed.) (1996) *Theorising a new agenda for architecture: an anthology of architectural theory 1965–1995*, New York: Princeton Architectural Press.

O'Hare, D. (1997) 'Interpreting the cultural landscape for tourism development', *Urban Design International*, 2(1): 33–54.

Peleggi, M. (2002) *Lords of Things: the Fashioning of the Siamese Monarchy's Modern Image*, Honolulu: University of Hawaii Press.

Roy, A. (2004) 'Nostaligias of the modern', in N. Al Sayyad (ed.) *The end of tradition?*, New York: Routledge.

Sattha, C. (2004) 'Replica temple at hotel draws local protest', *Bangkok Post*, Internet edition, 16 November 2004. Available http://www.bangkokpost.com/News/16Nov2004_news06.php.

Chapter 3
Between 'asianization' and 'new cosmopolitanism'
Housing in twenty-first-century Singapore

Xavier Guillot

Introduction

In Singapore, the diffusion of condominiums across the urban landscape has become more noticeable over the past two decades: a condominium is a type of housing characterized by a combination of apartments and various services and facilities for the use of residents. Condominiums can now be found in all the main cities of South-East Asia. First appearing in Singapore in the late 1970s, the construction of condominiums has spread to cities in Thailand, Malaysia, Indonesia, China and Vietnam, as well as in Indian cities connected to the global economy, such as Bombay and Bangalore.

Is there an 'identifying referent' or local antecedent?

The emergence of the condominium is generally associated with the growth of international mobility and the emergence of a so-called middle-class society (Robinson and Goodman 1996). In Singapore condominiums were first launched in the late 1970s, to accommodate foreign expatriates. Consequently, Singaporean media often see the condominium as a symbol of a 'cosmopolitan' way of life in contrast with the dominant way of life represented by local public housing and its inhabitants, the 'Heartlanders' (Long 1998). In academic literature, the growth of condominiums is also associated with the development of global financial flows generated by private developers and multinational capital (Dick and Rimmer 1998). Within this context, condominiums are often cited as part of a global 'generic city' (Koolhaas 2000), along with other types of buildings, such as shopping centres, office buildings or international hotels.

Does this process of globalization, however, necessarily mean that the local economy and culture do not take part in the development of condominiums? To answer this question, some preliminary remarks are needed on the matter of methodology. When

3.1
A typical bungalow of the colonial period.

looking at contemporary condominium design as a process involving foreign influences, two points of view are immediately possible: the first from the outside, i.e. the so-called global point of view; the second from the inside, i.e. the 'local' point of view.[1] Keeping these in mind, my analysis strategy will focus on how global ideas are received and translated locally by looking at how the condominium, as a 'transnational dwelling type', was 'received, decoded, domesticated or re-appropriated', in Singapore (Warnier 1999: 9).

The significance of the condominium in the transformation of the Singaporean way of living, and its relevance in the evolution/decline of its local dwelling identity are also evaluated. Drawing from the social sciences, our understanding of the notion of identity is necessarily subjective and interpretative (Muchielli 2002).[2] The following analysis of the condominium therefore takes into account the various factors which have intervened at the local level in the reappropriation process of this dwelling type by surveying past and present housing forms in Singapore – the dwelling antecedents that played the role of identifying referent in the design of the condominium and the intermediate agencies that facilitated its implementation.

3.2
An early garden residence outside the city centre.

Luxury and leisure in nature: paradigm of a colonial life

The first dwelling antecedent in Singapore is the colonial bungalow, introduced by the British in the nineteenth century, and one which is still continuing to develop.[3] The design of the bungalow is a combination of Malay and British architecture, and in Singapore the term 'bungalow' can be assigned to a variety of types based on the same model, reflecting the multiethnic nature of its inhabitants.

In terms of its setting, the colonial bungalow follows a logic totally different from the principal existing type – the shop-house. Bungalows were located outside the city centre. This location had a specific advantage – it provided a calm and healthy environment, far from the nuisances of the city, but it required its inhabitants to have their own transport: horses and carts at first, and then automobiles as soon as they appeared on the island. Bungalows symbolized the suburban approach to urban living. Prevailing at the same time in Western cities, this explains the use of the word 'bungalow' in the UK, North America and Australia. Although the whole territory of Singapore is now urbanized, the dream remains and is recurrent in the majority of condominium developments, where recreating a piece of nature as part of its setting is a common feature.

The design and location of the condominium is inscribed in this logic – living outside the city while benefiting from its advantages in terms of services. Beyond this desire for nature, one should see the bungalow as an identifying referent for the condominium through the cultural capital that bungalows embody in terms of social representation, transferred to the emerging local middle class by the elite. Originally, the bungalow was occupied by representatives of the British government or wealthy Asian merchants. In the past it acted as an indicator of social distinction; so, too, is the condominium in today's society.

High-rise living and self-sufficiency: the legacy of post-colonial housing

The second dwelling antecedent is the 'HDB housing block' promoted by the Housing Development Board, a government body established in the 1960s following the colony's independence.[4] The HDB housing block is now the most widespread dwelling type in Singapore. Its construction is associated with the development of new towns that are part of an island-wide planning strategy with large implications for the social and economic development of the city state (Goldblum 1987). Two fundamental aspects of HDB design are reviewed as architectural antecedents playing an important role in the development of the condominium.

The first is the fact that the Development Board introduced high-rise living. As Anthony King (2004) reminds us, in 1934 in Shanghai, high-rise building had become a 'metaphor of modernity' in Asia. HDB blocks are inscribed into this history as well as the condominium. The choice of going high-rise is closely associated with a fundamental urban planning option, inherited from the modern movement: verticality creates density. It is a principle that complies with a slogan of Singaporean planners, to create a 'tropical city of excellence', a so-called garden city.[5]

The second aspect is the idea of self-sufficiency. Each new town is provided with standard services and equipment such as shops, schools, recreation or sport facilities easily accessible.[6] The condominium uses this planning antecedent, developing the concept of self-sufficiency further by privatizing the facilities that it includes. Home becomes the focus of a larger number of activities that include both work and leisure.

The review of these two dwelling antecedents shows that various links exist between condominiums and previous housing types, whether by their design characteristics (HDB blocks), or by the images and

3.3
The main axis of a recent condominium complex with its recreational space and view to the landscape beyond.

symbols they embody (colonial bungalows). Regarding the nature of the process of globalization, it also shows the shortcomings of a reading disconnected from local culture and dwelling antecedents. Beyond this, the pluralistic nature of globalization in the evolution of dwelling design is revealed, as Anthony King (2004) rightly formulated. Further it supports King's proposition that such processes must be studied in an historical perspective, since similar processes had already occurred before the identification of globalization as a phenomenon, particularly during the colonial period.

In this sense, studying condominiums in Singapore leads to further questions about the implication of globalization in the evolution of contemporary dwelling forms. It suggests the need to be specific about the current processes of cultural interaction and to compare them with others already existing in the region and shows how, in Singapore, condominiums manifest a specific process of cultural hybridization (Pieterse 2004) or indigenization (Appadurai 1996).

3.4
The entrance to a recently constructed condominium complex through its garden.

Notes

1 As Jean-Pierre Warnier points out, 'the global point of view isolates the cultural products from their context, separates them into categories, quantifies the production and distribution at the scale of the planet' (1999: 95). It does not allow access to the activity of intermediate agencies, which sort out and recontextualize the products of industrial culture. Hence, we do not have the capacity to understand the way these 'cultural products' are 'received, decoded, domesticated or re-appropriated'. These intermediate agencies are the family, the local community, the political leaders, the clubs, the school. The impact of this cultural mix varies a lot according to the way these intermediate agencies work.
2 According to Muchielli, identity is always plural 'because it always involves several actors of the social context who have their own reading of their identity and of the identity of the others, in accordance with the situations, their task and their project'. Identity is always in transformation, adds Muchielli. It is always a 'bio-psychological and communication process' related to 'identifying referents' (2002: 5–41).
3 The term 'bungalow' finds its origin in the name of the traditional dwelling of the Bengali (*banggolo*). The first bungalows were designed and built by the British in India at the beginning of colonization in the eighteenth and nineteenth centuries. This is why the bungalow and colonial architecture are generally associated. According to K.L. Lee (1988: 42), as early as the 1860s, one can find several examples of this dwelling type on the island.
4 Although belonging to what is commonly called the post-colonial era, the HDB housing block has some antecedents in the colonial era, when British initiated public housing in the 1930s under the Singapore Investment Trust.
5 'Toward a Tropical City of Excellence' is the motto of the Urban Redevelopment Authority, the governmental body in charge of urban planning. Although the term 'garden city', borrowed from the vocabulary of English planning, does not comply with Singaporean reality, the fundamental intention remains: after independence, the future of the city state is not in the low-rise colonial urban model.
6 One of the key planning tools to reach this goal is the concept of the

'neighborhood unit', on which is calculated the level of services. A neighbourhood unit is defined by a group of 4,000 to 6,000 apartments, covering an area of 40 ha. Later, in the 1980s, the HDB introduced the concept of 'precinct'. The precinct is a micro-neighbourhood unit comprising 400 to 800 units gathered around a small square with communal facilities such as small shops or sports facilities) on an area of about two to four ha. It now constitutes the basic unit of the new town.

Bibliography

Appadurai, A. (1996) *Modernity at Large: Cultural Dimensions of Globalization*, Minneapolis: University of Minnesota Press.

Chua, B.H. (2003) *Life is Not Complete Without Shopping. Consumption Culture in Singapore*, Singapore: Singapore University Press.

Dick, H.W. and Rimmer, P.J. (1998) 'Beyond the third world city: the new urban geography of South-east Asia', *Urban Studies*, 35(12): 2303–2321.

Featherstone, M. (ed.) (1990) *Global Culture: Nationalism, Globalization and Modernity*, London: Sage.

Goldblum, C. (1987) *Métropoles de l'Asie du Sud-Est. Stratégies urbaines et politiques du logement*, Paris: L'Harmattan.

Guillot, X., (2003) 'Les élites professionnelles étrangères à Singapour. Du renouvellement à l'établissement d'une migration haut de gamme', *Les annales de la recherche urbaine 94, L'accueil dans la ville*, Octobre 2003: 71–80.

King, A.D. (2004) *Spaces of Global Cultures. Architecture, Urbanism, Identity*, London: Routledge.

Kong, L. (1999) 'Globalization, transmigration and the renegotiation of ethnic identity' in K. Olds, P. Dicken, P.F. Kelly, L. Kong and H.W.C. Yeung (eds) *Globalisation and the Asia-Pacific: Contested territories*, London: Routledge.

Koolhaas, R. (2000) 'La ville générique', in R. Koohlas (ed.) *Mutations*, Bordeaux: Centre d'Architecture Arc en Rève.

Lee, K.L. (1988) *The Singapore House 1819–1942*, Singapore: Times Editions.

Long, S. (1998) 'Cosmopolitan vs Heartlander', *Straits Times*, Singapore, 28 August.

Muchielli, A. (2002) *L'identité, Que sais-je?*, Paris: Presses Universitaires de France.

Murray, G. and Perera, A. (1995) *Singapore. The Global City State*, Folkestone: China Library.

Pieterse, J.N. (2004) *Globalization and Culture*, Lanham MD: Rowman and Littlefield Publishers.

Robinson, R. and Goodman, D.S.G. (eds) (1996) *The New Rich in Asia. Mobile Phones, McDonalds and Middle-Class Revolution*, London and New York: Routledge.

Warnier, J.-P. (1999) *La mondialisation de la culture*, Paris: Editions La Découverte.

Wong, T.C. and Guillot, X. (2004) *A Roof Over Every Head, Singapore's Housing Policies in the 21st Century: Between State Monopoly and Privatization*, Calcutta, New Delhi, London, Bangkok: Sampark.

Yeoh, B.S.A. (2004) 'Cosmopolitanism and its exclusion in Singapore', *Urban Studies*, 41(12) November: 2431–3445.

Chapter 4
Dissolved identity and disintegrated globalization

Steven Whitford

Progressive agendas

The issues of identity and globalization loom large in the general social discourse of the early twenty-first century. Conservative governments around the world embrace and extol the benefits of free trade and globalization for the major players in their economies, and the desirability of the pursuit and expression of individual identity is presented as sound collective wisdom with little critique. While both positions are generally presented as progressive, there are signs of discontent – ongoing demonstrations against the globalization of world trade; and concern from some about recent intolerant layers of collective identity, such as jingoistic nationalism or a faith of convenience – becoming increasingly prominent in cultural discussions.

An alternative position is discussed here, one where the ego associated with identity is 'dissolved', becoming an ego-free pre-identity (Deleuze 1998) and the power of global economics is 'disintegrated' by expanding its agenda to embrace the atmosphere (environment), the law and ideas of community (Singer 2002). Whether such a sensibility is evident in recent urban and architectural projects is then explored.

4.1
A *disintegrated* body squeezed under the existing rail line.

Dissolved subjects and disintegrated bodies

Dissolved subjects

Deleuze goes beyond merely agreeing that the meaning or the *subject* of any given object is brought to the object by those observing it, and is therefore multiple (Derrida 1976); he wants to dissolve the concept that there is an individual identity capable of constructing such meaning (Deleuze 1998). He argues that a more interesting position exists where the ego is dissolved and in doing so, will becomes a pre-ego, pre-individual, or pre-subjective identity. Deleuze argues that this condition, prior to the formation of an I, is full of potential – whereas the I or ego is potential acted out (Deleuze 1998). For cultural producers, including urban designers

4.2
The co-existence of *dissolved* subjects: ... and cafe and roof and floor and uninhabitable space and workstations and habitable space and....

and architects, this proposition suggests the question: what would the outcome be if this pre-ego/individual/ subjective identity full of potential was the focus of their design activity?

The scale and complexity of cities today are without precedent, and as a consequence Western cities have become the most highly regulated urban artefacts ever constructed. Most controls focus on the subjects of the city and deal with the articulation of such things as: circulation, land use, morphology, history, aesthetics, amenity and demographics. These are generally rationally identified and isolated, with particular strategies developed to control each.

Such particularization, however, stands in opposition to Deleuze's agenda for subjectivity and identity in the twenty-first century. Rather than particularizing the subjects of the city, his concepts suggest that we should dissolve these particulates to create a city responding to a pre-ego, pre-individual, pre-identity: an epigenetic soup full of potential. The questions for urban design in the light of such a challenge are: first, should such dissolution be pursued? Second, if so, how could it be achieved? And finally, how would it manifest itself?

Disintegrated bodies

Those nations with wealth and power have generally embraced the free-trade agreements that have contributed to the globalization of the world economy. These wealthy and powerful nations have been, however, less inclined to embrace the globalization of issues beyond their economies: for example, the atmosphere (making those who most pollute and exploit the atmosphere take the greatest responsibility); the law (ensuring that world best practice covering industrial relations, occupational health and safety, and human rights is globally applied to all areas of production); and community (redefining what is meant by words such as 'neighbourhood', 'district', 'region', 'nation', 'race', 'sexuality', 'gender') (Singer 2002). These arguments suggest that if globalization embraced these more difficult aspects of politics and culture, its economic hegemony would disintegrate.

It could be argued that the subjects of most Western cities are not dissolved; therefore, is the body of the city disintegrated? Disintegration is evident in the way in which free enterprise and individuality are directly expressed in the lack of cohesion or consistency of many urban forms, but are these urban conditions manifestations of a disintegrated body in Deleuze's terms?

This definition suggests, at best, a condition beyond integration, not to be confused with nostalgia for integration, a careless destruction of integration, nor a position of anti-integration – all three being often evident in Western cities. In such cities we seem either to freeze our integrated bodies out of respect (Paris, Berne,

Sienna, Venice); destroy any chance of integration by the unfettered embrace of market eclecticism (London, Sydney); or produce new cities that do not aspire to integration because to do so would be seen to contradict the rights of the ego and individual identity (Houston, Los Angeles).

Are any of these, then, disintegrated in Deleuzian terms? Are our cities full of potential, or are they manifestations of potential already acted out? A collection of egos, individuals and identities, all staking their claims on and in public space – the embodiment of investment capital and obsequious politics?

Approaching dissolution and disintegration?

Rem Koolhaas's description of New York's generic grid and the consequences of the Zoning Law of 1916 suggest a three-dimensional vision of the city as a highly integrated body full of potential. Within this integrated body, individual architects are free to explore the body's disintegration (Koolhaas 1978). However, due to the continual exceptions granted during development and, eventually, the elimination of these controls, New York as a disintegrated body in Deleuze's terms is yet to be realized.

Similarly, Koolhaas's City of the Captive Globe[1] project (Koolhaas,1978) adopts the generic Manhattan grid and also a three-dimensional proposition full of potential: every city block – even those containing parks – presents a bounded volume the height of which approximates the width of the adjacent main streets and avenues of the city. These volumes form a full-block podium aimed at achieving a Parisian spatial syntax at street level. Atop these podia sit a series of towers free to express the individuality or egos of their designers or owners.

It is unclear, and for our purposes unimportant, what other urban design guidelines may have been required to ensure a high urban amenity at street level among these towers. What is important is that via a series of clear and contradistinctive guidelines, an integrated three-dimensional plane of potential emerges from which various levels of disintegration can be achieved.

An architecture of becoming

While at an urban scale examples of dissolved subjects and disintegrated bodies are difficult to find, there are individual architectural projects that are beginning to investigate these issues. One such project is Koolhaas's first completed building in the USA, the McCormick Tribune Campus Center at the Illinois Institute of Technology (IIT) in Chicago.

The *form* of this project appears to have emerged from a series of forces rather than an exercise in orthodox composition. It is not the easy and nostalgic imposition of a highly regarded history, despite its location on the IIT campus, literally abutting Mies van der Rohe's Commons Building.

The form seems concerned about, and responsive to, a number of issues simultaneously, and without hierarchy. *Building economically* – the original formal gesture is a minimal rectangular shed or body. *Existing circulation systems* – student paths from the academic area to their colleges are the first extraction from this body. *The existing elevated rail line* – the body is simply squeezed under the existing rail infrastructure and in doing so is in the state of becoming a simple butterfly roof. *The historic fragment* – Mies's Commons Building is respected but not fetishized, given some space by the formation of a courtyard derived from the pathways and the removal of some of the body. *An economy of means* – the body is clad in a single-storey curtain wall infilled with clear and orange glass and a solid non-specific material given an almost animal-like camouflage in paint. *The overtly pragmatic accommodation of programme* – on the north side where the loading bay is located, the roof of the body has been simply cut and awkwardly lifted to ensure sufficient height for truck access to the loading bay.

All these subjects are embraced by a design sensibility of inclusion, resulting in an abstraction of the concept 'and' (Rajchman 1998) in design by the coexistence and eventual dissolution of subjects. This is not the accretion of highly articulated subjects of the constructivists or Koolhaas's earlier work (Koolhaas 1978). The subjects of the building are not particularized and expressed as elements but reveal a layered coexistence, with one subject often working against the agenda of another, compromising the result of each but in doing so gaining something beyond a clear and well-articulated orthodox formal resolution.

As a result of the initial design decision to maintain the existing external pedestrian routes through the building, the internal *space* lacks the hierarchy often associated with buildings of this scale. There seem to be a number of equally weighted internal circulation systems and main entrances and exits. In addition, the juxtaposition of programmes is refreshing, with cafe, bookshops, computer workstation areas, games space and the like smoothly connected visually, spatially, conceptually and (more importantly) in a number of directions simultaneously.

There are folded floors that form an amphitheatre-like space connecting the ground floor to the lower ground floor; a roof garden space at ground floor level; a roof that splits and drops, producing uninhabitable spaces before almost touching the ground floor surface; a space for computer use like a bloody incision half a level below the ground floor; and the ever present underbelly of the soundproof wrap around the existing elevated rail system. All suggest that the striated subjects usually associated with the making of architectural space – defined floor levels, spaces for the served and servant, rational clear circulation, and gradients of privacy – are understood, questioned and finally found to be irrelevant to this architecture. This is a smooth space where there is a sense that for this generation of students, work, rest and play are no longer separate activities (or subjects) that require specific, individual and identifiable spaces, but can and will occur anywhere, anytime, anyway. The boundaries between them have been both psychologically and physically dissolved.

The sense of *order* within and without the building would best be described as 'heterotopic' (Porphyrios 1982), where a multiplicity of ideal formal, spatial, structural and fabric systems co-exist. The first such system is the structural, for the elevated light rail; the second, an economic structural grid for the initial body. The third is an economical repeating glazing system for the curtain wall; the fourth, a seamless yet similarly economical ceiling system of stopped waterproof plasterboard left unpainted. Finally, there is the rational framing system for semi-translucent walling. The result: a contingent order, within which a series of systems co-exist equally in space-time.

All these decisions have an affect on *aesthetics* and it is here that Koolhaas extends his pursuit of dissolution – this time the particular subject of the beautiful. According to Lyotard, beauty results in pleasure for those in power, while the sublime results in both pleasure and pain, or specifically pleasure induced by pain (Lyotard 1984). The sublime is not, then, by definition, the particularization of beauty and its opposite the painfully unsightly, but the dissolving of both to become one.

As is elegantly argued by Graafland (2000), Koolhaas explores the sublime, rather than the beautiful. In this project, the ceiling is not painted; gaps between curtain wall and ceiling reveal insulation and air-handling ducts;[2] the painted pattern on the exterior is thin and two-dimensional. Would the exterior surface have been more beautiful if it had been three-dimensional, throwing shadow on the expanses of material and modulating the thinness? Possibly, but it would also have been more expensive. Such decisions exemplify an approach that avoids fetish in both the major and minor elements of the body of the building. All this is achieved with an apparent economy of means that avoids elements that might distract from the overall coexistence of formal and spatial achievements.

The work achieves a resolution beyond notions of good taste, good building, good detailing and achieves a position beyond the highly crafted and beautiful, inhabiting a place that 'puts forward the ... (concept of the) ... unpresentable in the presentation itself; that which denies itself the solace of good forms, the consensus of good taste [that] makes it possible to share the nostalgia for the unattainable' and has become 'that which searches for new presentations not to enjoy ... but in order to impart a stronger sense of the un-representable' (Lyotard, 1984: 84).

Neither indulgent nor beautiful, this building is not just pleasurable but simultaneously pleasurable and painful. More importantly, pleasure is gained from the most painful elements: the unfinished, the incomplete, the never being, the always becoming pieces, revealing a relaxed and robust body full of potential, so appropriate for a building at the service of students.

Conclusion

Deleuze and Singer have challenged cultural producers of the twenty-first century, including those producing the urban project. They demand that their concepts become tools to be used during the design process to produce projects that destroy the unethical aspects of the world; dissolve subjects of particularization and difference based on a datum of the same; disintegrate bodies of inequity, oppression, and isolation; shift the emphasis of politics from the powerful to the not powerful; and finally stutter grammar, not just speech.

Some individual architectural projects are responding to their challenge. We await projects at the scale of the city.

Notes

1 A project presented in the appendix of Koolhaas's book *Delirious New York*, which presents a integrated urbanism of grid, podium and tower disintegrated by an ego-driven market and consequent architecture of individualism – all focused on a sunken and therefore captive globe of the Earth. The globe, visible for all to see, grows in proportion to the amount of feverish thinking taking place in the towers. While this is an excellent example of the potential of a city of disintegration, the extent to which this project is a good example of dissolved subjects is less clear. At first glance it appears that each tower is a simple expression of a particular theme (modernism, surrealism, constructivism, etc.) and therefore does not present as dissolved subjects but rather as a highly particularized series of past subjects made manifest in the city.
2 Services in this project are generally concealed, which is perhaps inconsistent with the concept of dissolving the subjects of architecture. They might rather be in suspension, not made invisible.

Bibliography

Deleuze, G. (1998) *Essays Critical and Clinical*, trans. D.W. Smith and M.A. Greco, London: Verso.
Delueze, G., and Guattari, F. (1987) *A Thousand Plateaus: Capitalism and Schizophrenia*, trans. B. Massumi, Minneapolis: University of Minnesota Press.
Derrida, J. (1976) *Of Grammatology*, trans. Gayatri Chakravorty Spivak, Baltimore: John Hopkins University Press.
Graafland, A. (2000) *The Socius of Architecture*, Rotterdam: 010 Publishers.
Klein, N. (2001) *No Space, No Choice, No Jobs, No Logo*, London: Flamingo.

Koolhaas, R. (1978) *Delirious New York: a Retroactive Manifesto for Manhattan*, New York: Oxford University Press.

Lyotard, J-F. (1984) 'Answering the question: What is postmodernism', in *The Post Modern Condition: a Report on Knowledge*, trans. G. Bennington and B. Massumi, Minneapolis: Minnesota University Press.

Porphyrios, D. (1982) *Sources of Modern Eclecticism: Studies on Alvar Aalto*, London: Academy Editions.

Rajchman, J. (1998) *Constructions*, Cambridge, MA: MIT.

Singer, P. (2002) *One World: the Ethics of Globalisation*, Melbourne: Text Publishing Company.

Wines, J. (1989) 'The slippery floor', in A. Papadakis, C. Cooke and A. Benjamin (eds) *Deconstruction: Omnibus Volume*, London: Academy Editions

Chapter 5
The communal project and the reinforcement of values

Emmanuel Amougou Mballa

As societies become progressively more complex, the transmission of common values becomes increasingly important and the role of the urban project in the transmission process is called into question. For Jean-Pierre Boutinet (1990), for example, the project is necessary in communicating 'the situations of daily life'. More particularly, in discussing spatial planning or 'the project of building', Boutinet actually argues for the 'obligation of the project', not just to realize a practical programme of use but to reveal values. The project is a medium which represents the developer, the project team and other stakeholders. In short, any project, despite general conceptions to the contrary, manifests not only on its functional, creative and artistic dimensions. The project expresses the situational forces that mould it, and it is at the same time a determinant in the broader culture.

Considering the situational forces and determining conditions that influence and even make the basis of a project, as well as the role of the resulting project as an informer of culture, Boutinet (1990) focuses on the inherent cultural dimension. This cultural dimension, especially in the complex processes of heritage conservation that accompany contemporary urban projects, takes different forms according to the situation (Amougou 2004). Depending on the nature of work in each situation, the project reveals itself as a space of cultural expression, mobilizing many stakeholders and interested parties based on, (Boutinet would say) their respective capacities to access capital. Thus, the way a project values the historic or contemporary, the monumental or banal, the public or private, the conservation practices of the state (Amougou 2001), the development sector, the community or individuals, reveals the relative power of each and its position in the complex web of contemporary social relationships. Their very engagement in the urban project constitutes it as a space of contemporary cultural expression. From this position, therefore, it seems the relevant question for each of the many parties and factions involved is: to which 'culture', implicitly or explicitly, does it belong? Or which does it represent? In other words, if we see projects as spaces that express a whole range of practices and representations, inevitably they are also spaces of confrontation and competition that communicate values and culture. If this is so, how is it possible to speak about the values manifest as the material form of a project without revealing the relative hierarchy of those values?

Failing to rigorously question the contribution that various parties and their values bring to the process and outcomes of the project condemns cultural discourse to the anecdotal and denies its fundamental nature. The cultural dimension is unavoidable, particularly in understanding the strategies used by proponents to legitimate their positions and the elements of physical form that they choose to symbolize their contribution to, or role in, the outcome. In fact, it could be argued that representative cultural elements are often selected to justify the project in part or whole, and survive or are lost during the delivery process, according to the strength of the proponent in the inevitable battle of wills or consensus among the group. Such elements become instruments of legitimization, revealing the role of the proposing party.

Endowed then with their respective cultural capital, these elements transpose the values that underpin them, whether as veiled evocations of the culture of the 'Other' (Augé 1987) or as more explicit and overt messages of cultural belonging. In some projects, particularly those focusing on questions of heritage, urban designers and other actors refer to an array of cultures, for example: 'urban culture', 'country or rural culture', 'national culture', 'local culture' and 'ethnic culture'. Then, when specific cultures cannot be defined, particular social developments might simply be referred to in relation to the generic culture of the 'global' or of 'modernity'.

For many urban designers, architects, planners and landscape architects, the integration of the cultural dimension in the development process remains based on some widely accepted, often outdated presumptions about professional position, independent of their relative position in the universe of project production – even if these are no longer universally accepted. Such presumptions include: the autonomy (or increasingly, otherwise) of the architect (Montlibert 1995); the dominance of social and cultural function; the need to create space abstractly before building; and the necessity to locate new or historic objects in a coherent cultural context. Essential for those professional disciplines that are active in the production of urban projects now, however, is an understanding of the way that cultural heritage is valued by the many players involved in the process and how it is ultimately expressed and made manifest. This is increasingly the case, not only in urban projects that explicitly value cultural heritage but in all projects, given their role as spaces of cultural expression.

With the wide circulation of ideas and practices (Bourdieu 2002) and the application of international standards at the local level as a result of globalization, many international institutions are becoming involved in issues of local cultural heritage and the negotiations in urban projects that value and express it. The way projects manifest heritage values can therefore be expected to change, as cultural references will reflect different players and the differing dynamics of their interaction during the delivery process. Under these conditions, the institutionalization of heritage conservation at a local level, as a process that mobilizes different professional disciplines and many stakeholder parties, will necessarily be the subject for investigation to increase our understanding of the phenomenon of globalization and how it impacts on our cities.

This position, and its implications for the production of knowledge, will undoubtedly affect many aspects of the urban project and the process of its production along with spatial knowledge more broadly. How do projects happen? How are they conceived and understood? Ultimately, what do they mean? Such questions and their answers underpin the theory of urban practice, bringing it to the level of the urban project. They will also integrate the knowledge of the many contributing disciplines and the way, in turn, that they are understood in the urban domain.

Bibliography

Amougou, E. (2001) *La réhabilitation du patrimoine architectural. Une analyse sociologique de la domination des notables*, Paris: Éditions L'Harmattan, Collection 'Logiques Sociales'.

—— (2004) (Sous la direction de), *La question patrimoniale. De la 'patrimonialisation' à l'examen des situations concrètes*, Paris: Éditions L'Harmattan.

Augé, M. (1987) 'Qui est l'Autre? Un itinéraire anthropologique', *L'Homme, Revue Française d'Anthropologie,* École des Hautes Études en Sciences Sociales, No. 1003, July–September: 7–26.

Bourdieu, P. (2002) 'Les conditions sociales de la circulation internationale des idées', *Actes de la Recherche en Sciences Sociales*, No. 145, December.

Boutinet, J.-P. (1990) *Anthropologie du projet*, Paris: Éditions PUF, Collection 'Psychologie d'Aujourd'hui'.

Montlibert, C. de (1995), *L'impossible autonomie de l'architecte. Sociologie de la production architecturale*, Strasbourg: Presses Universitaires de Strasbourg et Maison des Sciences de l'Homme.

Chapter 6
Urban development and context
The traditional landscape and globalization in Marrakech

Jean-Noël Tournier

Introduction

The evolution of the urban landscape of Marrakech, the principal city of the south of Morocco, is comparable with many other examples of urban change in the contemporary world. It is, however, emblematic for several reasons, including the clear distinction between its different eras of development and the successive institutional and physical structures that have led to the city of today.

First era (eleventh–nineteenth century): surviving in an inhospitable environment

Marrakech is extremely unusual for a city of its size and importance since it has no river and its rainfall alone, at around 240 mm per year, cannot ensure sufficient water for the city and its agricultural areas.

When the city was founded in 1070 by the Berber dynasty of the Almoravides, water was supplied by a system of 'reverse drainage' based on a gigantic underground network of *khettaras*.[1] These underground galleries collect subsoil waters, fed in summer by the snow melt in the High Atlas Mountains and by draining the surface layers of the soil. These galleries, whose slope is slightly lower than that of the soil, collected water and conveyed it for several kilometres towards the surface, where they emerged in the form of artificial springs called *aïn*. From there, the water was stored in

6.1
The golden rampart of Agdal, the Palmeraie and the snow-clad Atlas mountains.

large reservoirs and used for people, cattle and for the irrigation of the food production areas by gravitational flow through a network of open ditches called *séguias*.[2]

This brief outline describes a very complex system that is, to a great extent, responsible for the social and spatial structure of the city.[3] As water is so precious, its control is a central tool of power, and a monopoly. In Marrakech, most of the collected water first fed the gardens of the Sultan,[4] the Agdal (in the south) and the Menara (in the west),[5] before being distributed towards the city and the surrounding productive gardens.

To the north, outside the ramparts and spread over several thousands of hectares, is a vast agro-pastoral space, or system of productive gardens, with the largest known *palmeraie*, or plantation specializing in palms, north of the Atlas Mountains. This space, protected from the sun by the canopy of the palms, is used for stock breeding and farming, and allows optimal use of the territory, in spite of the constraints imposed by the soil and climate. After the city ramparts, the Palmeraie of Marrakech is the second symbol of the city and one of its essential components – and created the luxurious green setting that so impressed many travellers to Marrakech.

Surrounded by the productive gardens and nestled behind its terracotta wall, the medina offered a protected environment to a population of approximately 70,000 inhabitants by the beginning of the twentieth century. The minaret of Koutoubia, the highest structure in the city and its emblematic religious symbol,[6] dominated the major public space, the Jemma-el-fna.[7] This traditional space simultaneously performed the functions of a parade ground, a commercial crossroads and a meeting place for all the cultures of Africa, situated between the sites of power and the popular city. Since the founding of the city, it has acted as the city's cultural and social centre.

Second era (1912–1956): the Protectorate

The Protectorate treaty was signed between the Sultan and France in 1912, and independence announced in 1956. The Protectorate was a particular form of colonization in which the two countries theoretically exerted power with parity. More than colonizing

6.2
An old inlet to the Khetarra network.

6.3
A more recent view of the Agdal and Palmeraie, with the Atlas Mountains in the background, here showing recent development.

through settlement or annexation, it aimed at development through French investments and bipartite economic relations.

Rather than political and military developments, the changes to the urban development are the focus here. When he arrived in Morocco, Hubert Lyautey (1854–1934, French soldier, town planner, humanist) found it had fallen prey to outside investors who were buying land and building without concern for the layout of the city, and without regulation. To remedy this, he established a department of town planning directed by Henri Prost,[8] giving it two principal instructions that illustrate his intentions as urban developer and the meaning he assigned to the term 'Protectorate'. First, respect and safeguard the artistic, religious and social integrity of the Moroccan culture and its cities; and second, create new cities that use the rules of the most modern town planning.

From 1917, at the request of Lyautey and on the advice of Jean-Claude Forestier,[9] Prost's team of town planners, architects, landscape designers, lawyers and engineers established and applied rules of protection to the cultural heritage contemporary with those of the French legislation.[10] Morocco's new cities[11] were created outside the old centres, generally on the least fertile, un-irrigated land and directly connected to the neighbouring medina by roads and avenues, simultaneously separate and yet belonging. The strongly regulated and authoritarian process of urban development manifested the power of both the social and urban ideologies.

Urban design was accompanied by a new architecture that was inspired by, but neither copied nor plagiarized, the forms and materials of the old cities. This new architecture, labelled 'neo-Moorish' and sometimes 'orientalist', influenced the Art Deco movement and though 'modern', is integrated through its colours and silhouettes. It achieved a continuity of form and ensured adaptation to local climatic conditions.

In the same way, rather than importing European models, the gardens of the new cities were inspired by traditional gardens, continuing their principles in perpetuity. They used local vegetables, little water and different layers of vegetation to protect from the sun. The neo-Moorish school initiated by Forester also influenced the art of garden design in the interwar years.

In Marrakech, the new city of Gueliz[12] was established to the north-west between the hill and the medina, on the least fertile lands,[13] preserving the southern pastures and the *palmeraie* to the north and the west. The master plan organized in the form of a star symbolically connected the new district to the existing city. The broad south-western triangle, between the two gardens of the Menara and the Agdal, was left open towards the Atlas, maintaining a panorama that is the common heritage of the Marrakchis, a symbol of the city's territorial roots.

The architecture of Gueliz follows the regulations decreed by

Prost with relatively low, simple buildings of a neo-Moorish style and of the same ochre colour as the medina and its ramparts, irrespective of materials. During this period the medina changed little with the few modern buildings inside the ramparts built mainly in open areas near the Jemma-el-fna.

Following Forestier's recommendations[14] the *palmeraie* and gardens were strictly protected using regulations theoretically still in force today, and housing estates were prohibited in both areas.

In 1925, however, Lyautey was recalled to France (probably because his activities were not considered sufficiently colonial) and through the 1930s the Protectorate evolved into a more traditional form of colony, marking the beginning of the Moroccan independence movements. The power of the urban principles his team established were gradually eroded until independence in 1956.

From independence to today: the urban crisis

After independence, the erosion of power, development control and management across urban areas accelerated. The country also experienced a population explosion, the result of the improved living conditions during the twentieth century and accelerated migration from rural areas following desertification and a consequent agricultural crisis in the country's south.

These led to rapid urban growth (the population of Marrakech more than tripled in 50 years, from 100,000 in 1921, to 330,000 by 1971), an often anarchistic consumption of open space and the beginnings of resource depletion. Outside the ramparts, new districts were created at the foot of the walls south-east of the city, on spaces that had been under the Protectorate, and so previously unavailable for development. Especially in the medina the uncontrolled development of open space consumed much of the Arsats, the traditional inner gardens.[15]

Further, the water resources of the *khettaras* were exhausted in the 1970s – a result of the drying climate, and public drilling for water to access the lowering levels of the water table fed by melting snow from the Atlas Mountains – which disconnected the traditional community-based system of controlling irrigation from its management.

In spite of this, the emblematic areas of the city, the *Palmeraie* and the panorama of the Atlas, resisted the pressure for urban development, protected by their traditional uses.

By 2005, Marrakech had approached one million inhabitants (from 750,000 in 1994). The urban crisis had not been solved, with the depletion of water a now familiar pattern. More and more housing meant there was never sufficient water and in addition, over recent years, the successful promotion of Marrakech as a tourist destination has imposed a new type of pressure.

The emergence of mass tourism and the popularity of the city among well-to-do foreigners have led the local authorities to develop infrastructure that is often out of scale with the vulnerable environment and cultural heritage of the urban area. For instance, to give the city a modern image, public spaces are now being developed using 'global' garden standards and forms with large lawns and European-style flowering plants that need irrigation, abandoning Forester's recommendations to Lyautey.[16] Further, to support tourist activities, numerous golf courses have been developed, or are under development, in the surroundings of the city which increase groundwater pumping and contribute to unsustainable consumption of the limited water resources.[17]

Recently, privatization of the *Palmeraie* has begun, with detached houses and enclosed residential estates, piece by piece, consuming this emblematic traditional landscape. This privatization of the communal space that supported the farming population has increased their impoverishment and social isolation. The disappearance of the *Douars*[18] has accelerated desertion caused by farming populations, increased rural migration and, perversely in its turn, increased the demand of land for residential development.

The panorama of the Atlas Mountains to the south-east, reliant on an area now abandoned by pastoral practices, is in the course of urbanization for housing estates and tourist facilities. Importantly, this new district for tourists and for affluent inhabitants will in the long term occupy a surface equivalent to that of the whole medina, cut its visual links to the mountains and, for the first time since the eleventh century, the walls of the Agdal.

At the same time, many houses of the old city have been bought by foreigners and transformed into second residences or guesthouses. While such acquisitions often enable their preservation and the rehabilitation of cultural heritage, they result in increased land values, forcing many original inhabitants, shopkeepers or artisans, to move to peripheral districts.

The Jemma-el-fna is also affected. This traditional space of cultural exchange, for this reason classified by Unesco, has become progressively occupied by tourist businesses and places to eat, limiting space for traditional uses which are, in turn, reduced to a spectacle.

These observations reflect the dichotomy that results from a central power responsible for protecting cultural heritage, landscapes and social urban policy, working with local economic interests who are implicated in development projects for short-term profits, based on a global liberal ideology. If it continues, this process risks, in the short or medium term, the destruction of the very value of Marrakech today – its cultural heritage, landscapes, gardens, way of life – reducing its appeal to those very investors and tourists who rush there today.

Conclusion

Marrakech has known centuries of traditional economic management, the result of the strength of the power structures, and intimate knowledge of the milieu. This combination allowed the city to survive through time in an unfavourable environment. The period of the Protectorate installed an ambitious and idealistic regime that effectively and strictly regulated conservation and development, oriented towards a sustainable outcome, traces of which are still present.

Today, Marrakech is involved in a process of globally driven standardization manifest as urbanization (or suburbanization) that is destroying its unique resources. This process is short term, based on short-term considerations, and uncontrolled by a sustainable vision or methods of control. This is not an isolated case and it reflects the situation in many cities and urban territories that are environmentally and socially fragile, but, because of their uniqueness, experience pressure from tourism and urban development driven by demographic changes in the broader environment.

Notes

1 During the Protectorate, early in the nineteenth century, a census of the network of *khetarras* identified 900 km, probably much less than originally built, since by then much of the network no longer existed or had escaped mapping.
2 This hydrological system was apparently imported from Asia Minor where it had been known since antiquity. Older *khettara* networks (some still functioning) are also found in predesert areas in the south of the High Atlas. During their conquests in the Middle Ages, the *Almohades* and *Almoravides* contributed to the diffusion of this technology even to parts of Europe.
3 If the system is complex technically, it is even more so in its management. *Khettaras* were created by private investors or by collectives (tribes or the ancient equivalent of trade unions or co-operatives); the rights of water were then sold to end-users or divided between the investor–managers, the whole being controlled by the Sultan or the power in office. The management of water rights was frequently at the origin of conflicts and wars between tribes.
4 The term 'garden' here means orchards and kitchen or market gardens feeding the population and producing for the market. Gardens were also organized according to aesthetic rules and had important religious and social roles as festival spaces. Water was displayed by a complex system of channels and fountains before they were used for irrigation, and in gardens such as the Generalife in Grenada.
5 The Agdal (500 ha) and the Menara (10 ha) are the two biggest gardens in Marrakech. Created at the time of the foundation of the city in the eleventh century, they remain royal property and are planted with citrus and olives with large central water reservoirs. They have hardly changed since their creation.
6 The Koutoubia is the principal mosque of Marrakech, and its minaret, at 77 m, was built in 1158 and used as the model for the Giralda of Seville.
7 The Jemma-el-fna has been classified by Unesco as 'a masterpiece of

the oral and intangible heritage of humanity', the organization's first recognition of the concept of the 'oral heritage site'.
8   Henri Prost (1874–1959) architect, town planner and winner of the Rome Prize 1902. Worked on the design of the new towns of Morocco, Algeria (1932–1939), Istanbul (1936–1951) and in the Paris region. In Marrakech, he was the architect of the hotel La Mamounia and an initiator of the new urbanism of the *Société Française des Urbanistes* (SFU).
9   Jean-Claude Nicolas Forestier (1861–1930). Landscape architect, town planner, technician, forest engineer. With Prost, one of the founders of the movement of new urban thinking and transformation in the early twentieth century. He worked in Hausmann's Paris and on the transformation and design of numerous cities in Morocco, Spain, Cuba and Argentina.
10 The Dahir (Moroccan law) of 1914 (derived from the French law on historic monuments of 1913) still regulates the protection of the architectural and cultural heritage. The Dahir of 1929 protected sites and landscapes and was adapted for France in 1930.
11 New towns include Casablanca and the imperial towns, Rabat, Fes, Meknes and Marrakech.
12 The hill of Gueliz is the only high land near the city, reserved for strategic military reasons by the French.
13 'Thanks to what was immediately and prudently made by the military authorities ... we will find on the old terrains of Maghzen the planned layout of a future city ... only using lands without vegetation and closely connecting the Gueliz, the Koutoubia with the existing gardens' (trans.) J.C.N. Forestier, extract from: 'Report on the reserves to be constituted in the environments of the capital cities of Morocco', 1913.
14 'It is an unexpected pleasure to approach the city by the long crossing of a green palm grove... it would be really annoying that land speculations and private housing estates could compromise this ensemble...' (trad. IA), (trans.) J.C.N. Forestier, extract from: 'Report on the reserves to be constituted in the environments of the capital cities of Morocco', 1913.
15 Traditional gardens inside the ramparts – generally for communal use, they form an important place for walks and meeting points in the social life of the medina. Many were destroyed, one exception being the Arsat Moulay Abdessalam, laid out as a park under Lyautey, and the gardens of the Mamounia, privatized by the establishment of the hotel.
16 'this arrangement appears the most logical and the most adapted to the conditions of these climates ... It would be very useful to respect as much as possible the old layouts of the gardens ... and for this reason to know, at least in its principles the system of watering which even justifies its existence.' And later, '...we have the occasion to see the gardening attempts made by the Europeans ... one is painfully surprised by the sight of the vegetation, which seems difficult, and by the arrangement, which seem to be out of place, we have a feeling of embarrassment.' (trad. IA) (trans.) J.C.N. Forestier, extract from: 'Report on the reserves to be constituted in the environments of the capital cities of Morocco', 1913.
17 Estimates put water consumption of a golf course here at around 1,000,000 m^3 per annum. In Marrakech there are three golf clubs and two under development, consuming ultimately approximately 5,000,000 m^3 per annum, for a relatively small number of users. Tourist water consumption ranges from 500 to 800 litres per person per day; there are an estimated listed four million overnight tourist stays annually in Marrakech, making a total of 3,000,000 m^3 per annum. Together,

the 8,000,000 m³ attributed to tourism alone, represents, on the basis of 10 m³ per person, per annum, the yearly consumption of approximately 800,000 inhabitants, almost the total population today or eight times that of 1920.

18 *Douar* indicates a traditional agricultural village. These were numerous in the *palmeraie*, with a population that supplied the city with fresh produce and collectively management and maintained it.

Bibliography

Abouessalam, Sabah (1992) *Pauvreté urbaine et comportements résidentiels à Marrakech*, Thèse de doctorat de géographie, Université de Paris I, unpublished.

Ahnouni, Abdelmajid (2000) *Aménagements hydro-agricoles et mutations socio-économiques et spatiales dans une région semi-aride du Maroc (le Haouz oriental)*, Thèse de doctorat de Géographie, Université de Rouen, unpublished.

Derdari-Lahna, Noura (2000) *L'eau et la ville: le cas de Marrakech*, Thèse de doctorat de Poitiers, Université de Rouen, unpublished, Atelier national de reproduction des thèses, 2003.

Deverdun, Gaston (1966) *Marrakech des origines à 1912...*, Editions techniques nord-africaine, (Thèse de 1912).

Douioui (1997) *Une ville du Maghreb au temps de l'ocuupation français: Marrakech (1912–1945)*, Thèse de doctorat d'histoire, Université de Nice, 2 volumes, unpublished.

Elamri, Jamila (1996) *Marrakech, ville touristique*, Thèse de doctorat de Lettres, Université d'Aix-en-Provence, unpublished. Atelier national de reproduction des thèses, 1998.

El-Faiz, Mohamed (2000) *Jardins de Marrakech*, Arles: Actes Sud.

—— (2002) *Marrakech. Patrimoine en péril*, Arles: Actes Sud.

—— (2005) *Les maîtres de l'eau. Histoire de l'hydraulique arabe*, Arles: Actes Sud.

Pascon, Paul (1977) *Le Haouz de Marrakech, histoire sociale et structures agraires*, Thèse pour le doctorat d'Etat en sociologie, Université de Tanger, unpublished.

—— (1983) *Le Haouz de Marrakech*, Paris: L'Harmattan.

Rossano, Jean (1954) 'La Colonisation européenne dans le Haouz de Marrakech', *Les Cahiers d'Outre-Mer*, 28 (10–12): 342–366.

Sebti Mohamed, (1984) *Les Douars de Marrakech: étude de quartiers péri-urbains*, Thèse de doctorat de géographie, Université de Tours, 3 vol, unpublished.

Tebbaa, Ouidad and El-Faiz, Mohamed (2004) *La place Jemâa-el-Fna, Marrakech*, Casablanca: Edité par Georges Naef/La croisée des chemins, collection Evasion.

Wilbaux, Quentin (2002) *La médina de Marrakech. Formation des espaces urbains d'une ancienne capitale du Maroc*, Paris: l'Harmattan.

Chapter 7
The urban edge
Bangkok *soi* as mediators of the global and local

Koen De Wandeler

Introduction

This chapter suggests that cities, rather than being reified, be viewed as a common realm of people's lived experiences, an expression of the collective unconscious, constantly adjusting to new experiences. Cities are part of everyday reality when they are imagined, remodelled, remembered – in short, when experienced and 'dwelt' in. The city is a context of real places where local time-space is produced.

Bangkok *soi* are such places. The word *'soi'* here denotes the small side streets that branch off a main road (*thanon*). Between the 1950s and 1980s, the development of this type of side street characterized urban expansion in Bangkok. Situated at the edge of the rural–urban interface, *soi* neighbourhoods became real places where the process of locality building and its material outcomes was most intense and could be best understood.

Inconspicuous side streets?

Soi typically run in parallel to each other, are less than 6 metres wide and lack sidewalks. The majority in Bangkok are cul-de-sacs and vary from a few dozen metres long to several kilometres, or branch out into a network of sub-*soi*.[1] *Soi* rarely connect to each other or to secondary or main roads and public transport is available only in *soi* that are either exceptionally deep, densely populated or connected to multiple *thanon*.

Since they do not function as 'distributor roads', they hardly contribute to an integrated road network or transportation system[2] for the city as a whole. With little in the way of comprehensive master planning or planning controls, the planning and construction of Bangkok's secondary road network was in effect given over to the private sector and property developers who made the most of land fronting *thanon*. This led to 'strip' development, often over considerable distances with *soi* emerging as the means to develop parcels beyond the road frontage.

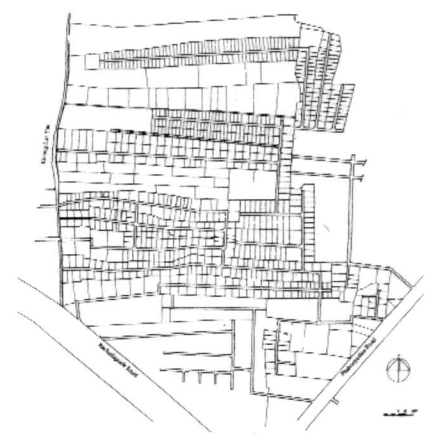

7.1
Land Holdings in Ban Soi Sukhon in 1955.

7.2
Land Holdings in Ban Soi Sukhon in 1970.

Vectors of lateral expansion

Once *soi* created the new frontiers, land-use conversion and construction activities could extend beyond the main road.[3] But without public transportation, areas beyond walking distance of main roads might remain virtually undeveloped for years, a hinterland spared from major construction but available to low-income households (Yap 1993: 154).

As most *soi* lead to vacant land, their natural condition was in sharp contrast with the bustling activity of *thanon*, and their relative isolation prompted Cohen (1985:19) to describe them as 'semi-autonomous ecological sub-systems'. He argued that they were important conduits of urban expansion channelling a 'penetration of metropolitan forces' and that progressively a *soi*'s physical appearance changed, eroding its semi-autonomous ecology and altering its social composition. Within the last decade, many *soi*, in particular where Cohen had conducted his fieldwork, evolved as he had predicted, despite his projections being too speculative to be generalized.

The study of Soi Sukhon in the northern expansion area of Bangkok illustrates that *soi* remain relatively secluded points of anchorage in the bustling city life of many Bangkokians. Residents return to that relative seclusion, not only to sleep and recover energies for the next day, but also because it is where their homes, schools and 'street-corner' shops are located, where they play with their children, gossip with their neighbours, pursue their crafts and ply their trade.

7.3
Hawkers deeper in the *soi* announce their approach to fixed stops by calling out or producing a typical sound signal.

A concatenation of places

Soi Sukhon branches off Phahonyothin Road and penetrates deep into an interstitial area, or 'super-block', girded by four major roads. From its single entryway (*pak soi*), it branches into 12 numbered sub-*soi* with a 6-metre-wide concrete road surface without sidewalks. Some sub-*soi* provide shortcuts to the surrounding *thanon*. The neighbourhood here is known as Ban Soi Sukhon.

Except for a few large tracts of fallow land towards the end of dead-end sub-*soi* (*sut soi*), land is subdivided into parcels of 400 square metres maximum. Some – particularly towards the deeper end – have been demarcated but remain vacant. Most parcels have been fenced off and built upon for residential purposes, Ban Soi Sukhon is housing at least 600 households.[4]

Besides a well-known technical college and a primary school, Ban Soi Sukhon has a few inconspicuous sites of home industry and a dozen or more local shops, its first stretches being lined with shop-houses. Deeper in, the buildings are less dense and more diverse with a lot more greenery and a variety of price ranges. Terrace houses are concentrated in two small housing estates (*mubanjatsan*) with several clusters of 'town-houses'. A few low-rise apartment blocks have also been built since 1995.

There is no clear segregation between households from the many and varied ethnic or regional origins, educational and employment backgrounds or social or economic levels. And yet inhabitants of the shop-houses distinguish themselves from the rest of the population and vice versa. Residents in the first stretches of *soi* (*ton soi*) consider themselves more fortunate because they have easier access to the main road. Those living deeper in consider their relative isolation enviable because it protects them from traffic, noise and dust.

Organized community life is all but absent with shop-house residents and inhabitants of recent apartment buildings keeping to themselves and other households living in carefully fenced compounds. People may have been living there for several years and yet remain unknown to all but a few neighbours and shopkeepers with social interaction among residents limited to petty neighbourly services, encounters at the local grocery store or barbershop and exchanges at street-corner food stalls. The number and distribution of such locations are limited and have remained practically unchanged throughout my fieldwork period.

7.4
Most shop-houses in the first stretches of the *soi* serve the practical daily needs of the residents further down the *soi*.

7.5
A line-up of motorcycle-taxi drivers is a familiar sight at the entrance and the important junctions of every densely populated *soi*.

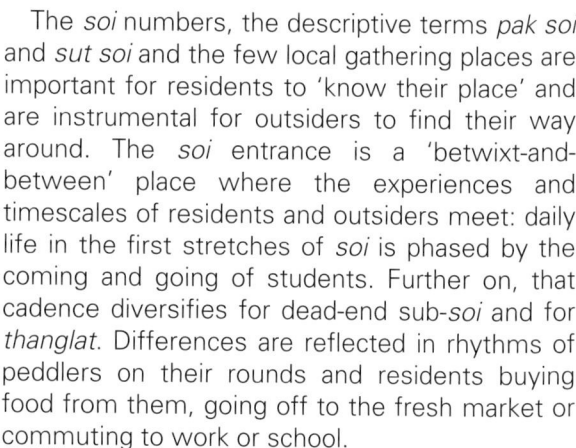

The *soi* numbers, the descriptive terms *pak soi* and *sut soi* and the few local gathering places are important for residents to 'know their place' and are instrumental for outsiders to find their way around. The *soi* entrance is a 'betwixt-and-between' place where the experiences and timescales of residents and outsiders meet: daily life in the first stretches of *soi* is phased by the coming and going of students. Further on, that cadence diversifies for dead-end sub-*soi* and for *thanglat*. Differences are reflected in rhythms of peddlers on their rounds and residents buying food from them, going off to the fresh market or commuting to work or school.

Such comings and goings make the *soi* a concatenation of 'practised' places, where the pathways of residents and outsiders intersect, slow down and daily routines are played out. Such practices of place materialize local time-space in a way impossible in the hurried reality outside. Such a myriad of trajectories do not set the *soi* apart from the city,[5] but weave a dense fabric connecting everyday practices, the texture of urban life and macro-processes.

A context-driven and context-generating environment

To know how this life-world came about, a social history of Soi Sukhon was re-constructed using both official records of property registrations and inhabitants' accounts of that official history.

Rice cultivation figured prominently in the 'myth of origin' among contemporary residents. In 1895 a few households clustering in hamlets along *khlong* Lat Yao had cleared grounds for cultivation. By 1903, 17 title deeds covered what is now Ban Soi Sukhon and rice fields covered only part of the area. From the late 1930s, cultivation was gradually abandoned and replaced by elephant grass.

In this mythological past, legend had it that the Sukhon family – who nowadays lead a low-key existence in the neighbourhood – were among the outstanding *jao thin* (or local inhabitants). In reality, the family first acquired a plot from original inhabitants in 1916, cleverly expanding their holdings in the area and exploiting their estate as collateral to pursue small-scale entrepreneurial activities. In 1934, construction of Phahonyothin Road entailed the expropriation and subdivision of large tracts of land, and the family gained control over several plots adjacent to or near the road track; other influential locals or outsiders purchased road-front plots. Except for this, land was largely unaffected for 20 more years and the neighbourhood remained sparsely inhabited. The next phase of development brought newcomers who engulfed the original inhabi-

7.6
Food vendors near the *paak soi* have fixed selling points to attract both resident and passing customers.

tants and wiped out nearly all remnants of the past. Hence few contemporary residents remember this recent past.

From the mid-1950s, most landowners had subdivided their land for sale. By 1970, there were over 700 new parcels and new owners with subdivisions sharing similar layouts – plots lining central private roads and plot sizes averaging 400 square metres. They were considered to be 'unserviced' with developers negotiating access passages across adjacent properties. Most were registered in the period 1965–1968, but the title deeds of private stretches of road were not transferred to the municipality until the period 1974–1976 when private *soi* became municipal roads, and drainage systems, road paving and street lighting were installed.

The Sukhon family had been among the first to join the subdivision business and effectively laid out the first stretches of Soi Sukhon in 1961, relying on their connections with the bureaucracy to identify buyers.

The proportion of vacant plots today indicates that some buyers had purely speculative motives, although the majority did move in eventually because of the lure of quiet and peaceful surroundings which became more attractive as urban density in the inner city increased. The converted land was also relatively inexpensive and welfare departments of different public agencies extended attractive housing loans to their employees.

As private access roads were transferred to the municipality, and paved public amenities extended deeper into the *soi*, the trickle of pioneer settlers swelled to a massive stream of immigrants. Housing construction proceeded incrementally: there was no large-scale construction during the initial phase of 'colonization' (Appadurai 1995: 208) when households called upon skilled relatives and friends to put together a makeshift structure or hired a contractor to build whatever they could afford. Later on, the original house was altered according to their needs. As traffic, congestion and environmental degradation encroached on their clean and healthy suburbia, settlers moved on and were replaced so current residents could offer only piecemeal recollections.

From the early 1970s, the original landowners became less inclined to engage in land-dealings and their role was taken over by professional housing developers. By 1985, Soi Sukhon's first fully-fledged *mubanjatsan* was ready for occupation, and in 1989 construction of a *mubanjatsan* in an adjacent *soi* made it an important *thanglat*. This increased exposure to through traffic coincided with the completion of the city's nearby inner ring road and lead to a re-evaluation of the area. Local and outside entrepreneurs flocked in to cash in on property development. Again, memories were overtaken by dreams and land prices soared. Absentee landowners offered their properties for sale.[6] One small-time entrepreneur got hold of adjacent plots, subdivided them and constructed townhouses for sale, others used a plot adjacent to their house to construct a low-rise apartment building. Professional property agencies launched a first low-rise condominium project in 1995, accessible from Soi Sukhon and the next *soi*. To maintain the private and exclusive character of the project, the management reserves access to the project residents. In due course, however, this new stretch of private road is likely to become integrated into the *soi*.

Conclusion

This social history shows a sharp break between the time before urban migrants 'invaded' the area and the time after. The *soi*'s development shows a progressive commoditization, densification and homogenization.[7] Cohen (1985: 14) portrayed this evolution as part of a 'penetration of metropolitan forces', but I prefer to view it as a trajectory. A *soi*'s history reflects a myriad of individual and household decisions rather than macro-economic trends or collective socio-cultural change, the result of 'tactics' rather than 'strategies' (Certeau 1984: xix); the result of personal, uncoordinated *modus operandi* rather than corporate, systematic blueprints.

Soi emerged in response to a context of unbridled urban growth, scarcity of available land and a laissez-faire economy. They originated from entrepreneurs' isolated initiatives to subdivide peri-urban land and sell it to middle-income groups eager to invest their savings. They provided a distinct trajectory for most Bangkokians. Successive waves of migrants blended with earlier inhabitants and *soi* became important sites for the material production of locality. Residents, visitors and passers-by, through their coming and going, made *soi* an integral part of their lives and created model for urban development, a model that proclaimed the triumph of urban lifestyle, global consumer society and 'universalized' middle-class values.

As *soi* histories unfolded, *soi* dwellers oscillated between facts and legends, between dreams and memories. They became reliably local subjects (*jao thin*) who negotiated 'local authority' by constantly questioning, re-presenting and reproducing their place within the urban context. True to their mission as builders of the urban frontier, residents constantly tried out new ideas and developed tactics that could improve their living conditions, consolidate their situation or extend their control over their immediate environs. By doing so, they implicitly built an imaginary city, an inverted reality constantly challenging local authority. Feld and Basso (1996: 11) argue that 'as people fashion places, so, too, do they fashion themselves'. Similarly, *soi* dwellers made their city, while the city was making them. Through everyday practices they created a context that exceeded the material and conceptual boundaries of their neighbourhood, actualizing their city as a 'horizon' where everyday life is experienced. It is in this situation, in-between, that the city attained its most concrete reality as the site of everyday practices, and became an urban space *par excellence* at the urban frontier.

Notes

1 In 1971, S. Yinyeod estimated the number of *soi* in Bangkok Metropolis at 2000 (*Bangkok Post*, 25 July 1971). Municipal authorities calculated the total length of *soi* in the Bangkok Metropolitan Area to nearly 1,900 km; *soi* constituted 67 per cent of the city's total road infrastructure. (See: Bangkok Metropolitan Administration, 1987. *Phaenthi sadaeng kan chai thi din rai khet khong krungthep* [Land use map per district of the Bangkok metropolitan area], Bangkok, City Planning Division BMA). Cohen (1985: 1) labelled *soi* 'one of the most ubiquitous and characteristic ecological features' of Bangkok. Yet *soi* are conspicuously absent in literature on the city.
2 In the late 1980s and 1990s, Bangkok's notorious traffic situation led to a series of studies with different suggestions for improvements to the urban transportation system. (See among others: (a) Japan International Co-operation Agency (JICA), 1990, 'The study on medium to long term improvement management plan of road and road transport in Bangkok in the Kingdom of Thailand'; (b) Halcrow Fox and Assoc., Pak Poy and Kneebone, Pty. Ltd. (HFA-AEC), 1991, *Seventh Plan Urban and Regional Transport (SPRUT)*, reports commissioned by the National Economic and Social Development Board, Bangkok.)
3 Durand-Lasserve (1976, 1980) illustrated that land prices in Bangkok varied not only according to distance to the city's central business district but also according to distance from the main road. Today, institutions such as the Department of Lands still handle different land price indicators for parcels near a main road or situated deep in a *soi*.
4 This estimate is based on a count of houses included in maps that were drawn up by the City Planning Department of the BMA in 1987 and are used by the BMA Revenue Department to monitor the collection of land and housing tax. See: Bangkok Metropolitan Administration (1987).
5 According to Certeau (1984: xviii), trajectories, 'although composed with the vocabularies of established languages ... and although they remain subordinated to the prescribed syntactical forms, ... trace out the ruses of other interests and desires that are neither determined nor captured by the systems in which they develop.'
6 In 1993, road-front land along Phahonyothin Road fetched 35,000 baht per square metre. Land in *soi* one was sold for 12,500 baht per square metre. Deeper in the *soi*, a land broker offered land for sale at 7,500 baht per square metre and deep into *sut soi*, land still fetched 2,000 baht per square metre. The conversion rate at the time was £1.00 = 42 baht (author's fieldwork data).
7 The use of these terms refers to Kopytoff's (1986) processual model. According to this model, commoditization assumes that things – *in casu*, property – are more frequently or lastingly being moved in a 'commodity state' (Kopytoff 1986: 13). Densification, thus, refers not only to population density but also to the frequency of exchange, the hallmark of commoditization. The last term, 'homogenization', refers to the flattening out of idiosyncrasies of distinct urban neighbourhoods as well as to the levelling of values due to exchange.

Bibliography

Angel, S. and Chuated, S. (1990) 'The down-market trend in housing production in Bangkok, 1980–87', *Third World Planning Review*, 12(1): 1–20.

Angel, S. and Pornchokchai, S. (1989) 'Bangkok slum lands. Policy implications of recent findings', *Cities*, May: 136–146.

Appadurai, A. (1986) 'Introduction: commodities and the politics of value' in A. Appadurai (ed.) *The social life of things: Commodities in cultural perspective*. Cambridge: Cambridge University Press.

—— (1995) 'The Production of Locality' in R. Fardon (ed.) *Counterworks: Managing the diversity of knowledge*, London: Routledge.

Certeau, M. de (1984) *The Practice of Everyday Life*, Berkeley, Los Angeles, London: University of California Press.

Cohen, E. (1985) 'A Soi in Bangkok – the Dynamics of Lateral Urban Expansion' in *Journal of the Siam Society*, 73(1)&(2): 1–35.

Dowall, D.E. (1989) 'Bangkok: A Profile of an Efficiently Performing Housing Market' in *Urban Studies*, 26: 327–339.

Durand-Lasserve, A. (1976) *Les facteurs et les mécanismes de la croissance de Bangkok à l'époque contemporaine, Travaux et Documents de Géographie Tropicale, 26*, Talence: CEGET-CNRS.

—— (1983) 'The land conversion process in Bangkok and the predominance of the private sector over the public sector' in S. Angel, R.W. Archer, S. Tanphiphat and E.A. Wegelin (eds) (1983) *Land for Housing the Poor*, Singapore: Select Books.

Feld, S. and Basso, K. (1996) *Senses of Place*, Santa Fe, New Mexico: School of American Research Press.

Kopytoff, I. (1986) 'The cultural biography of things: commoditization as process' in A. Appadurai (ed.) *The Social Life of Things: Commodities in Cultural Perspective*, Cambridge: Cambridge University Press.

Poungsomlee, A. and Ross, H. (1992) *Impacts of Modernisation and Urbanisation in Bangkok: an Integrative Ecological and Biosocial Study*, Bangkok: Institute for population and Social Research, Mahidol University.

Yap, K.S. (1993) *Low-Income Housing in Bangkok. A Review of Some Housing Sub-Markets*, HSD Monograph 25, Bangkok: Asian Institute of Technology.

Chapter 8
Eco-planning for development in northern Thailand

Thada Sutthitham

Introduction

The desire to modernize is leading the development of human settlements of all scales and in all locations, from rural villages to urban centres, and across many countries. In Thailand, community environments have changed, apparently spontaneously, as a result of this drive to modernize. Local communities, however, on considering the impact of such change, are now questioning its outcomes and the processes that lead to them. They are uncertain how their local identity might survive such changes and are seeking alternative approaches.

In this discussion, 'eco-cultural resources' are considered as nature-based cultural resources, or natural elements (land, water, forests, etc.) that have been altered by cultural activities. The study of human settlements in the north-eastern region of Thailand reveals that eco-cultural resources contribute to and even underpin the self-reliance and sustainability of communities (Sutthitham 2001). Failure to conserve such resources by disrupting their supporting systems, by lack of maintenance or by recent inappropriate development that interferes with their operation, reduces agricultural and material production, creating difficulties in rural areas and degrading urban and village environments. Typically, 'modern' development approaches have proven incapable of supporting the management of farmland so it continues to provide food in a nature-friendly way.

In Thailand, many successive layers of civilization have left their patterns on urban settlement. Between about 2,500 and 900 years ago, prehistoric Mon settlements in the flood plain commonly encircled their communities with rings of moats that protected them from flood in the wet season and collected water to use during the dry season. Between 1,300 and 900 years ago, the subsequent Khmer settlements began to construct rectangular ponds to collect water diverted from nearby natural streams. The latest cultural group to settle these areas, the Tai, migrated to Thailand in the thirteenth century from southern China, northern Vietnam and

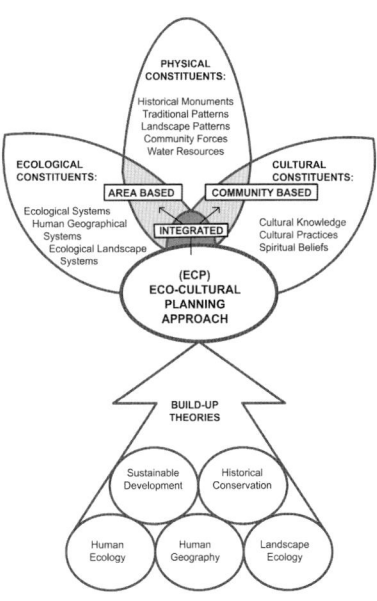

8.1
A lotus form, the Buddhist religious flower, symbolizes the Eco–Cultural Planning (ECP) approach for urban and rural development in Thailand.

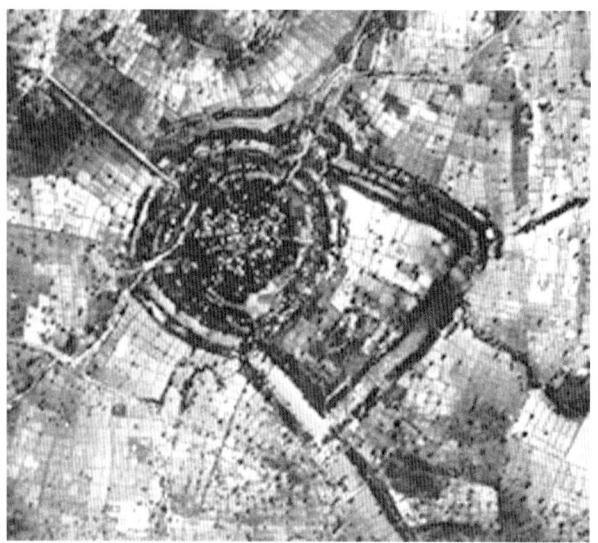

8.2
Ban Talung Kao, Buriram province. A prehistoric Mon settlement in a circular pattern.

Laos. The Tai are known for their upland irrigation systems which combine the building of small dams at the mountain elbows with systems of irrigation canal networks to irrigate their rice fields.

Urban form and the power of the spiritual

Most historic settlements in north-eastern Thailand were located on the basis of the spiritual power of their site (Sutthitham 2001). The diversity of patterns of settlement has resulted from the diversity of the perceived relationship between two forms of power – the natural and the human. That relationship is manifest differently at each location, and from analysis of the patterns that have resulted four types of settlement can be classified.

The symbolic

In the symbolic approach, urban settlements were planned to create the pattern of a *mandala*, or sacred urban area for their inhabitants. In Thailand such sacred urban forms follow Indian cosmological *mandala* including: the circle; the conch (an auspicious vessel of the god Visnu); the *sema* (a Buddhist marking stone); and the square. Accordingly, cities and settlements attracted universal power that would link its physical plan and form to that power. When the pattern of the city was deformed by the imposition of other development patterns, then that sacred power would likewise be deformed, or decreased, depending on the level of disturbance to the essential pattern of the *mandala*.

The adaptive

A symbolic or normative theory underpinned the origins of this type of urban form. When ideal configurations (such as the symbolic) were transferred to actual locations, different site constraints demanded more adaptive patterns. On the high plateau of the sandy north-eastern Thai region, for example, cities need to collect water during the dry season and divert water away to protect their cities from flood during the heavy monsoon season. In the mountainous north, however, cities are, by contrast, located in narrow valleys in the foothills, and networks of dams and canals were laid out to collect and slow down the running water while providing irrigation systems for farmland. Diverse urban patterns resulted with adaptations based on explicit recognition and acceptance of the natural constraints at each location. Such recognition is often signalled at sites of acknowledged concentration of power: as shrines or sacred pillars in the central public spaces, on the banks of rivers or ponds or in sacred forests. In the Thai language, river is *mae-nam* [mother water] and land is *mae-toranee* [mother earth], both of which express the respect people have for these fundamental environmental elements and their power. Spiritual ceremonies are performed to acknowledge these spirits communally every year and individuals also make offerings to them as often as they wish. To retain their spiritual power, those elements in the environment that manifest spiritual power must be retained and respected, using rules set down by the communities who care for and maintain them, as continuing resources.

The economic

The industrialized cities and settlements that have emerged during the past century have concentrated their attention principally on the systems of movement that support the transport of goods, especially roads. Transport time and distance have become the major factors that control urban plans and layouts and the idea of natural power has been neglected. In many situations, roads have blocked waterways, sacred green areas have been destroyed, land has polluted by chemicals and rivers and streams used for sewage. As trees have been removed, the salinity that they suppressed has been dispersed, especially throughout the north-eastern region. The cities that were built using the symbolic and adaptive approaches have been deformed by this approach.

The directive

City rulers have themselves created city plans and directed urban development in Thailand on the advice of spiritual mediums and, more recently, city planners. The star shaped fortified cities built to accommodate the canon wars during the eighteenth and nineteenth centuries and the urban beautification projects of the twentieth century exemplify this approach, which may use aspects of each of the other three. With the professional position of urban planners now established, more decisive city plans that do this are emerging. It may be possible to explore how the various approaches, especially the symbolic and adaptive approaches that call upon spiritual power to uplift the mental and physical strength of the inhabitants, can be utilized again for contemporary life.

8.3
Srakampangyai, Srisaket province. The eleventh-century Khmer city with a manmade pond. The perfect rectangular grid city has been bisected by the railroad cutting.

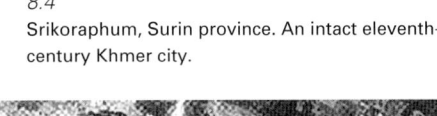

8.4
Srikoraphum, Surin province. An intact eleventh-century Khmer city.

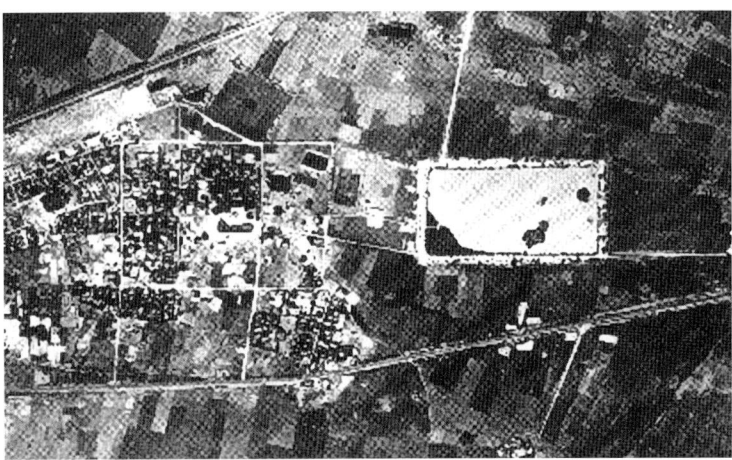

Eco-cultural planning as an urban development strategy

Many Thai villages and cities have organized and managed their own eco-cultural resources for centuries. By contrast, rather than being community-based, development planning in Thailand currently relies on a modern approach whereby planning is delegated to government agencies. These agencies have seriously overestimated their ability to manage these resources and as a result pre-existing local systems have been interrupted and local capacities undermined (Korten 1987). As many countries are now considering a sustainable development paradigm to address similar planning dilemmas, a strategic planning method is proposed that applies these ideas to the Thai situation and, in particular, its diverse urban settlements and cities. This method is called 'Eco–Cultural Planning'.

This method is based on three fundamental principles: conservation of the integrity of ecological and cultural resources, community-based resource management and integrated development planning. The revitalization of resources under such an approach is expected to improve and even re-establish the quality and integrity of ecosystems, landscapes and the historical and cultural values of communities. To achieve this, however, four challenges have to be confronted and change achieved. These are: explicit recognition of eco-cultural resources at a statutory level; acquisition of knowledge about resources and the ways that they respond to change; incorporation of community-based resource management in decision making; and, co-ordination between those parties using resources. In the domain of human settlements, three related constituents can be classified as resources that should guide such planning processes: physical constituents (buildings, infrastructure, farmlands, water), ecological constituents (landscape systems, ecological systems, human geographical systems) and cultural constituents (traditional practices, beliefs and knowledge).

Most traditional values and practices in Thailand encourage living in harmony with nature, including Buddhism which advocates, whether in Thailand or elsewhere, a gentle non-aggressive attitude towards nature as described in Sigalovada Sutta, one of the Buddha's scriptures:

> ... a householder should accumulate wealth as a bee collects pollen from a flower. The bee harms neither the fragrance nor the beauty of the flower, but gathers pollen to turn it into sweet honey. Similarly, man is expected to make legitimate use of nature so that he can rise above nature and realize his innate spiritual potential.
>
> (de Silva 1987)

8.5
Phimai, Nakoranratchasima province. The ideal city form of the Khmer: the twelfth-century stone temple is located at the centre. River fertility has been maintained by the inhabitants. Centuries old trees and water monitors still exist.

8.6
Khon Kaen, Khon Kaen province. The nineteenth-century Thai city. A natural pond was selected as the site for the settlement and natural elements respected. It remains one of the city's drainage ponds, but with many other uses as well.

Recognizing such values and incorporating them into contemporary planning approaches combines traditional values with modern systems, demonstrating how the two paradigms can beneficially converge. Historic urban forms, landscapes and architecture are assets for Thai cities, bringing them income from tourism and maintaining traditional social systems. They can be preserved under this planning approach along with their settings and ways of life.

Conclusion

The strategic planning method Eco–Cultural Planning is proposed here as the basis for development of settlements in urban and rural Thailand. It builds on both local traditional values and contemporary and international thinking about sustainability to emphasize the conservation of the integrity of eco-cultural systems, community-based resource management and integrated development planning. Best of all, it integrates the ancient Thai approach to urban development that recognizes the potential power of settlement form to link, spiritually, the mental and physical strength of the inhabitants to the power inherent in the environment. Inhabitants will, thereby, be strengthened in all ways. Further, eco-cultural planning may well be more broadly applicable, not only providing a sound environmental, economic and social foundation for Thai development, but possibly across other parts of South-east Asia where similar situations are encountered, assisting the achievement of sustainable development across the region.

Bibliography

Adhikari, P.K. (1987) 'Farmer VS Government Managed Irrigation System: A Comparative Study of Water Management Practices in the Mid Hills of Nepal', unpublished thesis, Asian Institute of Technology (AIT), Bangkok.

Agarwala, R. (1983) *Planning in Developing Countries: Lessons of Experience*, World Bank Staff Working Paper No. 576, Washington DC: The World Bank.

Bali Sustainable Development Project (1991) *A report on the Village of Buahan, Bali, Indonesia, Research paper No. 16*, University of Waterloo: Ontario, Canada.

de Silva, L. (1987) 'The Buddhist attitude towards nature', in K. Sandell (ed.), *Buddhist Perspectives on the Ecocrisis* (*Wheel* publication no. 346), Kandy: Buddhist Publication Society.

Korten, D.C. (1987) 'Conclusion: Community Management and Social Transformation', in D.C. Korten (ed.), *Community Management: Asian Experience and Perspectives*, Bloomfield, CT: Kumarian Press.

Lynch, K. (1990) *Good City Form*, Cambridge: MIT Press.

Menzies, N. (1988) 'Three hundred years of Yaungya: a sustainable system of forestry in South China', *Human Ecology*, 16(4): 361–376.

Parlin, B.W. (1991) *Farmer Participation and Irrigation Organization*, Boulder: Westview Press.

Rykwert, J. (1989) *The Idea of a Town*, London: MIT Press.

Siy, R.Y. Jr (1987) 'Averting the bureaucratization of a community-managed resource – the case of the Zanjeras', in D.C. Korten (ed.), *Community Management: Asian Experience and Perspectives*, Bloomfield, CT: Kumarian Press.

Sutthitham, T. (2001) *Settlement Plans in Thailand: The Land Use and Change in Khmer Settlements in the Northeast*, Khon Kaen: Pim Pattana.

Suttitum, T. (1995) *'Historical Conservation Planning'*, unpublished thesis, University of Waterloo, Canada.

World Commission on Environment and Development (WCED) (1987) *Our Common Future*, Oxford: Oxford University Press.

Chapter 9
Local identity in Bangkok's business districts

Ornsiri Panin

Introduction

From its establishment 222 years ago, Bangkok has been continually transformed and each of its districts now bears a diverse history, culture and physical character. Its very first district, Rattanakosin Island, was established on the east bank of the Chaopraya River. Although the areas along the west bank have changed, their development has been slower and the city's major business districts have principally developed eastward from this starting point.

During the past 25 years, most of the commercial areas in central Bangkok have been transformed in similar ways, with modern commercial and entertainment precincts superimposed over the traditional structure. Areas like Siam Square and Silom have continued to sustain their success, even through the economic changes that have ensued in Thailand. Consequently, many suburban commercial districts have employed similar models of development and transformation, resulting in countless suburban business and shopping centres of similar character. Only a few of these many developments in the suburbs have, however, survived, many being abandoned or transformed for other purposes.

Whether urban or suburban, however, none of Bangkok's districts are similar in historical terms. Their origins, cultures and physical circumstances differ, raising questions as to why so many new business and commercial areas of Bangkok have been developed along the same lines, regardless of their local identity. Must every commercial area be so similar? With the failure of so many new commercial centres, perhaps urban designers and professionals should take into account the local identity of each urban area, translating that identity into the provision of commercial and business precincts that are unique.

These questions are considered through the study of a specific case, Bo-Bae, one of the

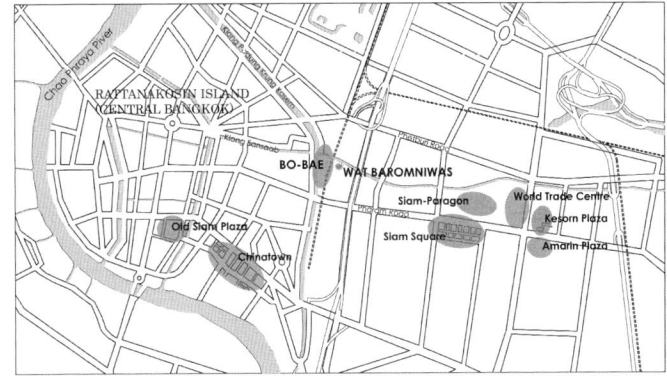

9.1
Bo-Bae area, located in relation to other commercial centres in central Bangkok.

9.2
Clothing vendors using the sidewalks during the day.

9.3
The same sidewalks converted to use by food vendors in the evening.

unique business districts located at the edge of Bangkok's Rattanakosin Island. Despite its location in the heart of Bangkok, Bo-Bae originated in the same manner as most traditional markets in the rural areas of Thailand. First developed 70 years ago, it has become a melting pot of Bangkok's diverse ethnic and religious groups including Thai, Chinese, Lao; Buddhist and Muslim, all of whom have sustained their ways of life and nurtured their social and cultural identities here. As a business district, Bo-Bae has gradually been transformed, from a traditional morning market to a complex mass market operating over 24 hours. With its Chinese population came the birth of a mass-produced clothing market that relates residential, business (production) and commercial functions. Bo-Bae has evolved into a market unlike any other in the city. Now confronted with rapid metropolitan growth and a new urban development plan for the city,[1] the crucial questions for Bo-Bae revolve around how it sustains its life and soul within this context; and can it develop further as a part of the city fabric while retaining its local identity? Can new urban development be founded upon the social and cultural, as well as historical, identity of the area? Answering these questions might suggest other ways of accommodating the many different cultures and contexts embedded within each and every city.

Bo-Bae and Rattanakosin Island

Bo-Bae is located at the edge of Rattanakosin Island between Banglumpoo, Pahurad and Yaowarad the old business districts of Bangkok and the new business districts and entertainment centres to the east (Siam Square, Ratchaprasong and Pratoonam). It fronts two historical canals, Klong Sansaab on the north and Klong Padungkrungkasem on the west, and is surrounded by four Buddhist temples, an Islamic mosque and four Chinese places of worship. Most of its land belongs to Wat Baromnivas, a Thai Buddhist temple. The Bo-Bae district has become a melting pot for Bangkok's diverse ethnic groups, all of whom have managed to sustain their social and cultural identities and their ways of life here. On the west bank of Klong Nahanark is the Islamic community. To the north, near Klong Sansaab, is the traditional Thai community market, Padunkrungkasem, which originated with the floating market. Bo-Bae itself has gradually evolved from a traditional morning market under the supervision of Wat Baromnivas to a complex mass market selling wholesale and retail products 24 hours a day.[2]

At present, Bo-Bae is well known as a wholesale and retail clothing market unlike any other in Bangkok. It combines residential, business and commercial functions with buildings covering 81 per cent of a site area of 26,600 square metres and open space covering the remaining 19 per cent. Building heights vary from one to six storeys and their age ranges from 20 to 65 years,[3] combining various functions and uses including shops, residences, food markets, banks, public facilities, Chinese places of worship, Chinese community associations and vacant buildings. Within its limited site area, Bo-Bae also accommodates service facilities and much space is utilized both day and night. Some functions, such as those occurring on the wide footpath, change with the time of day. From early in the morning until afternoon the footpath is the place for the many clothing vendors and service providers who give a special character to day-time Bo-Bae. In the evening, when the vendors move away, the area becomes an open space and a place to relax for local residents. During the night-time, the place once again becomes lively, transformed into night bazaars for visitors.

Religious beliefs play an important role in the daily life of the majority of the Chinese population in Bo-Bae. The many places of worship and the Chinese Association are used as community centres for everyone, not only ethnic Chinese. In addition to the shop owners and their families, there are also immigrant workers from the north-east provinces, known as E-Sarn, who work in the shops, as food vendors and as shopkeepers for owners who do not live in the area. Because the mass production and wholesaling of clothing dominates business here, many workers are required to work in the industry or to transport goods. The economic conditions are therefore generally good and support two banks, the Krung Thai Bank, Mahanark Branch,[4] and Kasikorn Thai Bank, Bo-Bae Branch.[5]

Despite the successful diversity of Bo-Bae, developers have attempted recently to impose their model, including high rise buildings and a new business centre, with the Bo-Bae tower appearing, just opposite to Bo-Bae market.

As a unique wholesale and retail clothing market with its own

9.4
Typical market activity in daytime Bo-Bae.

9.5
The streetscape at Siam Centre, Siam Square.

9.6
A typical conjunction of old and new Bangkok, combining residential and commercial activities.

physical and cultural characteristics Bo-Bae is well known in Bangkok and beyond. These unique and acknowledged characteristics create its public image and include: its 24-hour activity; its diverse ethnicities and religious groupings; the individual identities of its many residents; the way that religion influences local values including a commitment to prosperity and diligence; and the variety of its customers who come from all over Bangkok, other provinces and overseas.

Potential developers always compare Bo-Bae with the standard, highly successful commercial and entertainment precincts of Siam Square and Maboonkrong without considering its origins and the unique characteristics of its surrounding communities. In fact, it is highly likely that Bo-Bae would be completely transformed if it was privately owned. Its unique traditional life and physical form is sustained, however, because the property belongs to the temple, Wat Baromnivas, and the rector is concerned about the future way of life of the people who live and work there. If the rector were to resign or the policy of the Wat to change, Bo-Bae's future would be threatened.

9.7
The streetscape at Siam Paragon.

9.8
Clothing vendors and shoppers, Bo-Bae.

Conclusion

During the past 25 years, most of the commercial areas in central Bangkok have been transformed by superimposing modern commercial and entertainment compounds over the traditional urban structures.

Bo-Bae is unique because of its public image based on a character that combines the mass production of clothing with an intimate and unusual relationship between residential, business and commercial functions, along with a rich physical context. The district can sustain its unique way of life and physical form as a part of the urban fabric if developers and urban designers alike take into account its unique characteristics, rather than trying to transform it into a commercial centre similar to many others.

Notes

1 The Bangkok Urban Development Plan has been revised every five years. Observation of recent revisions shows that the old business districts, including Bo-Bae, have been expanded without determining individual characteristics and origins.
2 From an academic survey in June 2002 for the redevelopment of the old business district of Rattanakosin Island, Bangkok, conducted by 5th-year students of the Faculty of Architecture, Silpakorn University.
3 From an interview with Somsak Taveekul, an owner of a Bo-Bae shophouse, Soi Sapan 1, Bo-Bae Market, conducted in June 2002.
4 Krung Thai Bank, Mahanak Branch, is the biggest branch in the Bo-Bae vicinity, occupying the area of five shops.
5 Kasikorn Thai Bank, Bo-Bae Branch, occupies two shops.

Bibliography

Frey, H. (1999) *Designing the City: Towards a More Sustainable Urban Form*, London and New York: E and FN Spon.
Gruen, V. (1973) *Centers for the Urban Environment: Survival of the Cities*, New York: Van Nostrand Reinhold.
Lang, Jon T. (1994) *Urban Design: The American Experience*, New York: Van Nostrand Reinhold.
Lynch, K. (1960) *The Image of the City*, Cambridge MA: MIT Press.
—— (1981) *A Theory of Good City Form*, Cambridge MA: MIT Press.
Ward, S. (ed.) (1992) *The Garden City, Past, Present, Future*, New York and London: E and FN Spon.
William, K., Burton, E. and Jenks, M. (eds) (1999) *Achieving Sustainable Urban Form*, New York: E and FN Spon.

Part 2
Experiments in practice

Introduction
The dynamics of the urban design project

Guy Tapie and Darko Radović

With globalization, the interaction between societies and their territories has become more dynamic and complex then ever. The demands of the free market economy have resulted in an aggressive form of urban development that often disregards cultural and environmental particularities. Driven by a desire for efficiency that can be extreme, such development can lead to simplistic visions of a better future that, removed from local knowledge and aspirations, endangers the quality of local environments. Where culturally and environmentally sustainable urbanism is the goal, such approaches now deserve rigorous testing at the local level.

In some parts of the world, accelerated urban development is generated by accumulated wealth. In other regions it results from a combination of unbalanced economic development, unprecedented migration to urban centres, spiralling population numbers and increasing levels of poverty and social injustice. In all conditions there is a need to better understand the forces at play and the processes at work. Which aspects of the urbanization tend to be similar, and which are different? What can we learn from the sharing of experiences? How can the exchange of experiences enhance our capacity to achieve better outcomes in practice, to mediate between local and global imperatives? Such knowledge can lay the foundation for a contemporary professional culture more in tune with the demands of its times and attained in a number of ways: by travelling and observing similar processes in other environments; by attending international workshops, conferences and symposia; by studying abroad; by exploring international theories and practice; and by learning new professional methodologies.

This set of chapters illustrates and discusses some examples of learning such new professionalism through action-in-practice. Those directly participating in the process of urban development contribute essays that map and describe urban transformation – in a variety of cultures and locations – and speculate about possible and desirable changes to established practice. They base their reflections on actual experience of specific planning, design and research projects and the ideas underpinning them. The cases explore a variety of urban projects, the dynamic interactions between global forces and local values that influence their production and methods at play in their delivery. While not claiming that universal theories can be established from their analyses, a review of these cases does reveal that there are, broadly speaking, two types of experience that dominate the contemporary professional domain.

The first are broader-scale strategic urban projects implemented in metropolitan regions where the regulation of spatial development is already established – either European in approach where typically, public power is more evident, or Anglo-Saxon where typically, private forces appear more powerful. Because of their history and geo-strategic location, Barcelona, Bordeaux, Genoa and Montreal share a claim to originality. Barcelona leads through its capacity for reinvention and innovation and its successful approach to the development of public space. The experience in Bordeaux is of interest because of the way the views of decision makers and professionals there have evolved, particularly about the potential of urban design to generate a new urban culture. In this process they appear to abandon previously established planning processes that aspired to total control. Along with many cities, Genoa shared an ambition to use the activities of its harbour in a process of urban transformation that not only generated a specific urban quality there but was to influence development across its entire territory. Impregnated with a more Anglo-Saxon development culture, Montreal, by contrast, moves between two approaches to urban planning and design – the liberal, with its capacity for transformation without too many constraining rules, and the libertarian, with spontaneous appropriation of spaces by the local inhabitants. Equivalent experiences are not, however, apparent in the metropolises of the developing countries discussed here. Whether or not they are subjected to similar processes of change (and many are), the idea of strategic urban design seems less familiar or, consequent on the variations in local policies, less frequently implemented – for the lack, perhaps, of a supporting professional culture or legitimating political structures at the local level. This appears to be common across a number of such urban domains.

The second type of experience discussed here is local urban projects, many of which recommend more 'balanced' strategies for development, thus implying that much recent development has not been appropriate. It is also often implied, and in a number of cases even described, how certain approaches to development have caused serious cultural and environmental harm – because they have been imported directly without methodological adaptation to local circumstances; because they have focused on issues identified from too great a distance; or because they have reflected aims and aspirations that are foreign or even, in some instances, overtly colonizing and exploitative.

In Thailand, for example, two of the cases discuss the idea of 'eco-tourism', as both a much-desired source of income and a potential source of inappropriate development. The goal is, through greater understanding of local resources and the application of more locally appropriate planning techniques, to safeguard the country's natural and cultural wealth, a wealth already ravaged by unconstrained economic growth. Pollution, deforestation, lack of waste treatment and heavy industrialization have all resulted from development where the aims were established far from the place, generating an apparent polarization between 'us' (the local peoples) and 'them' (the distant developers). From the local perspective, the faraway 'them' are usually more powerful and much professional effort is focused on more responsible approaches to development that harnesses that power for development activity that is more locally desirable. The experience in Montenegro has similar ambitions. Suffering from the horrors of a recent civil war, the aim there is to direct international assistance towards recovery of local wealth through preservation and promotion of rural histories and heritage and protection of natural resources – all of which are seen as attractive to tourism. The Tunisian case was also formulated as local initiative supported by an international organization, saving the old, threatened medina from the massive destruction at the beginning of the 1970s. Thanks to the active co-operation of a successful local social and artistic elite and Unesco, this goal has in the main been achieved. The situation described illustrates a transformation that would have been, if imposed from outside, radical, resulting in the destruction of whole districts. In the end, the redevelopment accommodated the needs and aspirations of local people by maintaining, at a cost, much of the existing fabric and traditional typology.

As the chapters illustrate, a new generation of projects and practices appears to be emerging in countries that have, for reasons which were often beyond their control, paid little attention to their local spaces and places to date. The details of this trend however, remain uncertain, given the anarchistic character of much urban development that seems to promote physical fragmentation, amplify social hierarchies and avoid environmental criteria.

Given the diversity of experiences discussed and their limited number, it is not possible to generalize the impacts they have had on their cultural, economic and social contexts. These experiences do show, however, the possible range of situations in which urban design plays a significant role and where both planning and design can contribute. Reflections on experience suggest new meanings for practice and possible directions for its evolution. New interpretations of the idea of the 'local' emerge. Local qualities are, for example, considered as giving identity and value even to the broadest regions and agglomerations; the quality of 'the particular' defines and increases the value of spatial elements, making the city what it is – Bordeaux, Barcelona, or wherever. The regional qualities might be valued at the global scale (the Catalan, the West European, the Asian, the South-East Asian, etc.) or remain decidedly local, raising questions such as: who defines those values? What do we mean when we demand a certain 'value'? When does certain quality cease to be (only) local and start to acquire global importance?

A phenomenon of significance to contemporary practice is the planning, design and development of whole cities. The enormous scale and pace of new urban developments, (in China for instance), is fascinating and now expands the idea of urban projects beyond traditional definitions and influences to include city-regions, the cities-as-regions and even regions as cities. The urban territory now incorporates many domains and scales – the periphery, intra-urban rural, large natural spaces – and their relationships are more complex than ever, demanding new understandings of the role and interdependencies between parts. In such a context the accumulation of ideas, let alone reflection on international trends and experiences, is of value.

In the following pages, new urban (and urbanized spaces) and their interrelationships are discussed extensively from a variety of theoretical and practical perspectives. All contributing professionals put forward a case for recognizing the bonds of dependency operating at various scales, from the smallest land parcels or building units through to district and territories, whether regional, national or trans-national. While each territory or space discussed may not be seen to have equal value, level of local identity or potential for development, the contributors search for and demonstrate ways in which solutions to the problems of each might be found.

Taken together, the contributions suggest a transformation of urban design, from a discipline that delivers standardized conceptual and professional expertise, to one that changes according to the capacity of its professional practitioners to respond, with specific approaches and methods, to particular situations and issues.

Local identity: a shared interrogation

Urban design is always grounded in the desire to make change – ideally, to create a better world. Such desires are supported or challenged by the values, intentions and interests of those who are to a larger or lesser degree involved in the urban projects where urban practice is focused.

The need for change may emerge locally, seeking broader consensus and resulting in initiatives identified as strategic projects, operations and programmes. The need to implement such projects and programmes frames the resulting tasks: the adaptation of the harbour activities to tourist and recreational use, revitalization of old urban centres, creation of new collective transport. In some instances there may be the need to break with traditions that obstruct such change. Somewhat surprisingly, the very themes that legitimate such interventions may be similar, despite differences in cultural, economic or social contexts: cultural heritage, tourism, environment and, to a lesser degree, the economy. Whether this similarity between the selected cases is the consequence of a globalized professional culture, however, or coincidental, remains unclear. While urban design, as is illustrated by the cases discussed here, usually argues its position from the viewpoint of the local, global forces are also and in various ways at play, underlying values and the quality of outcomes and even explicitly manifest in project goals.

The value of the local is asserted strongly in the majority of cases. In the first group of examples from Montreal, Barcelona, Bordeaux and Genoa, the idea of the local is classified in three ways. In Montreal, an expression of local identity was sought through the hosting of exogenous events such as the Olympic Games, whose realization was a failure, both on urban and financial levels. Unlike Montreal, Barcelona used its hosting of the Olympic games to profoundly transform the city, co-ordinating the delivery of an international mega-project with numerous local initiatives that responded to local sensibilities, and were based on a desire to reclaim the public spaces of the city. Barcelona wanted to show, primarily to its own citizens, that the period of oppression experienced during the times of the dictator Francisco Franco, was over, by reinstating the intense, traditional vectors of urban life. Major international events – design competitions, international forums, political congresses and meetings – were orchestrated as economic, political and cultural forces for urban regeneration. Barcelona proved capable of establishing a unique synergy between two, usually opposing dynamics; events based on harnessing the benefits of globalization and low key urbanity, decidedly local and based on the Catalan spirit. Similarly, in Bordeaux with its 'multi-secular, historic, culturalist town planning' (Bergeron and Godier), aimed to maintain broader relevance in a regional and international environment increasingly based on competition between cities. While the success of the Catalan capital is already obvious, the French initiatives in Bordeaux aim to wake an innate, but dormant, urbanity. Some fear that the very success of Barcelona in becoming an acclaimed global city may even endanger its quality and achievements, manifesting yet another aspect of the complex dialectics between the global and the local.

The cases also show how Western metropolises claim historic and spatial uniqueness, using them as the basis with which to frame their urban aspirations. While remaining significant players in the global development – through their businesses, industries, service companies, project developers and international organizations – such cities also make sustained efforts against selected aspects of standardization and mass production. They resist globalization when and where it destroys their advantageous historic difference, whether cultural (linguistic, sociological) or architectural. It could even be said that some only resist globalization when it endangers their own advantage, happily exporting globalizing ideas that endanger 'the other' and effectively using the advantages created in the global competition for relevance and further prestige.

The interrogation and even outright questioning of local identity is more extreme in those places that now face accelerated change but honour traditional ways of life, some of which have also been subjected to direct or indirect colonial domination, such as Tunisia or Thailand. The necessity to operate between tradition and an aggressive hypermodernity (often nothing but colonial pressure in a new guise) is visible, intense and sometimes violent. In such cases globalization penetrates, inserting new dynamics that create more direct links between valuable local resources and global demand. Tourist activities, as conducted by well-organized and often highly exploitative agencies, offer good examples of this.

International institutions are also important, both as contributors to and referees or umpires in the game of globalization, including for example, the programmes mounted by Unesco and those of the European Community. The contemporary context is characterized by the mobility and flow of capital, information, technologies, images and symbols, all of which structure and define the bonds between a great variety of power brokers: companies, governments and individuals, spaces and nations, regions and localities. These flows are in constant flux and in what has become the informational city, influence the design of local space and place on a global scale. Carefully harnessed, such flows can contribute to positive outcomes, genuinely improving local conditions even at the smallest of scales, but examples of this appear to remain scarce.

Negotiating and mobilizing: project production

From the examples discussed it can be seen that urban design continues to address a great diversity of social, economic and cultural conditions and issues. Such issues are often manifest locally in unique ways: such as the abandonment of traditional economic resources (drugs); restraint of agricultural industrialization (north of Thailand); linguistic differences that translate into cultural oppositions (Montreal); and aspirations to higher levels of development to break the spiralling economic decline (Genoa, Bordeaux). Urban projects are increasingly culturally sensitive, characterized by terms such as compromise, negotiation, cosmopolitanism, multiculturalism and hybridization. When well informed and structured, urban design also manifests local memories in concrete form, where distant pasts combine with recent overlays and act as sediments deposited through time.

Almost regardless of the particular commissioning or institutional frameworks, certain approaches to urban practice now appear to be applied at all scales, including: long-term plans and strategies for broader areas; urban design strategies or frameworks for particular situations; and design responses to local demands for immediately visible outcomes. Such urban projects manifest new ideas programmatically and formally, and stimulate new practices, while challenging previously assumed, more 'scientific' certainties and the efficacy of existing urban forms. While some of the projects discussed here remain undeveloped and others are only partially so, all contribute to the composites that make up the urban design whole and are therefore important contributions to reflective practice.

Even the challenges mounted by local communities for example, successful or otherwise, are important repositories of experience from which to learn about how such urban projects actually work at the local level (Montreal, Bordeaux). The consensus or otherwise between many diverging interests (political, economic, social) ultimately determines the 'success' of any project now. Success, in contemporary terms, appears to result from the mobilization of local interests, using both strategic plans and programmes of activity including urban projects specifically targeted at local interests. The projects discussed demonstrate how such mobilization occurs in a variety of contexts.

For instance, while various modes of travel were proposed in Thailand to stimulate tourist activity (cars, bicycles, horses and elephants), decisions finally made were based on a compromise between the expectations of tourist operators and those of local communities, merging the economic imperative to assist the development of tourism with the desire to preserve established lifestyles. Such negotiations are typical of those required to preserve local landscapes, habitats, vernacular architecture and water use in the face of change. Some negotiations accommodate the ancient beliefs of villagers, and the need for these to be balanced by contemporary scientific knowledge (Anukulyudhathon in Chapter 10). Inevitably, the mobilization of multiple stakeholders has a political dimension and may well generate conflict. The cases where preservation of local values conflict with the provision of infrastructure to support mass tourism are typical. Many local authorities unquestioningly support development because of the immediate benefits it brings for employment, and local communities may remain unaware of the negative impacts of such projects until it is too late. In such cases the international exchange of knowledge about physically remote (but philosophically relevant) experiences can suggest alternative approaches. Such sharing of knowledge provides one of the most positive manifestations of globalization.

The achievements of some examples discussed, such as that of tourism development in Montenegro, are made more dramatic in the face of the other stresses that these regions face. In the case of the Medina of Tunis, a design strategy to rehabilitate, rather than totally replace, the historic fabric, made it possible to protect a site of great cultural value. That rehabilitation came, however, at the price of gentrification of the district and displacement of existing long-established communities that were economically and socially disadvantaged. Such a process is experienced in many places and is a reminder of the urgent need to learn alternative practices.

The complexity resulting from the multiple scales and modes of intervention discussed here now characterizes urban design, suggesting that both project outcomes and processes of delivery are of equal relevance to any reflection. If one can generalize, Western cities appear to use urban projects to seek strategic and political advantage. This, in turn, encourages them to address issues of identity and to focus on projects at various scales – the metropolitan, the district or the precinct. The power and capacity of local authorities is crucial here, including the availability of financial, organizational and professional resources to carry out plans or projects at a strategic level. Other societies appear to have greater difficulty in harnessing such resources. Royal support in Thailand, or that of the president in Tunisia, appear for example, crucial to achieving major urban projects in those countries, and such power appears to be as much symbolic as it is financial or organizational. In Thailand, the very name of the king may be sufficient to mobilize capacities. In other situations, international organizations such as Unesco underpin local capacity. The practicing professionals who discuss such examples, however, are principally concerned that the institutions responsible for implementing urban projects genuinely express local values. From an international perspective, such values provide a critical dimension to the discussions and warrant further analysis.

Professionals, disciplines, positions

Fundamentally, urban design is an interdisciplinary field and any investigation into the roles of the various disciplines in its practice provides valuable indicators of how it works and what it can achieve.

More than ever before, the manipulation of environments, including the engineering of biotopes and eco-systems, appears to be becoming more important in the production of urban form. Newly created landscapes, rehabilitated historic landscapes and recreated indigenous landscapes have all become active ingredients in the expression of contemporary social, cultural and economic values in urban areas. This mix suggests that landscape urbanism and landscape architecture will be among the disciplines critical to urban and environmental design in the future. Landscape design can be seen as a major vehicle for sustainable urban planning and design, because it determines the basics of land use and reuse, the limits of exploitation and proposes future characteristics. Such a vision is very different from common perceptions of practice, where 'landscaping' is confined to treatment of the leftover space after development, and demands the appropriation of new knowledge and capacity. Landscape architects can be expected to achieve a position of influence (and even notoriety) as they claim and occupy a central position in the systems that implement urban projects in the future. Their knowledge accommodates diverse values: the projects in Western metropolises that are discussed here have sought to break the negative spiral of urbanization that consumes the resources of land, energy, space and time; in more traditional societies, they have sought to preserve and conserve natural and cultural resources, identifying them as strategic resources for global phenomena (such as 'eco-tourism') as well as local survival. The knowledge of processes, policies and techniques made possible by such exchanges can promote a more equitable situation by reducing the divide between 'North and South' and 'East and West'. The central hope must be that the mistakes of one society are not repeated in the processes of development in another.

The essential quality of cross-disciplinary endeavour is explored in a number of chapters: for the Thai contributors, for example, who seek to understand the impact of the tourist development and to safeguard natural and cultural resources, several dimensions of professional knowledge are involved. These include the capacity to understand and analyse natural resources and the architecture, landscape and cultural life of settlements at the same time as accommodating the relationship between local and global economies. In parallel, it appears that more and more urban professionals integrate environmental data into their knowledge base to underpin design decisions. Analysis has become fundamental – to understand the process of change and the way the city is conceived, to spatial planning and to the various manipulations of space and place that accompany design. Such analysis has several characteristics and requirements, including the capacity to identify what information is necessary for a given project, to understand the processes that operate within and around it and, especially, to situate all information in an effective set of relationships at the project scale. From such a viewpoint, the urban designer 'would recognize the dynamics of a particular urban system; identify important flows and intensities; and, attempt a kind of organizational instrumentality. The designer of such a strategy would no longer be a master planner locating fixed installations … but rather a coordinator of complex systems' (Bradbury in Chapter 12). Urban design projects, regardless of their focus, now involve not only a number of professional disciplines but also the subject communities. This conjoining creates an additional level of complexity in the process and requires new kinds of urban professionals, capable not only of designing transformations of the physical environment but of resolving conflicts between competing interests, players and paradigms. Those involved in such processes (urban planners, urban designers, architects, landscape architects, engineers, managers) now act as 'shock absorbers', able to recognize, evaluate and react to new, untested opportunities and resolve the intersection between global ideas (such as sustainability) and local issues (Thailand, Tunisia). The urban design professional could be compared with a doctor who is able to diagnose the urban or environmental problem, provide treatment and prevent or, even better, help to eradicate problems at the source.

The cross-disciplinary approach and its ultimate effect on urban space through urban design projects presupposes a division of labour – a division guided by the complexity of the project and how it is framed as a series of questions to be answered or problem solved. In this way, the urban design project can be conceptualized as a kind of design–research endeavour where conditions are organized to support collective production, privilege organizational coherence and transcend competition between actors. Emerging theories of professional practice are explored, showing how professional networks are built and maintained, and how cross-disciplinary practice appears able to progress through successive compromises by employing multiple technical, material and regulatory programmes.

Within this overall structure, many of these contributors suggest the essential value of their relational abilities and their roles as strategists who shape the convergence of different interests at the service of an overarching ethical intention. That ethical intention can be described or implied as the idea of sustainable development (Margueritte in Chapter 16). The contributors suggest that urban planners and designers now need to be competent in connecting people and managing processes. They describe situations where contemporary professional activities shape space through complex negotiations and project processes. For communication beyond the cross-disciplinary team itself, models, three-dimensional images, reports, charts and films are all used to establish the sophisticated iconography of representation that is now required for professional and political communication. Beyond that, the quality of the person-to-person contact remains critical. It establishes two-way communication and, most importantly, trust – engendering an atmosphere upon which the quality of all project outcomes ultimately relies.

This collection of chapters aims to present and discuss a large variety of practices that relate to the contemporary delivery of urban design projects in many spatial domains and at many scales. It does this in order to explore how such experiences might inform future urban design practice internationally. Such analyses and comparisons are invaluable. They suggest that knowledge of other related experience can and should influence the transformation of urban spaces more generally, especially ways of responding to global influences in the local domain. Not only do these reflections on the experience of practice enable the identification of broader disciplinary and operational trends, they also provide tangible examples of how useful tools for urban design practice are used at the level of the urban project – tools that vary from the simple to the complex, from the latest technologies to time-honoured practice.

Chapter 10
Transparency in sustainable development
Nhong Han Basin, Thailand

Eggarin Anukulyudhathon

Introduction

Sakon Nakhon is one of the oldest provinces in the north-east region of Thailand with a history estimated to begin in the Paleolithic era (10,000 BC). The land area comprises about 9,605.8 square kilometres surrounding a huge basin of fresh water (Nhong Han Basin) which covers an area of 123 square kilometres (Forest Research Office 2002). This area has been urbanized in the last 50 years and 14 villages now comprise its main city. The form of development in these villages, which are located on the basin edge, had until recently been light, blending the settlement well with its surroundings. In particular it had maintained what is termed here, a 'transparent' waterfront, where the freshwater basin edge was always physically and visually accessible from the villages. Most of the land is used for commercial rice fields, agriculture and food production, including vegetables as ground cover. All of the wetland edges also support local life by providing space for food production with home gardening.

New settlement

Over the last 40 years, the people of the villages that comprise the city of Sakon Nakhon have become more conscious of the extent and impact of their activities and have searched for new land for settlement and agriculture. In the upper lands they have established new rice fields and agriculture including corn, tapioca, bamboo and also forestry, all of which rely on fresh water from the basin. With their agriculture expanding and the villages agglomerating as a result of population growth, the availability of sufficient fresh water from the basin has become a serious problem. Increasing consumption for urban and agricultural uses has challenged the capacity of the basin to supply sufficient water of good quality. Rice production techniques have changed recently, with the use of chemical fertilizers to increase outputs replacing the application of natural manure as used in the past. This new practice has impacted

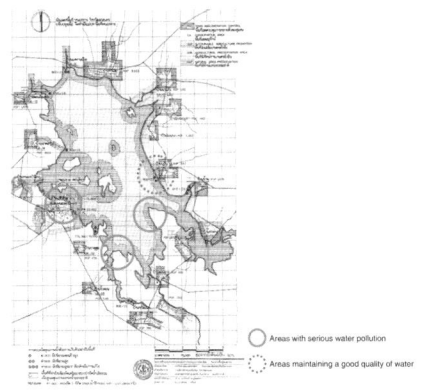

10.1
Master plan showing the implementation area of the Nhong Han Basin.

negatively on the quality of fresh water in the basin, combining with the impact of waste water draining from the surrounding village households, and contributing to what is known as 'bio-sprawl' and the explosion in numbers of water plants and weeds which decrease the dissolved oxygen in the water. As a result, human and natural impacts have combined to destroy water quality in the basin and have now affected the way of life of the people.

Saving nature

The Sakon Nakhon freshwater basin, or Nhong Han, is considered a major freshwater fish breeding area under the control of the national Department of Fisheries. It has also provided, until recently, a perfect supply of clean fresh water where people swim and relax. Unfortunately, however, these impacts have changed the local ecology of the water and marshlands that have been damaged by a combination of the increasing rubbish and other residues along the village waterfronts, the freshwater weeds and the polluted water from the villages. These are the cause of the worsening environmental conditions and are becoming progressively more serious.

Site surveys[1] that tested water quality in the summer period (May–June) showed levels of Biochemical Oxygen Demand (BOD) increasing at much greater levels than in other seasons while the Dissolved Oxygen (DO) was much lower, proving that water quality is now seriously affected by these residues.[2]

As an urgent solution to this problem, the municipality of Sakon Nakhon decided to clean the basin by cutting, digging in or removing all the water grasses, freshwater weeds and residues. Other measures were also taken that relied on technical and legal enforcement. A Sustainable Development Plan (SDP) was prepared to define and control the use of the land surrounding the basin; control waste water drainage; and control the use of chemical fertilizers and hazardous chemicals. This SDP requires a new setback alignment between the basin and development, a buffer zone as an easement for bio-protection of the environment. Such an easement keeps the area clean in an economical way, and involves the inhabi-

10.2
The existing waterfront of Nhong Han, polluted and covered by water grass.

tants, who participate in solving the problems of maintaining environmental quality. Each village now has to protect its own waterfront.

The transparency method

Most of the major impacts causing environmental damage in Sakon Nakhon have resulted from human activities, especially waste production and waste decomposition. To save the quality of the water in the basin and its environment generally, the municipality needed to employ what has now become known as the Transparency Method, which protects the bio-mass. This method protects nature by using natural processes such as freshwater weeds to treat waste water and dissolve residues. Water grasses are also then used as bio fertilizers for the plantations, gardens and rice fields.

Water pollution is the major environmental impact on the basin and water is caused by two major impacts. The first is nature itself, as imbalances occur from the cyclical over-population of water grasses and fresh-water weeds. The second is human, based in unconscious and thoughtless use. For both, the best solution is to use nature to protect itself by reusing the residues of dry weeds and water grass as a natural fertilizer to replace chemical fertilizers for plantation and agriculture. Dried water grass and weeds can also be used with other composite materials as the raw material for light weight partitions for housing construction. Green weeds are further employed in the buffer easements along the village waterfronts to dissolve the BOD in the basin. After treatment, all waste water has to be drained into weed ponds which act as filtration ponds and sediment collectors before draining into the basin proper.

The green buffer zone created between the village and the waterfront is a protected area, and requires the control of waterfront land use to prevent construction. The buffer can be used, however, as an open space and recreation area for the village as well as a marshland for green protection. In addition to the land-based or waterfront buffer, the water body in front of the villages is zoned for protection, and communities are required to protect it and promote environmental education of the inhabitants. Part of that education has

10.3
Basin surface survey measuring water quality.

meant creating a recycled packaging material to replace the plastic materials that, as residues and waste, damage this environment. Such packaging is made from locally produced tapioca flour.

Conclusions

Sakon Nakhon is recognized as an important producer of jasmine rice, sticky rice and many other famous plantation products including string beans, cucumbers, garden peas and tapioca. To maintain good production, the city has had to improve the quality of its environment and the body of water on which it relies.

The work discussed here commenced in February 2004 and ended in March 2005, concluding that solutions were required that satisfied physical, social and economic criteria and employed appropriate technologies. Such solutions combine together as the Transparency Method discussed above and summarized below.

For the physical solution the goal was to protect the environment and the water in Nhong Han Basin. To achieve this, an 'eco-protection', or bio-mass protection measure was required and proposed. Such a measure needed to re-establish the transparency of the waterfronts around the basin. The first step was to lay out a master plan for sustainable land use, dividing the area into conserved land to maintain natural processes as well as potential built areas. A green buffer was defined along the waterfront for green protection and as green linkage between the water and the wetland.

The social solution aims to involve every village surrounding the basin in the cleaning up process and protecting it in the future. Creating the zoning was to be a village responsibility along with local land use control, regulation to achieve conservation of the waterfront and promotion of environmental education among the community. Local volunteers acting as environmental monitors will also be testing and controlling water quality.

The goal of the economic solution is to increase local income. The proposals included reuse of previously unused raw materials and waste, such as the water grasses, which were polluting the basin; and recycling water grasses as light weight materials for the construction of partitions and ceiling boards for use as inside finishes for housing. This process could become a home industry and provide extra income. Such means of reducing water grasses in the basin and adding value to these raw materials will also create new areas of employment using accessible technologies and local knowledge.

All these proposals approached the environmental problems by using appropriate technologies and means. Sustainable approaches to planning and design proposed ways to improve the waterfront area, such as the green buffer along the waterfront and the promotion of bio-mass protection. To protect the environment, a system of recycling local raw material was proposed, such as the use of tapioca to replace plastics for food packaging and the creation of a new kind of construction material from dry weeds and water grasses mixed with other composites. All these would reduce the waste, residues, water grasses and weeds that are so damaging the environment.

The proposals that make up the Transparency Method need to be researched and experimented with further and the project developed in detail to approach a condition of sustainable development in Nhong Han Basin. The ultimate aim is to reach a situation where the people can live peacefully in the supporting environment, where nature is both clean and green.

Notes

1 The site surveys of water quality at the Sakon Nakhon freshwater basin were collaborations between the Faculty of Architecture and the Department of Sanitary Engineering, Faculty of Sciences and Engineering, Kasetsart University.
2 From an on-the-ground survey conducted in June 2004, which tested the water quality, residues and weeds.

Bibliography

Anukulyudhathon, E. (2003) *Report on Sustainable Development for a Rural Community*, Nhong Han: Municipality of Nhong Han, Udonthani province.

Buranasiri, P. (2003) 'City beautiful', presented at the Symposium on Community Development, Ministry of Economic and Social Development, Bangkok 16 July.

Chankaew, K. (2004) *Essence of an Aquatic Eco System*, unpublished thesis, College of Environment, Kasetsart University, Thailand.

Forest Research Office (2002) *Annual Report on the Forests of the Kingdom of Thailand*, Bangkok: Royal Department of Forestry, Ministry of Agriculture.

National Institute of Development Administration (2002) *Annual Report on the Environmental Situation of Thailand*, Bangkok: Office of Natural Resources and Environmental Policy and Planning, Ministry of Natural Resources and Environment.

Office of Research Studies, Kasetsart University (2003) *Master Plan of Sakon Nakhon Province*, submitted to the Office of Town and Regional Planning, Sakon Nakhon Province: Thailand.

Office of Research Studies, Kasetsart University (2004) *Final Report on the Environmental Situation Survey in Nong Han, Vol. 1*, Sakon Nakhon, Thailand: Kasetsart University.

Office of Research Studies, Kasetsart University (2004) *Final Report on the Sustainable Development Plan for Nong Han Basin Vol. 2*, Sakon Nakhon, Thailand: Kasetsart University.

Ruengpanich, N. (1994) *Forestry and Wild Life Conservation*, unpublished thesis, Faculty of Forestry, Kasetsart University, Thailand.

Chapter 11
Restructuring the medina in Tunis
El Hafsia

Wassim Ben Mahmoud

Introduction

In the thirteenth century, Abou Zakariya (1229–1249) was named Emir and founded the kingdom of Hafside, establishing its capital at Tunis. Tunis was influenced by the Turks during the sixteenth century and then, from the eighteenth to the late nineteenth century, by the Husseinite dynasty. It became a French protectorate in 1881, gaining independence in 1957, when Tunisia became a republic.

Originally, the town of Tunis developed between Lake Tunis to the east which is linked to the sea and another salted lake, or *sebkha*, to the west. The old city, or central medina, and its upper section known as the Kasbah, have traditionally been the seat of political and military power and are surrounded by ramparts. Two suburbs developed to the north and the south of this central precinct and, in their turn, these were also enclosed by a wall. The European area of the city developed on the reclaimed marshes between the central medina and Lake Tunis. After the period of the Protectorate, the city developed to the periphery of the medina adding new districts with names suggestive of French and European connections including Montfleury, Mutuelleville and various so-called garden cities. In general, however, the Beldis, or Arab inhabitants of Tunis, continued to live in the medina and Europeans settled outside.

In the medina, which has a population of approximately 150,000, there has been a recent change in the composition of the inhabitants. Most wealthy people now leave to settle in the European city, the new peripheral districts or the suburbs. In contrast, a new rural population squats in 'spontaneous settlements' around the city and the centre of the medina, transforming its traditional morphology. It has been said that the medina is 'gourbifying', a reference to the *gourbi*, the traditional form of rural settlement in Tunis. The Hafsia quarter (also called the Hara), the focus of this discussion, is located in the eastern, lower part of the central medina, and was originally the Jewish district. Abandoned by its well-off popu-

11.1
Plan showing the overall organization of Tunis in 1985.

lation who migrated to Tunis's European city, the district became run-down, insalubrious and fell into ruins. During the period of the Protectorate, the first attempts at urban restoration took place, focused on three buildings in Cassar Street.

After independence, demolitions continued within the framework of Immeuble Menaçant Ruine (IMR)[1] operations. Specifically, these were a college, a market and a social services centre, all of which were built on vacant land and required much demolition of existing fabric. The Souk el Hout, a very important commercial street running north to south and crossing the centre of the medina, was also demolished in this process.

The association for safeguarding the medina

After Tunisia's independence from France in 1956, grandiose urban projects were planned, one of which aimed to extend the main avenue of the European city of Tunis to the Kasbah. This project alone would have demolished a major part of the medina. Thankfully this operation was halted as a result of protestations by members of a jury selecting a project from a competition launched as part of a campaign to get the medina listed formally as a national heritage area, mobilizing artists and amateurs from the old city. This mobilization led to the creation of the Association de Sauvegarde de la Medina de Tunis, or ASM, supported by the municipality of Tunis.

A few years later, the ASM, now supported by Unesco,[2] developed a project called 'Tunis-Carthage', a study and plan for the rehabilitation of Tunis and the medina and the development of the archaeological site at Carthage.[3] Thanks to the team made up of Tunisian and foreign experts, a significant amount of research and analysis were carried out on the medina and the first large-scale rehabilitation project was commissioned by the ASM: the Hafsia project.

The purpose of the Hafsia project was the rehabilitation of around 10 hectares of the quarter. The project's goals included: overall organization of the renovation process, building restoration, rehabilitation of precincts, the provision of facilities; and improvement of the existing street systems to accommodate both cars and pedestrians. The first phase covered approximately 3 hectares and was focused

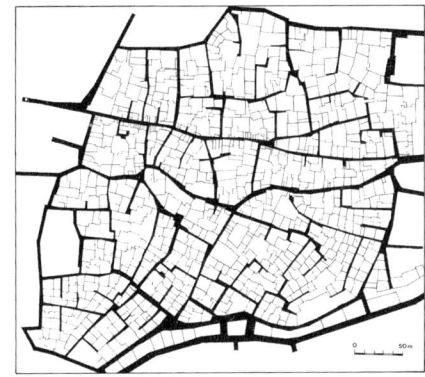

11.2
Plan showing the morphology of the circulation and lot layout in the original medina.

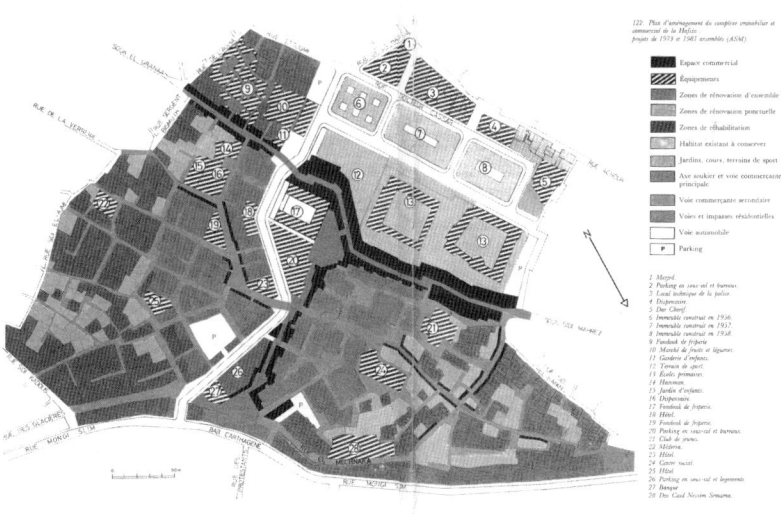

11.3
Plan showing the overall area of rehabilitation including rebuilt and retained fabric.

on vacant land. The programme included the reconstitution of the demolished Souk el Hout and the construction of a hundred housing units. A multidisciplinary team of town planners, sociologists, architects, economists and lawyers undertook the project.

The sociologists carried out a survey of future inhabitants to determine their requirements, which in summary indicated their willingness to live in the traditional courtyard houses, so long as the internal circulation was protected from rain, draughts and winter weather.

On the basis of these results, the architects developed several different house designs from a new form of courtyard house to a row house on a single level. The spatial typology and morphology of the existing medina was respected and reinterpreted in this process: the single level courtyard housing; separate living and work spaces; primary and secondary pedestrian networks; and houses arranged in cul-de-sac layouts.

The souk was treated in the manner of a movie with a missing film roll, with a new length spliced in. Using the techniques of analysis developed by Appleyard et al. (1964), the design team reconstructed the narrative and setting of the street using a consistent architectural vocabulary, exploiting among other things, the light and the variation of spaces. Such analysis appeared to create an appropriate sequential outcome.

The town planners debated at length the issue of whether the historic urban fabric should be accessible by car. The selected option, which discouraged access without resorting to an outright ban, resulted in what can now be seen as observable negative effects – and the absence of a multi-storey parking on the periphery of the quarter accentuates the problem. The new street layout reproduced the traditional hierarchical system, creating a continuity between the older fabric of the city and the newer areas of the medina, a kind of mending of the torn urban tissue, to such an extent that the new work is no longer visible from an aerial view.

The economists studied the balance between commercial spaces with high demand and sale price, and residential, with the goal of keeping low-cost housing and inhabitants with meagre means in the quarter after rehabilitation. As a result, purchasers have easy access to credit facilities: a personal capital contribution of 25 per cent with the remainder repayable at a fixed interest rate of 4.5 per cent over 15 years. To achieve this outcome, the government named the Société Nationale Immobilière of Tunisia (SNIT)[3] as its contracting authority, the ASM as project manager and, on behalf of the ASM, where research and follow up of the work is concerned, nominated the author as architect responsible for the process of delivery.

11.4
The interior of the new souk complex, integrated with the axis remaining from the original.

Evaluation

First, the Hafsia project, by being carried out on vacant land, allowed a part of the Souk-el-Hout to be reconstituted as an important contribution to the spatial and commercial organization of the medina. It made possible the repair of demolished urban fabric by re-establishing the traditional hierarchical street pattern, from the most public to the most private (street, lane, cul-de-sac). The typology of the new buildings was derived from and extended those that already existed to create an integrated whole. While inspired by the form of the traditional houses, they satisfied the contemporary needs of new inhabitants.

Second, the Hafsia project made it possible to retain and expand the social structure of the precinct by integrating a new population of similar socio-economic profile with a group of existing inhabitants of the medina, avoiding evacuation of the area for the benefit of a wealthier new population. While this positive outcome was achieved, it should be noted that what was considered an ideal economic balance between a very profitable souk and sufficiently varied housing units, was from a social viewpoint not so successful. An economic and social balance would have allowed more of the original and most needy of the medina population to be retained.

The rebuilding of the souk and the traditional commercial axes did, however, make it possible to maintain, even reinforce, the economic viability of the quarter of the medina and maintain its traditional activities such the trade in second-hand clothes.

The urban rehabilitation approach adopted in the first phase of the Hafsia project was widely considered a success, particularly by the World Bank which thereafter adopted the rehabilitation principle, because the project was successful in economic terms as well as in safeguarding cultural heritage. The first phase was also awarded the 1983 Aga Khan Award for architecture, not only for the formal quality of the architecture, but for the priority it placed on both rehabilitation and redevelopment (rather than on extensive demolition and reconstructive restoration), and for the new programmes that transformed the form and the socio-economic content of the area. A second Aga Khan Award followed for the later phases that were subsequently financed by the World Bank.

The most important outcome of this project, it is suggested here, has been the reversal of the expected evolutionary trajectory of the medina and perception of it. Rather than being a degraded, down-at-heel quarter doomed to restoration, the medina today is an organized, coherent urban entity, an integral part of the city's cultural heritage and worthy of preservation. Instead of spiralling inevitably towards further degradation that in turn would justify further demolitions, there is now a tendency to rehabilitate and improve. Such an inversion of process continues to be overseen by

11.5
A typical residential street in the rehabilitated medina in 2006.

11.6
Lane housing in the rebuilt medina area in 2006.

the municipality, which improves infrastructure, restores monuments and solves housing issues for the most needy, even outside the medina.

Conclusion

Today, the return of those who left the medina at the time of independence can be observed – its desirability is restored. The residential architecture, which is charged with history, attracts artists and liberal professionals, and many restored buildings have found new functions as restaurants, art galleries, handicraft shops and the like. In addition, the safe, restored, reanimated medina has become an important tourist destination in the city, one where its history is revealed. To date, such tourist activity has brought economic advantage without disturbing the traditional functioning of the old city.

The Hafsia project was originally intended for the low-income strata of Tunis society, including those still developing socio-economically. Houses were designed to be adaptable, allowing for extensions in response to the new needs of inhabitants as their circumstances changed. Through careful design the buildings have evolved along with the socio-economic evolution of the inhabitants, maintaining integration with their surroundings but still flexible enough to respond to the recognized need for appropriation and personalization.

In summary, at a time when total demolition and reconstructive restoration were the preferred methods of urban redevelopment, the Hafsia project demonstrated that the economic, cultural and residential values of historic quarters such as the medina, could be conserved with a different approach to design and development – one which favoured local rehabilitation and integration.

Notes

1 Immeuble Menacant Ruine (IMR) was the programme ostensibly implemented for the protection of buildings at risk of ruin or demolition.
2 UNESCO (1969) 'Mise en valeur du patrimoine monumental de la région de Tunis-Carthage en vue du développement économique', Paris.
3 The Société Nationale Immobilière of Tunisia (SNIT) is a national property company in Tunis.

Bibliography

Abdelkafi, J. (1989) *La médina de Tunis: Espace historique*, Paris: Presses du CNRS.
Appleyard, D., K. Lynch and J.R. Myer (1964) *The View from the Road*, Cambridge, Mass: The MIT Press.
Association Sauvegarde de la Médina, Institut National d'Archéologie et d'Art, UNESCO (1972) Rapport préliminaire *Sauvegarde et mise en valeur de la médina de Tunis*, Tunis.
Sebag, P. and Attal, R. (1959) *L'évolution d'un ghetto Nord-Africain: La Hara de Tunis*, Paris: édité par PUF.

Chapter 12
Garden urbanism in China and New Zealand

Matthew Bradbury

Introduction

In many parts of the world, the contemporary city no longer consists of a centre and periphery. Rather, it resembles a network, a mesh made up of nodes and connecting points which have been generated by infrastructure, often undifferentiated. This new city can be conceptualized as a field, or a landscape, crisscrossed by hundreds of networks; physical, virtual, digital. The most obvious networks are systems of infrastructure like transport or waste disposal but there are other invisible systems such as the internet, media, intellectual and social networks. This city is a thickened terrain, containing hundreds of layers of information.

The contemporary city can be conceptualized as a fluid complex system, constantly changing, evolving and moving. Any response that tries to fix it with some kind of certitude appears doomed. A more appropriate strategy might be, therefore, to develop an approach that can recognize the dynamics of a particular urban system; identify important flows and intensities; and attempt a kind of organizational instrumentality. The designer of such a strategy would no longer be a master planner locating fixed installations in the traditional sense but rather a co-ordinator of complex systems.

This emerging network city, as an undifferentiated network without borders or geographical limitations, also results in a loss of recognizably owned local place. One way to engage with the freedom it offers, or more accurately its inevitability, is to

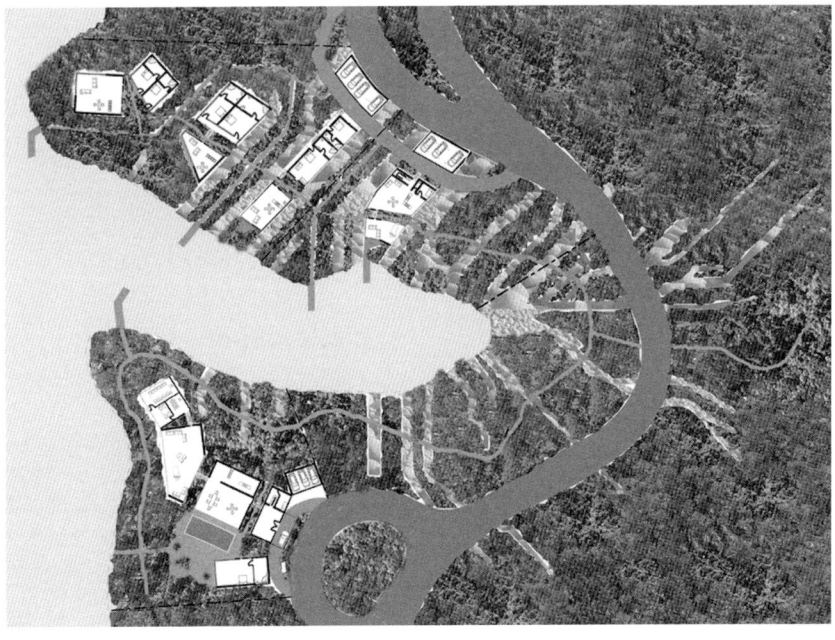

12.1
Plan of the proposed development showing the *parti* of house, flow paths and garden strips.

12.2
View from bedroom of family house to the lake. The bedroom also overlooks one of the overland flow paths and bamboo garden.

12.3
View from the living room showing the overland flow path, garden and neighbouring pavilions.

acknowledge the particularity of location and rethink this city as a landscape.

As a landscape rather than a plan, where it is conceptualized simply as figure (building) and ground (undifferentiated space), this city invites landscape architecture to contribute to a broadened discussion though its practice, techniques and theoretical work. Landscape architecture as a discipline, after all, has specialist ability in the reshaping of the terrain, knowledge of ecological systems and the selection of specific plants.

An exploration

Exploring the possibilities of how landscape architectural practice might engage with these ideas, a case study designed by the author is discussed to demonstrate how an urbanism might be generated from a detailed study of and engagement with the landscape conditions of the place. The case study is located near Beijing, Guangzhou, People's Republic of China. The brief presented many of the challenges that the network city presents. The client, a Guangzhou developer, had visited and lived briefly in New Zealand, and was very taken by the landscape and lifestyle of, in particular the residential subdivisions, in beach and bush locations to the north of Auckland. The client wanted to create the same relaxed feeling in a luxury subdivision around two lakes in the hills, north of Guangzhou.

How does a foreign designer reconcile the particularities of a local site with a brief that specifically calls for the adoption of a cultural and architectural model located many thousands of kilometres away?

To commence, two ideas were put forward. The first was to accept the condition of the New Zealand holiday house which has a sense of openness and an unforced connectivity between the house, the surrounding garden and the larger landscape, whether that is native bush or the beach and ocean. The second was to understand in as great a detail as possible, the particular landscape conditions of the site, taking cognizance of the existing environment, a lake surrounded by steep granite hills. The existing vegetation was a 'weedy' mixture of wilding pines and acacias and it was evident that any disturbance to the site would produce sediment runoff into a closed water body – a negative impact.

The site was a small inlet on the western side of the lake where water runs roughly east to west and the slopes face south and north. There we were asked to design five speculative houses and gardens of different scales and sizes.

The design strategy commenced with the gathering and ordering of the site conditions, such as overland flow paths and the aspect and slope of the site, all of which helped to determine appropriate areas of the site in which to position the buildings.

Importantly, the house sites were conceptualized as 'occupation zones' rather than as autonomous objects. Areas of the site with a low slope ratio that would require the least modification of the terrain were selected and formed into a series of low terraces staged down the slope and interleaved with the existing topography. These terraces became the occupation zones: the terraces nearest the road became entrance areas; the central terraces, the private area of each of the houses; and the lowest terraces by the lake became the living and entertaining zones. The areas between the terraces were treated as conservatories to be planted with species similar to those in the surrounding gardens. The platforms were covered to cause least disturbance to the site's natural drainage pattern, and the shape of the building roofs duplicated that of the unmodified terrain below.

When considering the landscape possibilities, the first consideration was the climate. While the site is on the edge of the tropical/subtropical climate zone it still receives the yearly monsoon, so the design had to ensure that the overland flow paths for water remained clear. These were excavated and laid out with riprap beds so that in winter their appearance will be a little like the traditional Chinese rockery. In the rainy season they would efficiently drain the site.

Further, the site was to be densely planted with native Chinese plants of types and species as determined by aspect, sun, shade, and wet or dry conditions. Ironically (at least for Westerners), those very species that are commonly conceived of as 'exotic', bamboo, magnolias and camellias, are actually indigenous to the Guangzhou province, which is where the first 'exotic' plants from China were exported to the West.

A complex system of paths runs through the site, from the road to the water, through gardens, alongside and across the streams and through the houses and conservatories, establishing a complex 'plaid' pattern of paths, linking the properties to each other and the public gardens.

Conclusion

This project demonstrated that new forms of urbanism could be generated by the intentional use of landscape techniques – considering topography, exploitation of natural forces and careful horticultural selection to determine the overall form of development. It also demonstrated, however, the limitations encountered when trying to use typological definitions and hierarchies such as the house, the garden and nature, or the local and global. These descriptions limit exploration and possibilities. In this project, the garden is both exotic and indigenous; paths are both movement systems and connections breaking down traditional property boundaries; streams are both overland flow paths and rockeries; and houses are more like living zones, with a range of occupational choices, than autonomous objects. The project is local – it acknowledges the particular landscape moments of the site, but it is also global, as it gestures to a new lifestyle, that of New Zealand in another land. All these possibilities open up new ways of living in the world, both local and global, or 'glocal', a combination of both, The result is rich and heterogeneous, opening up a new potential for an idea such as landscape urbanism.

Bibliography

Chapman, G.P. and Wang, Yingzheng (2002) *The Plant Life of China*, New York: Springer.

Deleuze, Gilles and Guattari, Felix (1987) *A Thousand Plateaus: Capitalism and Schizophrenia*, Minneapolis: University of Minnesota.

Fortune, R. (1847) *Three Years' Wanderings in the Northern Provinces of China*, London: J. Murray.

Howard, E. (1944) *Garden Cities of To-Morrow*, Fourth Edition. London: Faber and Faber.

Koolhaas, Rem and Mau, Bruce 1995 *Singapore, Portrait of a Potemkin Metropolis*, S,M,L,XL. Benedikt Taschen, Koln, Germany, pp. 1210–1237.

Le Corbusier, 1929 *The City of To-morrow and its Planning*, London: John Rodher, Reprinted 1947, London: Architectural Press.

Loudon, C. 1871 *An Encyclopaedia of Gardening Comprising the Theory and Practice of Horticulture, Floriculture, Arboriculture, and Landscape Gardening.* London: Longmans, Green and Co.

McHarg, Ian L. 1971. *Design with Nature*. Garden City, NY: Doubleday.

Valder, Peter. 2002. *Gardens in China*. Timber Press.

Chapter 13
Revitalizing the Montenegrin village
Gornja Lastva

Laurence Feveile, Marija Nikolic and Nicolas Petrovitch Njegosh

From diversity to fragmentation

The position of the Balkans, at the crossroads of the East and West, and Slavic and Mediterranean worlds, gives some clue to their animated history. Only one of the oldest principalities, Montenegro, has preserved its sovereignty over the centuries. At the end of the First World War, the collapse of the Austro-Hungarian and Ottoman empires modified the political maps considerably, and the kingdom of Montenegro became attached to Serbia before being incorporated into what was to become Yugoslavia. Where Slovenia, Croatia, Bosnia-Herzegovina and Macedonia then achieved their independence, Montenegro and Serbia agreed to stay together and, in 2002, formed a federation called the Union of Serbia-and-Montenegro, a federation already itself being called into question.[1]

The area around the mouth of the bay of Kotor has a strong identity and status in this region. Formerly inhabited by a Croatian population from nearby Dalmatia, the peninsula had known, until 1918, a period of Austro-Hungarian domination. Like Venice and Dubrovnik, Kotor had been a rich commercial port and the architecture of baroque palaces still competes with the inherent beauty of the peninsula site. The bay is listed as a Unesco[2] world heritage site. Coveted more than ever, the area at the mouth of the Kotor Bay has become a desirable target for investors seeking to conquer the littoral zone and colonize the heights.

13.1
The bay of Kotor with a typical village in the foreground.

13.2
Design by Grichka Martinetti, a workshop student 2003–2004, proposing the reuse of existing buildings and the revitalization of infrastructure.

The imbalance of the dynamic between these investors and the local population dramatically shows the fragility of Gornja Lastva and the other villages of the peninsula of Vrmac, and the imperative of the need to implement of responsible tourism development.

Sited at the mouth of the Kotor bay on the Vrmac peninsula, and at an altitude of 300 meters, the village of Gornja Lastva is part of the agglomeration of Tivat. This is a coastal city developed during the twentieth century as the result of its association with an arsenal – a now obsolete military establishment – and with a now disused Club Med resort located on the nearby island of Sveti Marko. The expansion of the city has meant that during the same period the number of villagers in Gornja Lastva has declined from over a thousand inhabitants to now total just five permanent residents.

The socialist period after the Second World War privileged industrialization and its related ways of living, including the development of the modern city and new cultural expressions associated with it. The village structure, therefore, corresponds to what became a devalued, almost pejorative concept – that of tradition. Mass tourism, already well established in the area, became concentrated in big, specially built hotel complexes, and neglected the villages, cultural heritage and tradition.

The search for a balance

The villages of the peninsula declined and fell quickly into ruins as they were abandoned. Gornja Lastva underwent the fate of many such deserted villages in the region, marginalized by the dominant economy and, especially, by its ideology.

Conscious of the rapid effects of degradation, the population of Gornja Lastva organized itself into an association called Napredak[3] with the following goals: to maintain the relations between people; to maintain the village infrastructure and public buildings; and, if possible, to continue land-related activities. The richness of its cultural heritage and traditions aligns with the principles of cultural tourism based on cultural exchange. According to such a concept, the visitor is received like a member of the family, and takes part in a society whose economy asserts the quality of healthy food, and the local production of fruit, vegetables and olives, bee-keeping and animal breeding. Such values are not always easily understood. Nor is experience of them generally available in the countries previously comprising Yugoslavia, where the civil war period of the 1990s was characterized by food shortages and the fight for survival. And while terms such as 'ecology' and 'sustainable development' may be used to harness local energies to better development elsewhere, they exert little force here. In fact these concepts are even brought into disrepute by the lassitude and scepticism of local people whose recent experience of life has been characterized by so many more immediate concerns.

Even if, supported by the vitality of the association, a project is proposed that might employ those locally unemployed and provide an occupation for elderly people, initial enthusiasm at the local level can turn into discouragement when the list of obstacles appears: the lack of accessible resources; the indifference of authorities; the inextricably complex problems of joint property ownership resulting from the patterns of inheritance for each house and its land; the difficulty of imagining alternative policies for, and forms of, development; and the insufficiency of infrastructure, particularly of water, sanitation and communications.

In 2002, however, the International Meeting of Contemporary Art of the Biennial of Cetinje[4] proposed a summer workshop focusing on the architecture and environment in the village. The topic, 'The Adriatic coast, a peninsula in danger', questioned tourism development in a context weakened by the passage to a market economy.

From pedagogic outreach to pilot project

In 2003, an agreement was signed between the Biennial of Cetinje and the School of Architecture Paris-Val de Seine to hold a workshop at Gornja Lastva to explore opportunities for new models of tourism for the village. There the students would find a challenging site for their theoretical and operational investigations and, supported by the local population, develop *in situ* a project inscribed in social, economic and cultural reality. Their regular exchanges with the inhabitants and the progressive adaptation of their proposals in a concrete situation reinforced the rigour of teaching in the field. Their reports and presentations initiated debates, disseminated information and brought forward technical proposals on many issues such as the water supply, networks of sanitation, the conversion of houses for supporting services such as reception and accommodation and discovery circuits for exploration of the village and its surroundings. They emphasized the importance of training local inhabitants to take autonomous responsibility by teaching them new skills – for instance, to become guides for excursions or alpinism, or to develop expertise on medicinal plants and by training gardeners and building professionals.

As the project progressed and the local population felt more supported, they started to generate their own initiatives. In the summer of 2004, Gornja Lastva accommodated its first eco-tourists. In the wake of the student workshops, the local people relearned the tradition of stone cutting in a masonry school called 'The beauty of the stone' that was held in their own village. The surrounding mountains are now equipped with more than 30 kilometres of hiking trails. The elected officials and those in charge of neighbouring communities and territories also began to re-evaluate their own cultural heritage and many who own property have

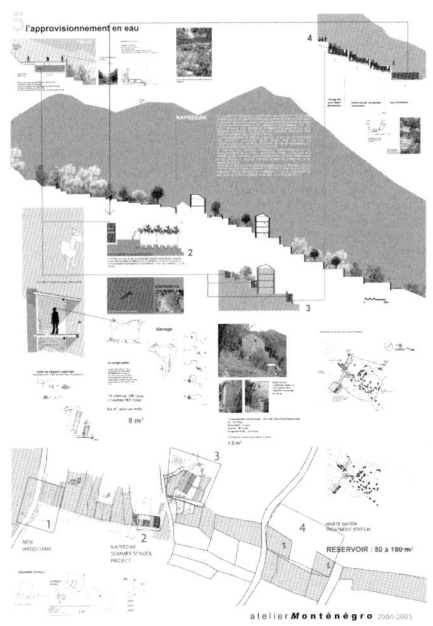

13.3
Design by Julien Mingui, a workshop student 2004–2005, proposing the recycling of buildings and materials.

started to restore their houses and recommence traditional activities that had been neglected, such as crafts and the production of fruit and other local produce.

The experimental project of Gornja Lastva is a useful reference for other locations and situations internationally. The programme was oriented towards the changing conditions of a society in transition. It encouraged originality and also moderated the discrepancy between the foreign concepts of tourism and economic development and the established habits of the locale. Further, it also demonstrated the capacity of both the local people and the students involved to consider the relevance of other geographies and other stories.

The workshop process in Gornja Lastva is a model that expresses how many diverging ideas – of tradition, of participation, of conciliation and of determination to change – can be successfully combined to derive a course of action in the face of a threat to a locality's survival.

Notes

1 The independence of Montenegro, obtained following the vote of 21 May 2006, did not change the major options for regional planning, already initiated thanks to the relative autonomy of the principality. The new statute of Montenegro, however, increased its visibility abroad and accelerated the process of urban development.
2 Unesco stands for the United Nations Educational, Scientific and Cultural Organization. The site of the Kotor bay as well as the town of Kotor are both included on the UNESCO World Heritage List.
3 'Napredak' literally means 'progress, evolution'. This word has other connotations, originally corresponding to a socialist idea of rural tourism in the former Yugoslavia which included organized visits to the 'typical' village, folk festivals and other 'traditional' events.
4 The Biennial of Cétinje, organized by Nicolas Petrovitch Njegosh, Prince of Montenegro, after the fall of the Berlin Wall, aims to bring together the artists of the East and the West, to open debates and to exchange experiments. The first Biennial was held in 1991. The most recent, 'Rebuildings' held in 2002, comprised various summer workshops in architecture and the environment. One of them was based in Gornja Lastva and carried out in association with Napredak.

Bibliography

Božović, G. (1986) *Naselja i kuće tivatskog zaliva*, Belgrade: CEP et la Mairie de Tivat.
—— et le groupe d'auteurs (1986) *Urbanistički projekat Gornje Lastve*, Tivat: Institution publique pour les sciences et la culture de la mairie de Tivat.
Braudel, F. (1985) (sous la direction de), *La Méditerranée*, 2 volumes, Paris: réédition Flammarion.
Groupe d'auteurs (1986) *Projekat oživljavanja seoskih naselja tivatskog zaliva*, Belgrade: CEP Belgrade-Centre pour la culture, les informations et les documents de Tivat.

Levy-Vroelant, C. et Levy-Vroelant, J.I. (1997) (présenté par), *La guerre aux civils, Bosnie-Herzégovine 1992–1996*, Paris: L'Harmattan.

Petrovitch Njegosh, A. (2004) *Voir dans le noir*, Podgorica: Club récréatif 'Café Europe'.

Popović, M. (2002) *Montenegrin Mirror, Polity in Turmoil (1991–2001)*, Podgorica: Nansen Dialogue Centre.

Yérasimos, S. (2002) (dirigé par), *Le retour des Balkans 1991–2001*, Paris: éditions Autrement, collection Mémoires.

Chapter 14
Strategies to support urban identity
Are there European models?

Carlos Gotlieb

Introduction

To position themselves to enter the global scene, many cities, particularly in Europe, now reinterpret the historical roots of their site and structure as the basis for both a new urban economy and as a distinctive amenity. Combined with the crisis resulting from the implementation of the modernist development model that characterized what the French describe as 'the 30 glorious years' between 1950 and 1980, this has forced cities to look for new drivers and processes of urban change. This investigation and discussion suggests that European examples of this process provide useful reference points for efforts toward urban regeneration internationally.

Genoa after the crisis

During the 1970s, Genoa was plunged into an urban crisis that was not easily surmounted. The port, which had been the principal source of prosperity of the city, suddenly came to be seen as a disturbing element within the urban scene. Deindustrialization exposed a number of urban problems until then ignored, such as the presence of harbour installations, often juxtaposed with heavy industries and expressways which severed the historic links between the city and sea. The old districts close to the port, with their Renaissance palaces, had become neglected and were now down at heel and often dangerous. In order to resolve this crisis, the city sought a new, unique identity that would use its history as the base from which to structure change and rehabilitation.

The first step towards attaining that new identity was to inject some dynamism into the local economy by recolonizing the historical centre with activities and developments that would, subtly, interweave forms that characterized both past and present. This process was accelerated by attracting and hosting events on a global scale: the Soccer World Cup; a celebration of the fifth centenary of the discovery of America; and a meeting of the Group of

14.1
The old harbour in Genoa, restored.

Eight (G8). Any such occasions were sought if they favoured the repositioning of the city in the corporate imagination as an attractive and amenable place. Starting in 1992, the most symbolic acts transformed the old port by integrating new developments, juxtaposing the playful with the commercial on the historic structure.

Such projects demonstrated the application of new philosophies to achieve urban change. The urban project was used as a means to develop consensus and dialogue among the many different actors who now took part in the overall process of urban development. Building on this, the new Strategic Plan of 1999 adopted an integrative approach that positioned the physical reorganization of key urban sites and territories as a driver of the region's economic and social transformation. The Plan specifies and encourages a series of strategic non-obligatory activities, whose influence is seen as emanating from a partnership between public and private actors.

In parallel, local plans were updated, applying these broader principles in a series of urban projects focused on the transformation of the three major sites of urban decay – the old centre, the port and the large post-industrial precincts. These plans are the major tools of transformation and various urban projects have been developed from them. In the old centre and the old port, the public projects implemented include the embellishment of degraded spaces; the reclamation and integration of major roads linking the downtown area to the port in time for the G8 summit; and the re-evaluation of the role of the Strada Garibaldi and its reconfiguration as a museum route in 2004, when Genoa was named European Capital of Culture.[1]

As part of this process, new modes of delivery were tested, based on public–private collaboration. These sought innovation in project programmes, as well as excellence in the design of the new buildings and public spaces proposed, such as the shopping centre of Ponte Parodi, which creates an unusual artificial topography at the sea front.

While these ambitious new programmes of conversion at the port and in the old centre were successful, the outcomes in the post-industrial valleys remain less convincing. There, perhaps,

14.2
The old harbour in Genoa, restored to combine recreational, residential and commercial space.

the overly simplistic distribution and apportionment of project process and excessive delegation of project management to private operators has resulted, in particular, in poorer quality community facilities and public spaces.

Barcelona as urban pioneer

In its search for a distinctive urban identity and in the way it has repositioned itself at a global level, Barcelona is Europe's pioneer city. Its mutation took place after an extended consultation process framed by several successive strategic plans[2] and a similar process of attracting and hosting events of international standing: the Olympic Games of 1992 and the Universal Forum of Cultures in 2004. Importantly, its planning tools framed the proposed evolution at a territorial scale, but also left significant room for manoeuvring at the scale of the individual urban project. Urban projects were concentrated on key sites, strategically levering the whole process of urban development and regeneration. First, the proponents of the plans included selected public spaces that met the immediate needs of the inhabitants. Second, was a round of projects that created new centres to relieve pressure on the historic city centre and to open the city to the sea. Finally, a series of urban projects was used to radically reshape the traumatized peripheral areas of the urban territory. These activities combined to support the emergence of a reinvigorated urban economy based on the concept of a city whose attractions would in turn attract a new range of different activities and industries.

14.3
The port entrance in Barcelona from the Cultural Forum.

The spatial quality of the resulting projects integrates several scales of urban planning and design. The urban project associated with the Universal Forum of Cultures of 2004 confirmed Barcelona's determination to open the city to the sea in an obvious way, by extending the Diagonal Avenue that had remained incomplete since its initial conception in the nineteenth-century Plan of Cerdà. The project, delivered by a public–private partnership, is organized around an esplanade with associated recreational spaces and major installations. In a courageous gesture, all combine to create a giant balcony that descends toward the sea, enveloping a sewerage purification station created in the 1970s. While the programme and building typologies, including high-rise buildings and a shopping centre, have been the target of some criticism, it should be recognized that these projects funded a subsequent project that fulfils the significant objective of reshaping the whole urban edge.

Conclusion

Urban projects of the size of those of Genoa or Barcelona are rich sources of experience. They demonstrate the scale of motivation needed to achieve significant change in the public domain and the level of consensus necessary to achieve a commitment to collective action and legitimate that change. They also demonstrate the need, in the contemporary city, for urban planning, design and delivery processes that not only structure the evolution of overall urban form but remain flexible enough to support encourage strategic urban projects at the local scale so that they incorporate valued elements of their sites in the process of their redevelopment.

14.4
The bathing area and playground, Barcelona port (and 14.5 below).

14.5

Notes

1 The European Union annually names one or two cities as European Capitals of Culture. This enables cities to showcase their cultural life during the year, and often acts as an impetus for cultural development and transformation both locally and internationally.
2 The first Barcelona Strategic Slan was approved in 1990, the second in 1994, and the third in 1999. www.bcn2000.es/en/2_plan_estrategico/antecedentes.aspx (accessed 10 March 2007).

Bibliography

Gotlieb, C. (1997) 'Barcelone, cinq ans après' *Diagonal*, No. 127, Paris.
—— (2001) 'Barcelone réaménage ses confins à l'horizon 2004', *Diagonal*, No. 151, Paris.
—— (2002) 'Gênes: un projet urbain pour redécouvrir la ville', *Diagonal* No. 144, Paris.
—— (2004) 'Plan stratégique métropolitain de Barcelone', *Diagonal*, No. 164, Paris.
—— (2005) 'Barcelona 2004', *Diagonal*, No. 167–168, Paris.
Masboungi, A. (2004) (forthcoming) *Penser la ville par les grands évènements: Gênes*, Collection Projet Urbain, Ministère de l'Equipement, des Transports, de l'Aménagement du territoire, du Tourisme et de la Mer de France, Paris: éditions de la Villette.

Chapter 15
Mediating global and local
The Montreal experience

Daniel Latouche

Introduction

Can a city participate effectively in the process of globalization, maintaining its sense of difference while partaking of its benefits and positioning itself among the select group of influential cities recognized in the new global domain? These questions set the agenda for urban design today. Is the urban project part of the problem, contributing to a global wave of urban homogenization? Or is it part of the solution, where healthy and vibrant cities contribute to a common sense of identity and self-confidence?

An unexpected success

Built between 1958 and 1962, the Place Ville Marie (PVM) quickly became the emblematic building of Montreal's business district. Designed in the New York atelier of I. M. Pei and Partners, the building of 42 floors with its cruciform plan would not have achieved this status based solely on its architectural qualities. Cruciform buildings already existed in a number of North American cities, notably the Gateway Center in Pittsburgh. What makes for the success of PVM is the ease with which it inscribed itself into its immediate political and urban surroundings. When the American property developer William Zeckendorf commenced the project on a site belonging to the Canadian National Railway, Quebec was about to enter a period of unprecedented change, both politically and socially. Times were not particularly welcoming for new banking headquarters, especially one with a direct tie to the British monarch – PVM was and has remained the official headquarters for the Royal Bank of Canada – and built by an American architect with cadre of English-speaking engineers at that.

Place Ville Marie was the second stage of development of an immense empty space adjacent to the central railway station. It was intended that a hotel, designed in the tradition of the American hotels of the 1950s, would fill part of the space. Montreal's mayor at the time, Jean Drapeau, of Expo 67 and Olympics 1976 fame, suggested that the new hotel be named 'The Chateau Maisonneuve' or 'The Ville-Marie', in honour of either Montreal's 'discov-

15.1
A view of Place Ville Marie dating from the early 1960s.

erer' or its initial colonial name. The promoters of the development refused, proposing instead the name 'The Queen Elizabeth', a move which initiated a linguistic revolt in Montreal. Nationalist movements, dormant since the early 1930s, collected a petition of 250,000 names (including those of several elected officials) which was dismissed out of hand by the federal authorities who had the final word in selecting the name of the publicly held hotel.

The demonstrations that followed were not lost on the Zeckendorf team, who insisted on finding a more suitable name for the office building, more suitable in any case than the 'Queen Elizabeth Complex'. Zeckendorf was quick to jump on Mayor Drapeau's 'Ville-Marie' suggestion, going so far as to suggest to the Archbishop of Montreal, who visited the site, that the cruciform plan was a clear reminder of the Christian origins of the city.

But the success of the Place Ville Marie came about not only because of these political events in its history. By simultaneously building parking facilities, a railway and an underground shopping mall, the property developers conformed to the modernistic ideal of separating urban functions. They also borrowed from traditional urban design forms such as the gallery Victor Emmanuelle II in Milan, and the Rockefeller Center in New York. Without realizing it, however, they laid the foundations for what was to be one of Montreal's principal urban innovations of the decade, the underground city with its 40 kilometres of walkways, hundreds of shops, cinemas, hotels and convention centre, all of which are connected by subway.

Fifty years later Montrealers remain convinced that this *mélange de genres*, where urban functions get to be mixed and where the meaning of buildings can literally be highjacked, a form of hyperconsumerism with a human face, is Montréal's unique contribution to modern urban design.

15.2
Place Ville Marie by night.

Conclusions

What constitutes an urbanistically and politically successful design, one which pretends to be both local and international? First, it can be said that any such design must propose both a remodelling or at least a serious reorganization of the urban form, while working with what is already there. Adaptation requires the designer to consider and respond to the actuality of the site. To adapt is not to destroy, and gaining respect starts with respecting what is. Humility has a place in this process.

Second, adaptation requires the designer to make way for improvisation and opportunism, taking the time to pay attention to details, however small, especially those of a symbolic nature. Sometimes even a simple change of name can make all the difference. In the end, Place Ville Marie demonstrated how global ideas and local ideals can be made to create new meanings.

Perhaps, despite their 'internationalist' credentials, urban projects, not unlike politics, are always local. This is where their contemporary success ultimately lies.

Finally, where there is success, there is also failure. One unhappy lesson to be learnt from the experiment at the Place Ville Marie is that it is often difficult to take lasting lessons from large-scale projects, especially those with a large dose of improvisation. Fifteen years after Place Ville Marie, Montrealers woke up to two new urban catastrophes, both initiated by the same mayor: the Montreal Olympics with its flamboyant, fast-decaying and over-priced Olympic Stadium; and the Radio-Canada Tower whose insertion in the urban grid required the removal of more than 2,000 residents.

Bibliography

Borja, J. and Castells, M. (1997) *Local & Global. Management of Cities in the Information Age*, London: Earthscan Publications.

Levine, D. (1990) *The Reconquest of Montréal. Language Policy and Social Change in a Bilingual City*, Philadelphia: Temple University Press.

Marsan, J.-C. (1990) *Montréal in Evolution: Historical Analysis of the Development of Montréal's Architecture and Urban Environment*, Montréal: Mcgill-Queen's University Press.

Piché, D. (1991) 'Le design urbain: le cas de Québec', in A. Germain (ed.), *L'aménagement urbain. Promesses et défis*, Québec: Institut québécois de recherche sur la culture.

Chapter 16
New practices in urban development

Jean-Claude Margueritte

Planning and urban strategies no longer anticipate singular outcomes. Nor do they anticipate systematic, linear processes to achieve their outcomes. In fact, it could be said that the entire process of urban development has been inverted, with processes and outcomes entangling, rather than proceeding predictably as they have in the past, from planning, to project, to outcome. This can be considered a reflection, in the urban project, of broader changes in society, where disagreements among stakeholders and unexpected contingencies affect projects along the way. Paradoxes now abound, not only influencing the process of delivery, but how the discourse around urban projects is framed to support project realization. In such a context, urban evolution is increasingly the result of short-term considerations, decisions and actions.

On the other hand, a strong desire for urban planning, urban design and indeed, urbanity itself, appears to emerge from this context of increasing uncertainty. Desire, however, as is recognized, is not enough to realize intentions, and the delivery of actual projects requires that those involved reflect on contemporary processes of urban development, identifying and disentangling impediments.

Urban professionals, therefore, must consider recent experience, anticipate change and problems

16.1
The tram system as it fits within the urban structure of the city of Bordeaux (populaton 22,000 people). This shows the tram's relationship to existing roads, and the historic and residential centres of the city. The Garonne River is to the west. (Image redrawn from material provided by the author.)

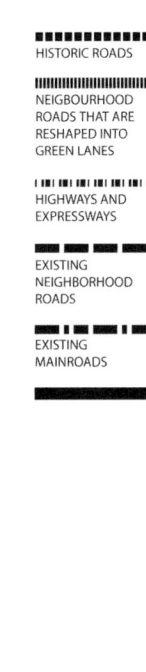

as they emerge, and find alternative methods. Especially, it would seem, in the existing context, they must accept the working reality of multiple, even unforeseen, futures both in terms of projects on-the-ground, and delivery processes, in order to fulfil their goal of achieving urban outcomes that can be considered excellent. Reflection on theory must be balanced by reflection on action.

The contemporary working environment requires urban planners and designers to react rapidly to immediate (often short-term) requests from many stakeholders, while maintaining their awareness of the broader strategic goals and possible long-term impacts. The management of project champions, or local leaders, has become integral to the urban project, and the separation of reflection from action is less and less possible. Urban planners and designers are, therefore, forced to practise action research, or reflection-in-action.

It is argued here, that this increasingly uncertain context, in turn, forces urban professionals to be increasingly sensitive to local demands and to consider or even involve project champions and local leaders in their reflections and decision making. Such stakeholders can even be considered as the drivers of urban projects with the power to impact significantly on the dynamics of project delivery. Because of this, it is often necessary to anticipate, seek out and avoid confrontations by incorporating their involvement in the broader planning and delivery processes, especially through iterative decision making. Decision-making sequences need to be methodical and clear, neither overly intellectual, nor just 'flying-blind'. The process of community involvement is a project in itself, requiring careful project management.

Through such involvements the city becomes, again, a collective work based on diversity and mobility, a kind of work-in-progress. Within this collectivity, the guiding principles of the urban project must encourage the involvement of many stakeholders, and so urban professionals must confront this reality, renewing their practices at the same time that they are renewing urban forms.

While on the one hand the urban planning and design process must now aim to go beyond sectoral interests and the demands of individual stakeholders and project champions, on the other, it must accept the uncertainty of their influence. Urban professionals must also keep control of the

16.2
A sketch of a proposed new tram stop and its relationship to the existing fabric.

process, adjusting it repeatedly and progressively to achieve overall project goals. As well as needing access to more than the few previously accepted methods, urban professionals are now required to respond in a great variety of ways to the inherent realities of the contemporary city which can be seen as a site subject to slow sedimentation and accretion, where each urban project, however complex, becomes just another part of the evolving work-in-progress.

This complex reality must be confronted and worked with. The focus must be on involving and guiding stakeholders and project champions and on harnessing their power and influence via robust decision-making systems. The management (or governance) of all of this at the level of the project must in turn operate within the systems of governance operating at the level of the city, suggesting that greater knowledge of urban management is now necessary. In order to be effective, urban professionals also need advanced knowledge of project management processes, to involve and gain commitment from all stakeholders, be they ultimate decision makers or local residents. The techniques that guide planning and delivery processes must be readable, accessible and motivating. They must focus on issues and outcomes that are widely recognized as important so as to capitalize on local experience and knowledge, and to build a shared sense of what is achievable in the communal imagination.

The idea of the contemporary city as a work-in-progress to which each urban project contributes does not deny the role of many subjective realities in its making. In fact, it is openly acknowledged that there are many interests to be managed and many contributions to be made to the process. Some contributors will use opportunities for involvement as opportunities to play and to egotistically advance their own agendas. Some who feign indifference may actually take advantage of unclear processes and momentary confusions for their own ends. Yet others who have anticipated outcomes early on may lose interest in what are necessarily protracted processes. Others again may subvert decision making, and even whole urban projects altogether, refusing to accept that prevention is in itself a decision that ultimately affects urban quality. Caught in the eddies of contrasting positions and viewpoints, it is easy to forget the overall drift of the tide and the need for urban

16.3
The new tramway as constructed to integrate with the historic fabric of old Bordeaux makes the city centre accessible again.

planners and designers to harness this multiplicity of views, so that the urban project contributes to what is an improved strategic direction for the city as a work-in-progress.

The complexity of the contemporary planning, design and delivery process can be even more destabilizing for decision makers, suggesting why urban professionals are increasingly needed and why their roles are expanding. Recognizing the city and the urban project as works-in-progress rather than finished entities, however, helps them to imagine how their particular Utopia might progressively be approached.

Bibliography

Loinger, G. and Spohr, C. (2004) *Prospective et Planification territoriales*. Rapport commandé par les Directions de l'Urbanisme, de l'Habitat et de la Construction, de la Recherche et des Affaires Scientifiques et Techniques, publié dans la Note du CPVS No. 19.

Lion, Y. (2000) 'Editorial', in *Transformaction, Actes des Rendez-Vous de l'Architecture, Paris, 15–18 novembre 2000*, Editions du Patrimoine: 25.

Margueritte, J.C. (2000) 'Lormont, recomposition urbaine autour du tramway' in *Transformaction, Actes des Rendez-Vous de l'Architecture, Paris, 15–18 novembre 2000*, Editions du Patrimoine: 82–87.

Chapter 17
Sustainable tourism for local identity
The hill-tribe villages of northern Thailand

*Wandee Pinijvarasin and
Pasinee Sunakorn*

Introduction

Tourism has become a significant influence on the areas around what are known as the Royal Projects[1] in Thailand. It is especially significant for the hill-tribe villages in Chiang Mai. Many of today's tourism problems, however, can be attributed to an overemphasis on the business aspects of tourism activity, that promote negative impacts on the cultural and natural resources of a locality. To reduce and even prevent such impacts, a project was established to guide tourism development around the Royal Projects in Chiang Mai. In early 2004, a unique collaboration was established between the Faculties of Forestry, Agriculture (Department of Home Economics), Economics and Architecture at Kasetsart University in Bangkok with the express aim of developing a concept plan for tourism development and landscape improvement for the whole network of Royal Projects, especially around the site of Ang Khang.

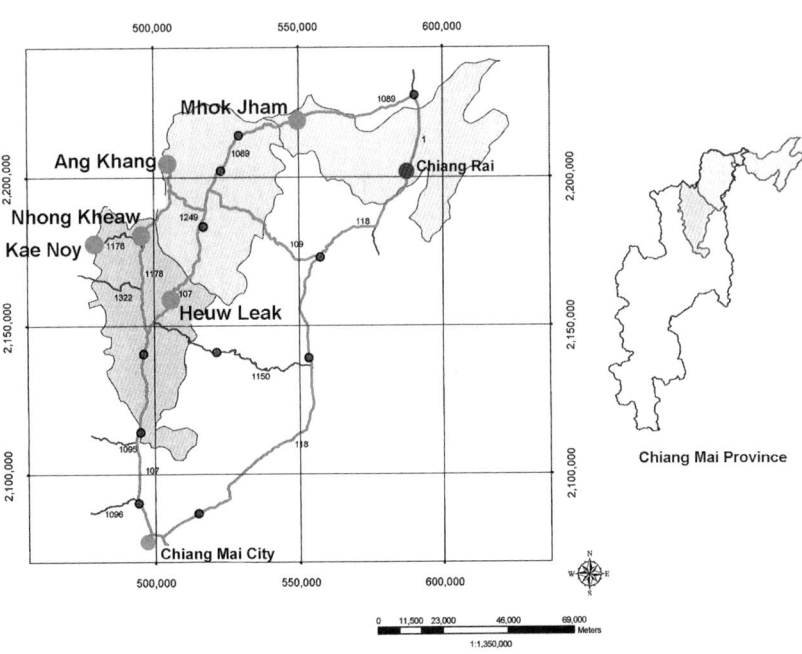

17.1
The network of five Royal Projects at Ang Khang.

The project at Ang Khang

The Royal Project at Ang Khang is located in the northern part of Chiang Mai province, in an area of river basins and mountains which varies dramatically in elevation, ranging from 400 to 1,400 metres above sea level.

17.2
Khob Dong village in the Royal Project at Ang Khang.

The area has a relatively cool climate with an annual average temperature of 24°C (with a range of 21–27°C). The network of Royal Projects covers three districts (Fhang, Chiang Dao and Mae Eye), and includes five Development Centres (Ang Khang Agricultural Centre, Heuw-Leak, Nhong-Kheaw, Mhok-Jham and Kae-Noy). These five projects include 30 hill-tribe villages composed of 10 ethnic groups: the Karen, Hmong, Yao, E-kaw (or Akha), Musue (or Lahu), Lawa (or Lua), Haw, Tai Yai, Palong and Kachin (Kerk University, 2003). Each ethnic grouping is composed of hill-tribe people from many villages, each identifiable by their dress, language, folkways and rites and rituals, which are usually associated with their belief in animism. Most hill-tribe dwellings in the areas manifest as a village. Typically one village is composed of many households, and villages are self-governed. The characteristics of each hill-tribe dwelling and its landscape type are unique, reflecting their particular ways of life and beliefs. The regional weather and picturesque scenes of hill-tribe dwellings, and the natural environments around the five projects at Ang Khang, are considered one of the most spectacular tourist attractions in Thailand.

After interviews with members of 18 villages, it became clear that while most local residents were ready to make themselves available for tourism activities, they did not wholeheartedly understand tourism as a type of business. It is commonly accepted that tourism is an industry that can enrich the life of host communities and that it can help to expand the local and regional economy. If tourism around the hill-tribe communities is to succeed in such a goal and achieve economic benefits and minimal impact on cultural and natural environments, the question arises: what should appropriate tourism planning and strategies be so that local identity and well-being can be sustained in the process?

According to the World Tourism Organization (WTO), ecotourism or community-based tourism is the fastest growing market in the tourism industry. Salobol (2004: 17) for example, states that community-based tourism is an alternative form of travel that stimulates economic development opportunities in local communities while preserving the essential aspects of place, as well as minimizing cultural and environmental impacts. In our collaborative proposals, three steps were included as guiding principles for community-based tourism for the hill-tribe villages around Ang Khang.

The first step is to identify appropriate tourism programmes for each specific locality. To sustain local character and to create a distinctive and recognizable tourism identity, it is vital that the hill-tribe people themselves identify those tourism destinations and the programmes that they consider appropriate to their local history, community and cultural and natural resources. This requires collaboration – between hill-tribe villagers, the staff from the Royal Projects and other participants, who can identify and articulate what individual communities have to contribute to the tourism industry.

The second step was either to generate new facilities, or to improve those already existing, in an appropriate way. Different localities may well have different tourism programmes, and therefore require different facilities. Facilities can network the community with other places, especially the Royal Projects, using landscape, buildings, utilities and signs. While some facilities can be developed from the existing fabric, some need to be created to suit the specific tourism programmes of the place. There are, however, at least four basic principles and concepts that were proposed for creating tourism facilities for the hill-tribe communities. These include such activities as the planning of movement networks using the offices of the Royal Project as the first gate, in order to change transport to non-polluting modes in accordance with local ways of life; landscape improvements using local knowledge, local materials, indigenous plants and local techniques; regenerating old buildings and creating new ones while maintaining vernacular quality and using appropriate technology; and developing sanitary systems while still maintaining the existing cultural practices of the community.

The third step is to plan action programmes to manage negative impacts. Appropriate tourism programmes and the physical development of facilities need planning for a continuing series of actions, based on identification of potential impacts. Action programmes, however, need experimentation and monitoring with a small number of visitors before opening to a larger mature tourism market. Such an approach, in turn, needs many processes and procedures to be developed for testing and evaluating the programmes, activities and facilities. It does, however, improve the likely satisfaction both of local residents or hosts, and visitors, ensuring the long-term sustainability of tourism and the village structure.

17.3
Houses of E-kaw or Akha people at the Mhok Jham Royal Project.

17.4
E-kaw or Akha people at the Mhok Jham Royal Project.

Conclusion

The guidelines and principles for sustainable tourism development of hill-tribe communities around five Royal Projects developed through this collaboration are not limited to creating new built environments. Rather, they emphasize the improvement of existing conditions of all facilities in the locality to fit the tourism industry while maintaining vernacular quality. The proposal encourages the hill-tribe people to realize that tourism is only one supplement to their way of life, rather than a replacement and that to be sustainable it needs to reflect their local past in their particular tourism programmes, as well as responding to tourism markets. In such a form, community-based tourism can not only support but also reinforce a local community and the diversity of local characteristics and identity.

Note

1 Hill-tribe minority peoples in northern Thailand are nomadic; as such their living activities have resulted in drug problems, a perceived threat to the nation's border security, deforestation and destruction of the water resources of the country. In 1969, His Majesty King Bhumipol conceived and launched a Royal Project in order to assist in improving the quality of life of these hill-tribe communities. Thirty-six Royal Projects have since been established in five provinces of northern Thailand. The establishment of Royal Project Development Centres has helped to stop the nomadic way of life of the hill-tribe villagers and in turn to revitalize the natural environments in their areas.

Bibliography

Gunn, C.A. (1994) *Tourism Planning: Basis, Concepts, Cases*, New York: Taylor & Francis.

Kasetsart University (2004) *A Study on a Master Plan for Tourism and Landscape Improvement: the Tourism Network of Angkhang and Inthanon Km.31*, Report commissioned by Highland Research and Development Institute, Ministry of Agriculture and Co-operatives, Chiang Mai, (unpublished).

Kerk University (2003) *The Conceptual Planning for Tourism Development around the Royal Project*, Report commissioned by Tourism Authority of Thailand, Bangkok, (unpublished).

Office of Economic and Social Development in the Highlands. <www.geocities.com/hesdp/hilltribe03.html?200517.html> (accessed February 2005).

Panin, O. (1999) 'Yhou Yen Pensook' in *Proceedings of the Conference on Back to Basics: Thai Lifestyle*, Bangkok: Association of Siamese Architects under Royal Patronage.

Payakeaw, S. (2003) 'The application of thatch over corrugated galvanized steel/corrugated cement roof tile for rural houses in Thailand' in *Proceedings of the 1st International Conference on Sustainable Energy and Green Architecture, SEGA*, Bangkok: Building Scientific Research Centre (BSRC), King Mongkut's University of Technology.

Salobol, S. (2004) 'Community-based Tourism', *Research Community: Newsletter of the Thailand Research Fund*, Vol. 57, September–October: 15–21.

Srinivas, H. 'What is Sustainable Tourism?'. <www.gdrc.org/uem/ecotour/whatis-sustour.html> (accessed February 2005).

World Tourism Organization. <www.world-tourism.org/sustainable/top/concepts.html> (accessed February 2005).

Chapter 18
Making the city
The Bordeaux experience

Michel Bergeron and Patrice Godier

Introduction

The experience of urban projects can be understood in two ways. The first relates directly to the project objectives, how they are set and whether they are achieved. The second relates to the context from which the project emerges. In Bordeaux, the making of an urban project at the city scale emerges both from the city's history and from a context of perceived competition between it and other cities in the region and internationally. Analysis of the experience that comes with the progress of an urban project is valuable, not only for what it shows about the principles that underpin the goals of that particular project but for the lessons it suggests about the way a project might best be implemented.

In Bordeaux, for example, despite the presence of a pluralist, culturally embedded form of town planning, a process of urban transformation has taken place in its agglomeration over a period of more than 40 years. This process is reflected in the considerable peripheral urban sprawl occurring since the 1960s, the result of the construction of a ring road that confirmed the car as the principal means of individual transport for the city and its region. Even with this process, however, the historical and traditional fabric and form of the city centre has remained an essential rampart against such excesses of urban functionalism based on the automobile. Quite simply, its existence prevented the penetration of new roads, and quite recently a network of tram lines was chosen as the new means of development, not only of transport but of the city's public spaces. Implementation of this project was to demonstrate how the centre could be restored to its position of centrality in the face of such aggressive decentralization, by re-establishing an urbanity of proximity that respects human scale and gives priority to pedestrian movement over vehicular.

A similar goal and development process can be observed in many cities across Europe. As a consequence, there are now numerous action plans and strategies put in place and being implemented by those actors who are responsible for deciding, designing and delivering the resulting projects. In this way, a more global phenomenon can be observed, a new frame of reference for urban

18.1
The historic quayside opened up to pedestrians and incorporating the new tramway.

transformation that characterizes the contemporary way of making and remaking the city, wherever it occurs. Such transformations mark a return of the importance of urban planning and design as the means of implementing on-the-ground, broader concepts of urban change. They also demonstrate the emerging influence of project management on implementation at the scale of the urban project. Elected officials, professionals, inhabitants and communities, and those who are driving economic development, are all engaged at a local level in new processes that deliver projects and that are often global in their instigation and conception.

Transformation and continuity in the historic city

The impact of urban sprawl across the surrounding territory, and the consequent increase in car use have, importantly, been accompanied by the movement of economic activity and residents to the city's periphery. The central areas of the historic city have been, as a result, confronted by the emergence of vast post-industrial wastelands, empty historic buildings and a general degradation of environmental conditions (congestion, noise and air pollution).

The major urban projects of the last decade have been undertaken to redress these impacts of sprawling urban agglomeration and include: the introduction of the tram; the rediscovery of the river and waterfront; and the revitalization of the historical centre and old dock areas. All are based on the desire for a symbolic cultural centre, as much as for the achievement of political and economic urbanity. Indeed, whether or not Bordeaux recovers its particular and local urbanity developed in the seventeenth, eighteenth and nineteenth centuries, through these projects, nevertheless their emergence in itself signals a renewed interest in the city's past, adding a new dimension to the growth of the overall agglomeration. Both are, in their own way, driven by the globalizing forces of the late twentieth century. The tramway project, now with a network of three lines of 45 kilometres, is in continuing development, based on a policy of urban consolidation of the various city centres, and aligned with public transport routes through a policy of residential densification. This policy aims at creating an economically attractive urban area with the recognizable status of a European metropolis of one million inhabitants by 2020.

The metropolitanization of Bordeaux has overtaken its historic urban structure by imposing its own logic at the different temporal and spatial scales that operate across its many urban institutions, including its 27 communes. This expansion of institutional structures presents a new challenge to the whole metropolitan territory, which will now have to face a new proposal for further ring roads to bypass the city. Like any project that must operate across this expanded urban domain with its many stakeholders and interested

18.2
The new tramway, constructed to integrate with the historic fabric of old Bordeaux, makes the ancient city accessible again (and 18.3 below).

18.3

parties, this project too will be constrained by its capacity to gain support for its realization, compromising with them all and modifying its form during implementation.

A new system of action

Some of recent experiences of urban projects in Bordeaux suggest patterns of experience emerging internationally. There appear to be strategic goals that are common to many cities (typically being a competitive destination) that suggest fundamental shifts in the way that collective action in city centres is framed. These include, for example: the re-emergence of local political action; new modes of professional practice; and new modes of control.

Local political action in urban centres now appears to have a new logic based on complex networks of numerous participants, including local inhabitants. Such networks dominate urban projects and their implementation. The dominance of local communities in the process of realization shows that the political dimension is important again, in contrast with previous decades where implementation was more a result of established systems of governance and negotiation within these.

The role of professionals is also being redefined. While it has long been recognized that the modes of action, scales of reference (city centre/agglomeration) and debates diverge, this has in the past been accompanied by diverging disciplinary traditions. Today, however, with less certainty in the operating context, the technical organizations involved in and responsible for urban projects are being forced to be more adaptable in their strategies and their processes for implementation. They are responding by updating their expertise, and putting priority on processes that encourage co-operation between and the management of input from the many stakeholders involved.

The final challenge is that of integrating and harnessing the many divergent views and different activities that now, typically, characterize the making of the urban project at the city scale. New mechanisms are put in place to create greater solidarity among actors and participants and diminish the tensions between them. Typical is the reliance on procedures such as planning controls, design competitions and the urban project itself. There also appears to be recourse generally to a more purposeful rhetoric that repeats, in the public forum, common principles that should apply to urban development, including references to shared history, the value of built heritage and sustainable development. Finally, there appears to be a collective desire to acquire new systems of action that create and reflect shared these intellectual attitudes, particularly concerning the reclamation and transformation of public spaces. In Bordeaux such spaces include the old quay areas along the river, but similar activities can be seen in many cities.

Conclusion

Analysing the processes of formulation and implementation that accompany contemporary urban projects presupposes that it will be possible to identify some principles that shape the action. Such reflections on the recent experiences in Bordeaux suggest some emerging trends. First, urban planning and design need to be based on an understanding of the synergy between the overall process of urban agglomeration in the metropolitan territory and the potential for re-establishing the pre-eminence of a revitalized historic centre for the future.

Then, once the urban project at the city scale is underway, a whole set of changing organizational features and aspects can be observed to achieve its implementation. The first is the need to work politically with an increasingly diverse range of actors and participants (stakeholders) – politicians, technical experts, local inhabitants – by focusing their attention on projects which they agree will achieve their shared goals. The second is the introduction of project management to break down professional segregation and enhance co-operation between parties. Finally, fundamental values must be sought and redefined. This is achieved by using techniques such as competitions that articulate values and build a shared rhetoric that focuses on underlying philosophies and how the urban project might express them. These explicitly include sustainability, heritage, the role of public space and, implicitly, the end of the automobile in the central spaces of the city.

Bibliography

Bergeron, M. (2006) 'Bordeaux, moderne et eternelle' in *Revue l'Ingénieur constructeur*, No. 498: 28–31.

Godier, P. and Tapie G. (2001) 'Les nouvelles logiques d'action de la maîtrise d'ouvrage: le cas du projet urbain de Bordeaux' in Bonnet, M. (ed.), *La commande ... de l'architecture à la ville*, Vol. 1, Paris: Éditions du Plan Urbain Construction Architecture (PUCA), Ministère de l'Équipement.

—— (2002) *Rapport sur les cultures urbaines et les expériences d'acteurs dans la ville de Bordeaux*, Paris: report commissioned by PUCA and Institut Français d'Architecture.

—— (2004) *Recomposer la ville, mutations bordelaises*, Paris: Éditions L'harmattan.

Part 3
Learning cross-cultural practice

Introduction
Reflecting on cross-cultural interactions

Catherin Bull and Davisi Boontharm

The experiences discussed in this section confront complexity in contemporary urban design and planning practice by presenting the results of a range of experimental programmes in teaching and learning. These experimental programmes were created specifically to enable critical reflection on contemporary cross-cultural and in some instances, cross-disciplinary practice. The creators of these programmes and authors of these chapters are committed to better understanding how such teaching works and how it can be improved. On reviewing their contributions, the editors propose that these discussions demonstrate how the findings of such experiments have the power to inform not only teaching but also the larger domain of disciplinary practice. This section, therefore, presents a summary of their research (or reflective practice) in the realms of the studio and the workshop, field studies and in the theory seminar. In all these, the world of ideas is explored in relation to the realm of practice. The research that is reported can therefore inform both education and practice about cross-cultural and cross-disciplinary interactions, recognizing, given the international nature of much of their work, the increasing importance of these and the complexities they present.

The focus is, in the main, the workshop – as the design studio (Singh in Chapter 22), the field studies elective with its project base (Thomas in Chapter 23) and the design workshop (Boontharm, Bull, Radović and Tapie in Chapters, 20, 24, 19 and 25). Being central to the pedagogy of the teaching of urban design and planning, and the model for practice, the results can be generalized across both work domains. The ways that ideas are communicated across and between cultures are also discussed (Singh and Thaveeprungsriporn in Chapters 22 and 21). In each of the cases examined, participating students were taken on experimental, if guided, journeys. It is their activities, experiences and views that are discussed, along with and those of their guides (or teachers). Operational issues (such as time, working language, working technique and group composition) are also considered to the degree that they were found to constrain or enhance delivery in unfamiliar environments and cultures.

What stands out from these reflections is the power of difference. While difference generates complexity for work and learning, challenging assumed modes of thinking and working, it also motivates. The idea of experiencing and working with difference – different views, different places, different professional methods – inspires students and teachers alike, just as it inspires practitioners. Access to alternative views is seen as assisting critical reflection on established patterns of behaviour and the fundamental value of cross-cultural practice, despite the challenge it presents to those norms. All the chapters deal with this in their own ways asking: what supports the experience of difference or inhibits it? And what helps us understand and work with it?

In her chapter, Davisi Boontharm discusses an issue of interest to all designers: how to define what a place is and move from analysis to a concept proposing intervention. Observation of the cross-cultural and cross-disciplinary workshops leads her to explore the power of words and the science of signs that underpins the very notion of design ('de-sign'), especially in the cross-cultural and cross-disciplinary domain. This supports the proposition by Catherin Bull that, contrary to expectations, the use of a common working language, even where it is not the primary language of the majority, actually assists group interaction rather than hampering it. Time spent in negotiating the meaning of words and their relationship to place and experience is valuable, in and of itself, because such negotiations build cross-cultural understanding and the capacity to clarify expectations and resolve issues. Boontharm's findings however, further extend the issue of communication, going to the creative act itself. She discusses how skill with the use of words underpins what urban designers normally think of as primarily their expertise in spatial manipulation.

The conscious use of semiotic games, of language and of words in urban design and planning, is proposed therefore as a tool to generate shared meaning and purpose among diverse groups. While it is recognized that such negotiations undoubtedly add time to the process of negotiating the design and planning of complex territories, it enhances the understanding and acceptance of different contributors and ideas. It also enhances the likelihood of moving from that understanding onto mutually agreed actions to effect change. This is a lesson for practitioners and teachers alike. It confirms the need for practitioners in the international domain to challenge the normal expectations for rapid resolution of complex urban design problems and propose more, better structured time for negotiations and discussion to achieve higher orders of interaction. Out of this will come, the research indicates, stronger resolution of complex cross-cultural problems, and greater acceptance of and commitment to outcomes.

The idea that games and play make a positive contribution in cross-cultural and cross-disciplinary work is explored by more than one author. Radović (in Chapter 19) discusses the need to create what he calls a 'thematic narrative' to guide the evolving relationship between the different parties involved. Such narratives are proposed as another means of involving all, and encouraging shared, poly-vocal participation while developing a higher order of interaction. Thaveeprungsriporn (in Chapter 21) extends the discussion on this idea by discussing how in Thai culture, in stark contrast to the West, work is approached playfully. She suggests (as indeed does Bull, albeit from a different viewpoint) that play and work are actually of equal importance in building understanding between parties and creating acceptance of new ideas. These related ideas of narratives, drama and play interact and are proposed as ways to encourage reflective practice and explore (as they have traditionally in other fields) our assumptions about accepted ways of thinking and acting. There is even the suggestion that such activity assists participants to perceive higher truths in the differences they experience. Radović goes on to suggest that to gain the most from the unavoidably dramatic situations that cross-cultural work presents, it is helpful to move beyond the traditional structure of dual protagonists (what he terms 'dialogues'), and construct 'tri-alogues' or even 'multi-logues'. These he points out, assist the cross-cultural or cross-disciplinary interaction to move beyond the usual 'us and them' dualities to another, more constructive working domain.

Such an emphasis on alternative modes of interaction leads to discussions of the issue of time and whether time for play (and its equally important partners, interaction and reflection) is more important in the domain of cross-cultural practice. Since a higher order of interaction and acceptance across diverse participants appears to be a shared goal among contributors, there are many suggestions as to how this can be achieved. These include specifically constructing processes for work that concentrate on teasing out the dimensions of difference (in thinking, in meaning, in place and in ways of working) and time for critical reflection as well as action. A number of authors present and discuss the issue of time and its influence on their work in an era characterized by compressions of both time and space, the twin foci after all, of urban designers, whose principal interest is in the manipulation of space for our time and the future. In summary, they argue that, quite simply, the difference inherent in international practice and cross-cultural work needs more time to negotiate. This is, perhaps unsurprisingly, a major finding of their experimental work. To accommodate difference in the face of the standardizing effects of internationalization and the global market demands that we reconsider the contribution that time makes and make more of it available for what they consider are key contributors to success – recognition, understanding, accommodation and acceptance of what is different and, usually, new.

While it appears that the hot-house atmosphere that characterizes much cross-cultural interaction in urban design work generates drama and intensity and therefore creativity, this needs to be balanced. Such balance, it is suggested, can be achieved by time for more diverse activities. Time should be allocated within cross-cultural interactions – for preparation, for systematic reflection to generalize experience and, just as importantly, for play. This is necessary to develop higher levels of understanding and acceptance and the capacity to work appropriately with difference.

While the chapters reveal that the strength of motivation is to experience difference in place, culture, discipline and work practices, there is less interest apparent in ubiquitous everyday reality, especially among students (but also among professionals). Very often 'the everyday', whether present in ideas or attitudes, places or processes, simply remains invisible. This book – in its title *Cross-Cultural Urban Design. Global or local practice?* and content – suggests that one of the benefits of cross-cultural practice is that the particularities of the everyday condition, especially in urban places and practices, is revealed to the host culture by the very processes of its exposure to others (or outsiders). Working across cultures enhances the capacity of participants to appreciate their own difference as well as that of others and also to observe the standardizing affects of much contemporary urbanization. The processes of global benchmarking undertaken by global clients in development and government may even seek such standardization. Clearly, however, that is not what the students, teachers, communities and practising professionals discussed here seek. They want, as is particularly evident in the chapters by Singh and Bull (Chapters 22 and 24), to have access to the best of global thinking, work and education but to experience, understand and learn how to accommodate difference as well.

Irrespective of cultural background, it appears that participants in urban design projects, whether communities (see Thomas) or students (see Bull and Singh) need to be taught how to see the difference in their own everyday reality and conditions. In the experiments reported here, participants were given the capacity to see by those from other cultures, their guests, who cast a new eye on their home environments as workshop colleagues (see Bull and Thomas, Chapters 24 and 23), or in some instances, as teachers and researchers with a critical capacity to translate the often invisible processes at work around them. While students used their own everyday experience to provide models for alternative approaches in new situations where they were acting as cross-cultural practitioners, unless they were specifically guided, they did so somewhat uncritically (Bull, Chapter 24). This suggests that for the urban design and planning professions, the capacity for reflection on and understanding of 'the ubiquitous', whether local and specific or global in character, requires conscious encouragement and nurturing. This is unlike 'difference', which brings with it its own motivations and enthusiasm for critical exploration. Skills need to be strengthened, then, in reflective practice and the capacity to better understand one's own cultural milieu, global or local. Such skills will enhance the capacity of practitioners to mediate between, and use to advantage, all their working domains and more skilfully articulate their value and potential now and in the future.

By working co-operatively and consciously in cross-cultural and cross-disciplinary teams, the exploratory studios, workshops and fieldtrips discussed here were able to achieve, to varying degrees, their goals of 'higher levels of interaction' or 'greater dialogue' among participants. Their mode of working enabled them to shed new light on what was happening in the territories they addressed – both culturally and environmentally – and, just as importantly, to identify ways to change those processes for the better. By working more closely with local participants, often as partners, the changes they proposed had more resonance and potential to mediate the dynamic interaction between global forces for change (standardization) and local specificities. Such design process can be seen as a form of cultural practice. It is a conclusion of this work that such practice can and should be taught as a skill required of urban designers and planners in the global age, and that the experiences reported here demonstrate how that can be better achieved (Bull, Radović and Thomas, Chapters 24, 19 and 23).

More specifically, where such experiments went further and students worked directly with those who would implement the proposals generated (see Thomas, Chapter 23) it is clear that cultural sensitivity and skills do influence the ownership of outcomes and should influence the workshop method. In his discussion, Tapie (Chapter 25) confirms this, observing the specifics of one kind of cultural interaction (between French and Australians), claiming that the workshop itself is culture.

Authors such as Thomas and Bull in their chapters and Singh in his discussion of a specific experiment in English language teaching, discuss the need for students to actually experience the complexities that go with difference, rather than just finding out about them in theory. That experience is needed in order to gain the skills to confront them in practice. While much policy and theory on international education already promotes the value of experience, the student participants in the various experiments discussed here explicitly confirm those views. They know real life experience of difference and its complexities is important for them and they are motivated by it – not just for their broader education but because it increases their knowledge about what matters most to them, their future work. They want to know more about how their work in urban design and planning can contribute in many places and in many cultures. And while they want such educational programmes to be part of their standard, assessable education, they also want them to retain their fundamental experience of difference. In itself, the complexity of maintaining the experience of difference in a standardized system provides educators with a challenge.

To the views of these students we add our own – that urban design and planning practice in complex situations, characterized by difference, requires specific skills. While these skills need to be both technical and cultural, in the contemporary world it is the cultural, especially, that needs to be developed through learning. The complexity we see needs to be recognized, experienced and confronted, not only by practice but also by education. Modes of practice need to be enhanced by explicitly teaching cross-cultural skills that respect difference and demonstrate ways to work with it. In the world of global practice such skills are needed urgently to balance the standardizing forces that accompany globalization and to turn these to advantage. To acquire those skills our graduates need additional education. Specifically, they need access to theory about what global culture and globalization are, and how they influence their disciplines. It is that culture, after all, that generates the world of international or cross-cultural practice where they will work as urban designers and planners. They need the skills to observe and generalize the elements of place and the processes of change in the spatial domain, at home or abroad, whether that change manifests global or local culture, or both. They need the skills to practice in any place characterized by difference, whether that difference is cultural or disciplinary. And finally, they need to gain experience in reflective practice and learn its value as a skill. In summary, their education needs to prepare them better for their future as urban designers whose practice is not only cultural but, more often than not, cross-cultural.

Chapter 19
Casts, roles and scripts of otherness

Darko Radović

> It may be a mistake to mix different wines,
> but old and new wisdom mix admirably.
>
> Bertold Brecht

> It may be mistake to mix different wines,
> but Eastern and Western wisdom mix admirably.
>
> Bangkok-Melbourne-Bordeaux (BMB)[1]

A third way

The beginning of this millennium was notable for two prevailing views of the future, both extreme. One of those sees the approaching 'end of history'. Following the collapse of the Berlin Wall, Francis Fukuyama (1992) coined that phrase, announcing the victory of free-market capitalism and American-style democracy. In his view, there was no alternative force that could even attempt to change the newly established global status quo of power. His was a vision of the world in which political and economic systems and values, due to a process which dictates 'a common evolutionary pattern' for all societies (Saul, 2005), would converge to the extent that all fundamental differences would disappear. At the same time, Samuel Huntington (1996) formulated an opposing view, with an equally catchy motto, 'the clash of civilizations', envisioning drastic societal divergence rather than convergence. For Huntington, the ever-growing differences in values and world views will lead to irreconcilable positions, which will inevitably result in fierce conflicts between the East and the West, Islam and Christianity, rich and poor and so on.

While these world views arise from different positions, as often happens with radical concepts, neither precludes the other. Both express an important aspect of our times – a dominating vision of a world of clearly labelled winners and losers, a confrontational attitude probably best illustrated by the tragically simplistic statement: 'You are with us, or against us'. While directly corresponding to the Huntington's vision, this in its own way asks

Darko Radović

us to see the end of history by freezing the current distribution of power and its fruits. Fukuyama and Huntington essentially share the same values.

Between the extremes, however, there is a whole spectrum of options and, as always, a third way of thinking that goes beyond those that can be expressed by a single slogan. Our experiment, the BMB, was in essence an effort to find the third way within the practice of urban design that would be environmentally and culturally responsive and responsible.

A personal(ized) theory

The focus of the experiment was on practising urban design in cultures and places that differed radically from those of the majority of the designers involved in the project. Methodologically, the experiment was defined by mature partnership between three very different cultures and approaches to urbanism with an ethos of sharing. The project was conceived collaboratively, and all activities were negotiated carefully. The idea was to enter the process critically, consciously aware of the difference of the participants, to open up to 'the other', to learn about other environments, other urban design cultures and other models of design and design teaching and learning. That broad idea defined the complex relational identities of everyone involved. Very early on, both staff and students started referring to themselves as 'the BMB staff' or 'the BMB students', while at the same time becoming increasingly conscious of their own differently grounded group and personal identities.

In this spirit, at the end of the three-year-long experimental journey, there is a need for multiple theories, personalized theories of the experiment. All players entered the field with their own agendas, expectations and aspirations. During the process, all drew diverse experiences and benefits. Some experiences questioned usual boundaries and stereotypes, and brought the participants closer to each other, while others only exposed how far apart we were destined to remain. Importantly, differences were never flattened, and that probably constitutes one of the most important achievements of the project. That attitude frames other lessons

19.1
A pre-workshop exercise: one Melbourne student imagining Bangkok.

crucial for all cross-cultural investigations and for international design generally.

The classic Confucian text *Zuozhuan* metaphorically explains the subtleties of Chinese philosophy by describing how 'a good cook blends the flavours and creates something harmonious and delicious. No flavour is completely submerged, and the savoury taste is due to the blended but distinctive contributions of each flavour' (Nisbett 2005: 7). That is how, from its initial stages, I saw the full potential of the project.

Such composite quality is 'dramatically constructed' (Karahasan 1994). In his *Exodus of the City*, Dzevad Karahasan, also uses a culinary analogy to describe *dolma*, a Bosnian specialty which is

> a dish of the female principle – internal, closed. Because of that it is tolerant, accepting and embracing all flavours, so much that it is considered a failure if a single one of its ingredients loses its original taste during the process of cooking.
>
> (Karahasan 1994: 10)

He then translates that observation about a particular meal into a much broader explanation of the whole Bosnian cultural system as decidedly 'dramatic'. In such a system, Karahasan argues:

> the fundamental relationship between elements of the system is oppositional tension, which means that its elements are poised against one another, and mutually bound by that opposition, wherein they define each other. These elements enter the system – which is the totality of a higher order – without losing their primordial nature or relinquishing any of the properties they possess independently of the system to which they belong. Every element enters the system by acquiring new properties, instead of losing any of those it possessed from the beginning. Every one of these elements is itself a complex whole, composed of two parts, mutually connected by their oppositional relationship.
>
> (Karahasan 1994: 7)

19.2
A pre-workshop exercise: one Bordeaux student imagining Melbourne (left), and one Bangkok student imagining Melbourne (middle and right).

That principle provides the logic underpinning our experimental approach to urban design workshops and frames the potential of each individual contribution. The fundamental quality of our collaboration, as with any dramatically constructed system, was sought in the pluralism of ideas, contexts and backgrounds, in 'the tension in which its elements confirm their primary nature.... The most pronounced trait of a dramatically constructed cultural system is an exciting interplay of dialogue and opposition between the open and the closed, the external and the internal' (Karahasan 1994: 7). In terms of our methodological orientation, that meant a pronounced sense of poly-versality, the need to establish ways of seeing sharedness rather than sameness (Eisenstein 2004).

While the quality of such an international project was built upon careful implementation of this orientation, its key achievements come from the initially accidental inclusion of the third party, and from the resulting movement from a common bipolar to a multilateral exchange of ideas.

What follows is a reflection that frames one possible theory of urban design in culturally complex situations. That view emerged from my involvement in the BMB experiment from its very beginning – from the initial meeting in 2001 in Bangkok, in which I proposed the vague idea of a tripartite collaboration, through conception of the project and the long process of executing the design workshops, to the conclusion in Bordeaux 2005.

My road

A definition of any personal(ized) theory demands a clear individual position. I became sensitized to the issues of cultural otherness in the early 1990s, developing an interest and then a passion for that theme through three, now clearly discernible, waves. First, it was the tragedy of my (now non-existent) country of Yugoslavia that made me realize the significance of cultural difference. That understanding came about in the most drastic fashion with the belated realization of our collective failure to comprehend the importance, the beauty and the fragility of 'the other'. In the multiethnic, multi-confessional, dramatic society of former Yugoslavia, cultural difference was a part of everyday life. With the emergence of radical, nationalistic exclusiveness in late 1980s that system collapsed into the chaos. Cultural complexity was lost, because it was taken for granted.

My immersion in another multiethnic concoction, that of Australia in the early 1990s, generated the next wave of this fascination with difference. A decision to move to another world turned out to be a decision to become 'the other', to put difference and otherness into the very centre of my own existence. That dramatic, enriching and complex experience was probably best encapsulated in the tantalizing, often repeated question of a friend, who asked: 'Have you started dreaming in English?'

The early 1990s were, for me, also a period of rigorous investigations into cultural difference that became central to both my research and teaching. The third and, for a change, a very (self)consciously staged immersion into the culture of otherness was through my encounters with the cultures of South, South-East and East Asia. Through research, design-research and educational projects in the region, I began first-hand explorations of those fascinating cultures, so different from my own.

These three steps sharpened my sense of responsibility towards the environments and cultures in, and with which, I was increasingly expected to work. They formed a significant part of my starting position for the experiment.

'Thirding as othering', a central concept

For me, the dramatic culture of the BMB experiment was framed by theories of difference and positioned within the post-colonial discourse on orientalism. My own approach to 'the other' is one of respect and implies a strong anti-colonial attitude.

I wanted to test a hypothesis based in Geertz's recognition 'that other cultures are as "deep" as our own, just as well thought out and rich in meaning, but perhaps "strange", not easily fitted into our own way of thinking' (Watson 2000: 675). Through encounters with 'the other' of China, Japan, Vietnam or Thailand, I became a cultural relativist (Radović 2003). My version of the relativist position indeed 'casts doubt not on the existence of local truths, but rather on the ability of an external observer to apprehend and translate those truths completely' (Augé 1989: 32). And, importantly, it also 'casts doubt on the existence of a superior point of view from which these truths might be ordered in relation to each other' (ibid.). Those encounters confirmed to me what Geertz presented in his research of Balinese culture – that there simply are matters that

> can not be compared to their Western equivalents ... because there *are* no Western equivalents. That is the point. A relativist ethnologist does not refuse the exactitude of his or her colleagues' descriptions but rather the generalizability of such descriptions.
>
> (Watson 2000: 675)

That is what I wanted to learn and, as a teacher and practitioner, to share. Cross-cultural design projects offer great opportunities to question stereotypes.

Our cross-cultural project was an occasion to acknowledge that the East and the West, in their many forms and within their multiple boundaries, touch, overlap, influence each other, but remain different. That at certain levels they remain forever totally alien to each other, and that 'the fact that the other cannot be thought directly by no means ... forbids thinking or speaking about it' (Hillis Miller 2001) as Derrida's work abundantly shows.

My primary question was, therefore, how the West (embodied in the French and Australian teams) was going to deal with the cultural otherness of the East (represented by our Thai partners) both as host and as guest.

All teams entered the experiment with rich and highly successful experience in cross-cultural education. What was new about this exercise was the above-mentioned departure from bilateralism, and the inclusion of 'the third'. By that seemingly simple and initially accidental addition, the communication and exchange of ideas was dramatically multiplied. That facilitated a remarkable qualitative leap. In each encounter with otherness, there was always the third, the viewer, the observer – who was also observed. The main difference between this trilateral and those previous bilateral exercises was that original tripartite character of the partnership that, through the constant presence of the third, undid the dualism which is often implied in cross-cultural projects. Each team rotated through various interrelated positions – from being (intentionally or not) dominant, a part of the dominating two, an observant, or often (willingly or not) the Hegelian, frustrating, 'excluded middle' (Sartre 2000: xiv).

In that sense, the rich opus of French meta-philosopher Henri Lefebvre, together with that of his interpreter to the English language Edward Soja, are of importance for understanding the BMB experiment, both as process and as product. At the first meeting in 2001, when only a possibility of a joint project was first tabled, I used a term 'trialogue' and thus, 'secretly' (because I did not want to influence the process, which was to be co-owned by all partners) referred to Lefebvre's (1996) obsession and excitement with 'the third'. As Edward Soja pointed out, 'for Lefebvre, reductionism in all its forms, including Marxist versions, begins with the lure of binarism, the compacting of meaning into a closed either/or opposition between two terms, concepts, or elements.' (Soja 1996:60). It was in that sense that I wanted my own experience of the other to be enriched – by adding the third party. Typically, in cross-cultural situations it is too easy to get to simplistic comparisons between 'us' and 'them' because they facilitate learning. Those comparisons can, however, also establish dangerously simplistic oppositions that impede the capacity to understand and identify the truly different, especially our own difference.

In practice, the experiment gave a positive dimension to the term 'othering' and, centrally for our collaboration, the term

> was coined ... for the process by which imperial discourse created its 'others' ... Othering describes various ways in which colonial discourse produces its subjects. In Spivak's

explanation, othering is a dialectical process because the colonizing *Other* is established at the same time as the colonized *others* are produced as subjects.

(Ascroft *et al.* 1998: 171)

In that sense, throughout the three long years of the experimental process, especially during the three workshops in Bangkok, Melbourne and Bordeaux, we were rediscovering and reframing both our partners and our own identities – as 'the other' – by constant redefinition of our relationships. The key task was and remains: to make difference obvious, to expose and to celebrate difference and to stay aware of our own otherness. That is where Lefebvre and, now in particular his translator into the post-modern, Edward Soja, provide a framework for theorization of the experiment in 'thirding as othering' and as an exploration of 'thirdspace'.

It remains important for us how

> Lefebvre consistently sought to crack ... (the binary oppositions) open by introducing *an-Other* term, a third possibility or 'moment' that partakes of the original pairing but is not just simple combination or an 'in between' position along some all-inclusive continuum.
>
> (Soja 1996: 61)

Thirding-as-Othering 'is much more than a dialectical synthesis *à la* Hegel or Marx, which is too predicated on the completeness and temporal sequencing of thesis/antithesis/synthesis'. Importantly, thirding introduces 'a critical "other-than" choice that speaks and critiques through its otherness' (Soja 1996: 61). In its various forms that ranges from casual discussions among the staff (including misunderstandings as well as acceptance) to the place-, time-, and culture-specific lecture programmes and presentations; that logic permeated both the 'experiment-as-philosophy' and the 'experiment-as-practice'.

As in the Lefebrian method, the BMB thirding 'recomposes the dialectic through an intrusive disruption' (Soja 1996: 61). That 'intrusive disruption' in our project was often embodied in the very presence of the 'third', of 'another other' (which, in many situations, proved to be our own self). The existence of the 'third' in the experiment multiplied all possibilities – possibilities of collaboration, possibilities of (mis)understandings, those of alliances, the frictions and the dialogues (within a trialogue), because 'thirding produces what might best be called a cumulative *trialectics* that is radically open to additional otherness' (Soja 1996: 61).

To stay true to its philosophy and practice, with theorization of this experiment the dynamic nature of othering does not stop. Open-endedness is the very nature of cross-cultural situations and has to remain open to continual redefinition. This, book, for example, sees the tripartite BMB project as an opportunity to both act and contemplate practising and learning in culturally complex environments that are 'not meant to stop at three (to construct a holy trinity) but to build further, to move on, to continuously expand the production of knowledge beyond what is presently known' (Soja 1996:61). This book is a contribution to that process.

A game in othering

Such was our third way. In concrete terms, the three workshops explored three different approaches to (the teaching of) urban design. In each workshop, the host was expected to select the site and thematic focus, to organize the workshop and to provide methodological leadership, at least in critical, opening stages of the process. Even from those first steps, our methodological differences became obvious. The sequencing of particular exercises, the character and the foci of briefings, the pace and many other elements of intensive design workshops, all exposed significant variations in design approaches. The relationship between the analytical and design phases of projects, for instance, turned out to be one of the most discussed issues.

Five snapshots from the workshops focus on key aspects of the project and encapsulate its contribution to the process of cross-cultural design in practice:

Imagining and encountering the place

Prior to each workshop, I conducted a small warm-up exercise. Before leaving for the fieldwork, I asked our postgraduate students, practitioners in the fields of urban and landscape design and architecture, (and, before their visit to Melbourne, the French and Thai students) to present, on a single sheet of paper, their own, personal summary of the place–city–culture they expected to experience. The tasks were simply formulated as 'Imagine Bangkok', 'Imagine Melbourne' and 'Imagine Bordeaux' exercises. The main purpose of that request was twofold: to record individual starting positions, and to amplify the inevitable culture shock.

That exercise coupled neatly with the subsequent phase, investigated and discussed by Davisi Boontharm in the following chapter – the first encounter with the site and the recording of immediate reactions to that experience. In both exercises we were playing with metaphors. One was placed at the naive stage before actual encounter with a place of radical cultural and environmental difference. The other captured what is probably the single most exciting stage in the process – the moment of that encounter. The dialectization of the expected and the real held a potent charge for an efficient start to the workshop, even the key moment of inspiration.

Not surprisingly, the general conclusions from those opening exercises point in same direction. They agree with Low that we now need

> quite other metaphors for imagining our worlds and our responsibilities to those worlds. Localities Specificities. Enactments. Multiplicities. Fractionalities. Goods. Resonances. Gatherings. Forms of craftings. Processes of weaving. Spirals. or ices. Indefinitenesses. Condensates. Dances. Imaginaries. Passions. Interferences ... Metaphors for the stutter and the stop. Metaphors for quiet and more generous versions of method.
>
> (Low 2004: 156)

The issue of language(s)

As a matter of convenience, BMB partners agreed that the working language would be the *lingua franca* of the era, English. The impact of the use of English on cross-cultural encounters remains largely unexplored. Language is never an innocent tool of communication. At one end, each language is marked by strong cultural belonging. At the other pragmatic but not banal end, such a choice positions the native speaker in the position of (sometimes undeserved) advantage.

Languages are culture. In the BMB experiment it was necessary to be aware of that fact, both within and beyond our word games. Our only trilingual staff member, Boontharm, points out the various ways in which the three cultures spontaneously saw words and capitalized upon their power. The very imprecision of our readings of those words was a sometimes critical contribution to the creative process. In the way Wittgenstein and Lacan

> believed that words are imprecise, meaning both more and less than they appear to mean to either the speaker of the hearer, and that it was the job of psychoanalyst to understand this question of meaning, as revealed through language, in the light of the unconscious.
>
> (Watson 2000: 626)

While participating partners never pretended to be psychoanalysts, to degrees that vary depending on the organizer of a particular workshop, they were able to let words linger within and between their diverse cultural frameworks and carve out their contribution to the design process. That contribution often held strong ideolects and kept on resonating with the culture of its origin, and thus identified the team member who introduced a particular theme in an otherwise exemplary team effort. It was fascinating to find that some initiatives, regardless the place of particular workshops, were distinctly Thai, French or Australian. Some of those culture-specific propositions blended into a composite quality, while some remained exotic. All of them had their place in a cross-cultural studio situation.

As further explained by Boontharm, words are central to design communication. Here, it is sufficient to remember that they are always culturally mediated. The words are signifiers of complex situations in and for which we use them, and they also reflect the complexity of our cultural backgrounds.

This opens a field of immense importance for cross-cultural communication in general. The results of Nisbett's empirical research shows how, for instance, in Japanese schools ' "How" questions are asked frequently – about twice as often as in American classrooms', while ' "Why" questions are asked twice as frequently in American classrooms as in Japanese classrooms' (Nisbett 2005: 127). That leads to our next snapshot.

A culture of (non)debating

The role of debate in the workshops that involves participants from cultures of the East and the West holds an important message for cross-cultural collaboration. Cultural studies show that 'debate is almost as uncommon in modern Asia as in ancient China. In fact, the whole rhetoric of argumentation that is second nature to Westerners is largely absent in Asia' (Nisbett 2005: 73). Any participant in cross-cultural communication between the East and the West must be aware of that fact.

Within the Australian learning system, in particular at the university level, debates are encouraged and highly valued in the education process. It was noticed that in various situations our overseas students tended to step back, and discussion started to be dominated by the locals. The reason was not simply better command of the working language. It goes much deeper, and is an issue that is profoundly cultural. For Australians, as 'for Americans, this rhetoric is constructed bit by bit from nursery school through college. By the time they are graduate students, it is second nature. But for the most part, the rhetoric is new to the Asian student and learning it can be a slow and painful process' (Nisbett 2005: 74). The combative, rhetorical form is also absent from other spheres of Asian culture.

There was, therefore, another issue much larger than our workshops that lent itself to close, trilateral examination. All institutions with multicultural populations, like the University of Melbourne, address on a daily basis questions that result from Nisbett's research:

> How should one educate Asians and Asian Americans [or, in our case – Australians] in American [or, in our case Australian] classrooms? Is it a form of colonialism to demand that they perform verbally and share their thoughts with their class-

mates? Would it have the effect of undermining the skills that go with a holistic approach to the world? Or is it merely common sense to prepare them for a world in which verbal presentation skills, even if it might be difficult to achieve them, will come in handy?

(Nisbett 2005: 212)

Design practice, potentially, provides potent solutions to this impediment to communication. Design-as-language on its own can help span not only linguistic but also cultural barriers, and enable meaningful communication and even debate of equals (Radović 2005). The outcomes of our experiment confirmed such a position.

Hierarchy ... or not?

The next snapshot comes from the workshop that was methodologically framed by the Thai team in Bangkok. It illustrates both the complexity of cultural difference and the threats of cultural domination that exist within any cross-cultural project. During the Bangkok workshop, the teaching panel suggested the students establish a clear spatial hierarchy within their interim design proposals for an area south of central Bangkok.

While that advice aimed to facilitate faster understanding of the very complex site and to help further refinement of initial ideas, it soon became obvious that our Thai students needed assistance. It was puzzling to us foreign teachers why local knowledge, an obvious advantage for Thai students, did not seem to be of much help. Our assumptions ranged from blaming difficulties with the language, to questioning their education in urban design. We could almost sense the Orientalism at work.

The problem lay elsewhere, however. Our well-intentioned advice was grounded in, for us, commonly accepted theory, and lots of practical experience. The problem was that both the theory and the experience communicated to the Thai students were alien – not only to their understanding of the project, but also to Bangkok as a place, and to the Thai urban culture as a philosophical concept. The theories evoked in our advice came from the dominant Western paradigm. Our practical experience was also conditioned by the urbanity (or rather, urbanities) of the West. Within the cultural context of our site, the design approach and the implied spatial solutions which we encapsulated in a single word – hierarchy – were highly questionable (Radović 2005).

A desirable chaos?

To explain the magnitude of cultural difference between the urbanism of the East and that of the West, we can use the example of Japanese urbanism.

> When exploring another great city of the East, Tokyo, Augustin Berque discusses how its 'spatial order, which is *characterized by juxtaposition rather than hierarchization*, is fairly typically far-eastern. One can already see its principles in Chinese gardens: interlocking, superimposition, juxtaposition, terracing, the succession of points of view rather than general views etc (my italics).
>
> (Radović 2004: 176)

To the Western mind and to an eye trained by the lived experience of European, or any other Western urbanity, that order might be elusive (Ashihara 1989). Those less flexible among us could even cry that there is no order at all in the cities of East and South-East Asia, that they are a pure chaos. And, *chaos* might be the word that both Eastern and Western urbanists would gladly accept.

In the cultures of the East, the word 'chaos', as a signifier, does not necessarily denote what we foreigners, the *farang* of Thailand and the *gaijin* of Japan, expect. Evelyn Schulz (2003), in an essay which presents the prominent Japanese intellectual Koda Rohan, explains why. 'For Rohan Tokyo is in general state of "chaos" (*konton*) and looks like an unfinished product (*miseihin*). This is due to the fact that even the idea of what capital city should be is "chaotic and without shape" (*konton musho*). In Rohan's thinking chaos is the means for describing Tokyo's contemporary condition and serves as the image of the crisis' (Schulz cited in Radović 2004: 176).

A summary

What should be concluded from these experiences in the games of othering? It is suggested that they illustrate the care that foreign designers need to take when practising in places and cultures that differ significantly from their own. In many, the West may be seen as superior, not only by Westerners but also by participants from elsewhere, including the East. Approached from a position that recognizes cultural difference, however, such perceptions can be exposed as superficial. Nisbett, for instance, sees that at least

> two advantages of Asian cognition stand out: (1) the fact that Asians see more of a given scene or context than Westerners do; and (2) the holistic, dialectic, Middle Way approach to problems. Leaving aside for the moment the question of whether one should attempt to teach these skills to Westerners, there are some hints from the work of cognitive psychologists David Meyer and David Kieras that it might be surprisingly easy to open 'bottlenecks'.
>
> (Nisbett 2005: 212)

Learning to immerse oneself in the ways of significantly different ideolect is an important feature of cross-cultural practice. One can learn from radical difference, and

> to do this we will need to unmake many of our methodological habits, including: the desire for certainty; the expectation that we can usually arrive at more or less stable conclusions about the way things really are; the belief that as social scientists we have special insights that allow us to see further than others into certain parts of social reality; and the expectations of generality that are wrapped up in what is often called 'universalism'. But, first of all we need to unmake our desire and expectation for security.
> (Low 2004: 9)

The conclusion – the precious *other*

In *Towards Culturally Responsive and Responsible Teaching of Urban Design*, I used a painting by Salvador Dali to explain the overall philosophical framework of this experimental approach. That painting also encapsulates some of the key conclusions of relevance to the practice of cross-cultural urban design.

Portraits usually represent the object as seen by the artist and are analogues for how most Western philosophers see the world. They

> start with subject-object opposition and see the object from the subject – that is, they grasp the world from the standpoint of the self. From such a subjectivistic perspective the self is understood to stand, as it were, outside the world

says Abe Masao in his introduction to Nishida Kitaro's *Inquiry into the Good* (Nishida 1987: xxiv). In *L'Angélus de Gala*, (1935, now at MoMA) Dali takes an important step back, towards us as viewers, and focuses our attention on the observer, the observed and their relationship. We become an extension of the field. Abe would translate that into the realm of philosophy by stressing how 'the world is not something that opposes the self but something that envelops it' (Nishida 1987: xxiv).

Dali included himself, the painter, into the frame of a portrait of his beloved Gala. Here, we have not only the observer, the observed and their relationships, but also the viewer, ourself, as 'the third', the one who becomes an extension of the field. She or he is outside, extending the totality of the experience into Bakhtin's 'exotopy', 'outsidedness' 'which is not simply alienness, but a precondition for the ... ability to understand and formulate a character, a precondition for dialogue itself' (Ascroft *et al.* 1998: 12).

19.3
Van Delft's *Atelier* or *The Art of Painting*, Dali's *L'Angélus de Gala*, and graphical elaboration of the positioning within the BMB experiment.

Dali's complex (self)portrait depicts an ideal situation for the culturally sensitive exploration of 'otherness'. Rather than simply framing the exotic object, we must remain aware of the whole situation, investigating at once ourselves, the objects of our interest and the field of forces within which we interact. Dali was an eclectic. That composition was not new in the history of art. A marvellous Johannes Vermeer van Delft's painting, *Atelier* or *The Art of Painting*, from the Kunsthistoriches Museum of Vienna, is a good example. There we also see the painter sitting in front of a young woman, as realistically depicted as one would expect from the seventeenth-century Dutch master. He also hybridizes two traditional categories in painting – portrait and self-portrait. This painting could be used to support my finding. But, *L'Angélus* was selected over the *Atelier* because of Dali's cynical depiction of himself and the implied self-criticism, which is an essential ingredient for a reciprocal relation with the other. After entering the expanded field of the other, our existence becomes fundamentally relational. In the BMB experiment we strove to achieve true relationship among equals. The portrait of Gala and Dali is a metaphor for the way in which we composed the cross-cultural design workshops. Such direct experiences are fundamentally trans-individual. As Nishida said, 'knowledge, feeling, and volition are undifferentiated ... The unity of intellectual knowledge and practical emotion-volition is the deepest demand of human beings, and it indicates the living ultimate reality' (Nishida 1987: xviii). In these studios we wanted moments of 'pure experience' to occur and facilitate encounters with 'the other'.

L'Angélus remains the best summary of the whole BMB experiment, one that contains the single most important message for practitioners involved in cross-cultural urban design. Together with the above-described resonance of the post-colonial theory within the BMB and the founding concept of 'thirding as othering', the message of *L'Angélus* completes my theoretical framework of the experience.

Note

1 BMB – or 'Bangkok–Melbourne–Bordeaux' – as already described in the Introduction to this volume, was an international, experimental teaching and research project conducted by the Faculty of Architecture at Kasetsart University, Bangkok, the Faculty of Architecture, Building and Planning at the University of Melbourne and École d'Architecture et Paysage, Bordeaux over the three years from 2003 to 2005.

Bibliography

Ascroft, B. Griffiths, G. Tiffin, H, (1998) *Key Concepts in Post-Colonial Studies*. London, New York: Routledge.

Ashihara, Y. (1989) *The Hidden Order*, Tokyo, New York: Kodansha.

Augé, M. (1998) *A Sense for the Other – the Timelines and Relevance of Anthropology*, Stanford: Stanford University Press.

Berque, A. (1997.) *Japan, Cities and Social Bonds*, Northamptonshire: Pilkington Press.

Dale, R. (1986) *The Myth of Japanese Uniqueness*, Oxford: University of Oxford.

Eisenstein, Z. (2004) *Against Empire: Feminism, Racism and the West*, London, New York: Zed Books.

Fergusson, N. (2003) *Empire: How Britain Made the Modern World*, London: Allen Lane.

Fukuyama, F. (1992) *The End of History and the Last Man*, London: Penguin.

Hillis Miller, J. (2001) *Others*, Princeton and Oxford: Princeton University Press.

Huntington, S.P. (1996) *The Clash of Civilizations and the Remaking of World Order*, New York: Simon & Schuster.

Karahasan, D. (1994) *Sarajevo, Exodus of a City*, New York, Tokyo, London: Kodansha International.

Lefebvre, H. (1996) *Writings on Cities*, Oxford: Blackwell.

Low, J. (2004) *After Method, Mess in Social Science Research*, Albingdon, NY: Routledge.

Nisbett, R.E. (2005) *The Geography of Thought*, London, Boston: Nicholas Brealey Publishing.

Nishida, K. (1987) *An Inquiry Into the Good*, New Heaven: Yale University Press.

Radović, D. (2003) 'Celebrating the difference – design, research and education for cultural sustainability', in R. King, O. Panin and C. Parin, *Modernity, Tradition, Culture, Water*, Bangkok: Kasetsart University Press.

—— (2004) 'Towards culturally responsive and responsible teaching of urban design', *Urban Design International*, 9 (4): 175–186.

—— (2005) BMB – the basis, lessons and inspirations: teaching design vs. teaching *about* design' in *Identity and Globalization: Design for the City*, Bordeaux: EAPdB.

Sartre, J.-P. (2001) *Colonialism and Neocolonialism*, London: Routledge.

Saul, J.R. (2005) *The Collapse of Globalism and the Reinvention of the World*, London: Penguin Books, Viking.

Schulz, E. (2003,) 'The Past in Tokyo's Future', in N. Fiévé and P. Waley, *Japanese Capitals in Historical Perspective*, London: Routledge Curzon.

Soja, E.W. (1996) *Thirdspace, Journeys to Los Angeles and Other Real-and-Imagined Places*, Cambridge, MA, Oxford: Blackwell.

Watson, P. (2000) *A Terrible Beauty, A History of the People and Ideas that Shaped the Modern Mind*, London: Wiedenfeld & Nicolson.

Chapter 20
Analysis, concept and the value of words

Davisi Boontharm

Introduction

Etymologically speaking, the word 'design' relates directly to the word 'sign'; sign comes from the Latin, *signum*, where the verb *designare* means 'to signify'. The connection between usages of these words now frames a question of interest to all designers: what is the importance of 'sign' and 'signification' in the process of 'de-sign'?

Since understanding and interpreting existing signs and an ability to produce new signs and signify new relationships are central to the everyday reality of designers, it is important to make that process explicit. Equally it is important that designers are aware of their capacity to (re)locate, (re)discover and (re)create both the signified and signifiers in the environments they create. Design combines both rational and imaginative, intuitive processes. In urban design, the analytical and the intuitive needs to be in balance to make good proposals.

Signs have a symbiotic relationship with language. Semiotics even places them before language as the entities that enable interpretation, relating the meaning of one phenomenon to another. Thus, a sign is not just an object, it evokes a process. Through signs we present and interpret, we develop knowledge and signification. Pierce even proposed that there is no thought without signs (Ockerse 1991), suggesting their importance for human communication and existence.

This discussion is about the relationship between 'de-sign' and 'sign', a relationship most clearly demonstrated during the second workshop of the BMB experiment in Melbourne, where the 'key words game' was a part of the opening stages. Words were used to signify the phenomena, the facts and the activities observed at the site, as well as to frame the initial responses to those phenomena. The aim was twofold: to describe what was observed; and to trigger the creative process of design. The complexity of issues, the fast pace of the fieldwork and the quality of participants offered an ideal opportunity to better understand some critical questions, including: when and how creativity enters the design process; whether there were significant methodological differences in approach to this issue between the Australian, French and Thai participants; to what extent differences reflected broader cultural differences between those cultures; the effect of cultural difference on the balance between the analytical and the creative; and whether word games, specifically the key-words game generated better design or communication, especially at the early stages of the design process.

Within the experiment, words were used not only for basic communication, but also as affective triggers of imagination, as tools for early openings and to introduce creative concepts, and as potent signifiers of issues and qualities to be explored through design. It is argued here that it was the power of words as used in the early stages of the design process that made a significant difference to communication among design teams and the overall quality of their proposals.

The project

The focus here is on methodological differences and the way that these affect learning and design quality in cross-cultural urban design work, particularly within the workshop. The collaborative protocol for the BMB experiment (introduced elsewhere) included an agreement that the workshop method was the responsibility of the host institution and that all participants would follow the method selected. The key questions (*problematique* in French) for the design outcomes were, therefore, established in advance.

Analysis of the process of thinking and the development of ideas within the BMB workshops revealed that all three had some methods in common: all had an introductory phase of lectures, discussions and site visits by land and by boat. Students were then divided in mixed groups to experience a variety of cultures, disciplines and schools of thought. They were expected to react to the information provided through the series of assignments, brainstorming sessions and debates, both within their

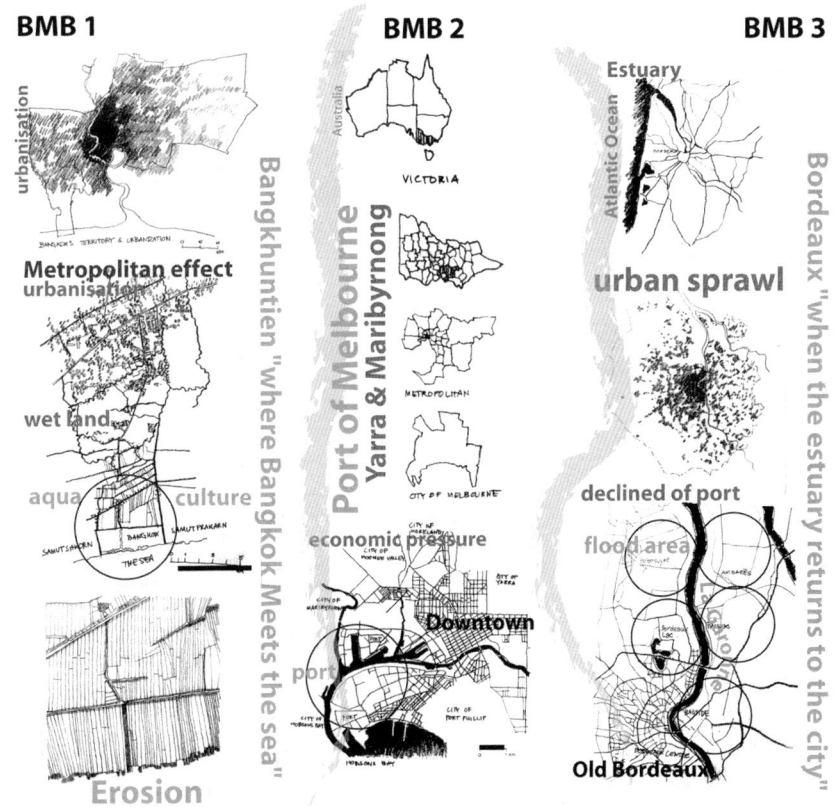

20.1
Bang Khun Tien (Bangkok), the Yarra River (Melbourne) and the Garonne (Bordeaux) – a schematic representation of the main issues for each of the three sites.

group and between groups. The task was for each group to produce, in due course, design proposals for specific spatial interventions. The teaching process was shorter than the usual full semester, and this condensed and concentrated experience offered interesting insights into the ways students respond and develop their ideas about urban design processes.

My interest was in the role of analysis and the formation of design concepts within those intensive workshops, starting with several questions. How does the 'concept', which is mostly imaginative and intuitive, relate to the analysis, which is rational? How do analysis and the formation of concepts interact and assist progress? What catalysts can accelerate that process? These questions were eventually refined to focus on an exploration of the power of words, and this discussion explains my understanding of the role that words played in those studio workshops and, in particular, how words can facilitate strong design responses. It also attempts to convey the intensity and ambience of the experiences in order to describe how words emerged, were used and contributed, to both analysis and synthesis of design concepts.

Learning in urban design requires concrete situations and sites. In October 2003 we explored a remote area of Bangkok for the first workshop in the BMB experiment, a site which raised some complex and important questions about the relationship between the city and water in Thailand. That site is Bang Khun Tien, one of 50 districts of the Bangkok Metropolitan Administration, an area of special environmental quality, and a place 'where Bangkok meets the sea'. It exemplifies the conflict between the natural environment and integrated local cultures and various, often imported, planning doctrines, models and patterns of development. It is an example of how political and planning systems are insufficiently prepared to deal with the severe environmental problems that result from urbanization. The environmental condition of the site is unique, and in its scarcity of land and abundance of water, it is 'very Thai'. Almost the whole of the Bang Khun Tien area is covered by water: canals, shrimp farms and the encroaching sea. Erosion is eating up the coast at a staggering pace and the remnants of the once rich mangrove forest now hardly resist the tides. A memorial column, which elegantly marked the point on the coast where Bangkok and the sea used to meet, is today accessible only by boat. In Bang Khun Tien one can feel both the power of nature and the devastating impact of human development on the environment.

In Melbourne in 2004, the workshop explored the lower stretches of the Yarra River, where it feeds the busy Port of Melbourne. Today this place is decidedly industrial, but the rapid urban development of Melbourne poses inevitable questions about its future. The Melbourne Docklands, an area between the site and the downtown Melbourne, is a successful large-scale urban renewal project on post-industrial brown-fields land, suggesting a possible (even likely) future for Melbourne's other waterfronts.

In a less dramatic but no less significant way than Bang Khun Tien, the Melbourne site is also exposed to severe environmental threats. Dangerous chemicals and other cargo incompatible with human settlements are transported and stored in close proximity to the emerging urban area. Commercial water traffic increasingly threatens the bay and river ecologies, suggesting the need for a serious rethink of the role and future of the port in such close proximity to the city.

In Bordeaux, the Garonne River has played a vital role in the history of the city. The Port de la Lune flourished from the eighteenth to the mid-twentieth century, but today it is largely a forgotten, vast, abandoned land, a true brown-field site. The stretch of the river from Bordeaux to the estuary is now used exclusively for industrial and cargo shipping, but the sites along the riverside show diverse and often incompatible uses. La Garonne was always considered a part of the ocean that entered inland, but today it is very much an undesirable, brown rather than blue, body of water.

The constellation of socio-economic powers can change urban environments in many ways. One of the roles of urban design is to provide and test alternative visions for the future and help to direct both social and financial capital towards a better outcome. All three sites have their established characters. The first, Bang Khun Tien, is marked by both a strongly cultural dimension and dangerous exposure to the destructive forces of nature; the second, the Port of Melbourne, is a key location for the local economy where the industrial areas, the port and the areas increasingly popular for living come together. The third, the Garonne riverside, demonstrates the determination of urban authorities to revive the waterfront. These sites exemplify that the interplay between the city and its water, with all their common and local nuances and their futures, is of

20.2
Comparative schedules/workshop programmes for BMB workshops 1, 2 and 3 which detail the activities conducted over the allocated time.

critical importance for the future of each city. The dangers for Bang Khun Tien are coming from the sea to the south and from the expanding city to the north; Melbourne's expansion is pushing urban development downstream to the estuary, as it is along the Garonne at Bordeaux. In all three water is the key ingredient, one which holds the potential for a pleasant urban lifestyle and encourages urbanization that in itself brings threats.

In Bang Khun Tien water is an agent of damaging erosion, but still remains central to Thai cultural identity. The Yarra River in Melbourne was, until recently, seen only as a route for shipping. Changes of attitude towards urban living have, however, made water an important part of the economic and experiential value of river-front land, and urbanization there is rapidly changing the morphology of the city.

In contrast with both, Bordeaux has its unique 3-kilometre-long facade of eighteenth-century buildings on the river. Like many European cities, cars, urban sprawl and a decreasing inner-city population are causing negative impacts. The port activity is shifting toward the estuary, causing a rupture between land use and activities on the water. The city centre is the main focus of Bordeaux's urban strategies, with a major public space created to improve access to the river. The waterfront not only recalls a glorious past but seeks to establish a new interface between the river and the city.

The central question explored within the three workshops was how architects, landscape architects and urban designers can react and contribute to such complex situations and their evolution through design. How can they bring together and expose both the positive and the negative aspects of urbanization, which are both globally recognizable and locally defined?

The workshops

Learning urban design through intensive workshops (in academia, as well as in practice) condenses the usually lengthier process of design into short timespans. In the case of the BMB, the process lasted only ten working days. Workshops must start fast, with decisive

20.3
The words from the whiteboard session of BMB workshop 1, and the keywords workshop of BMB 2.

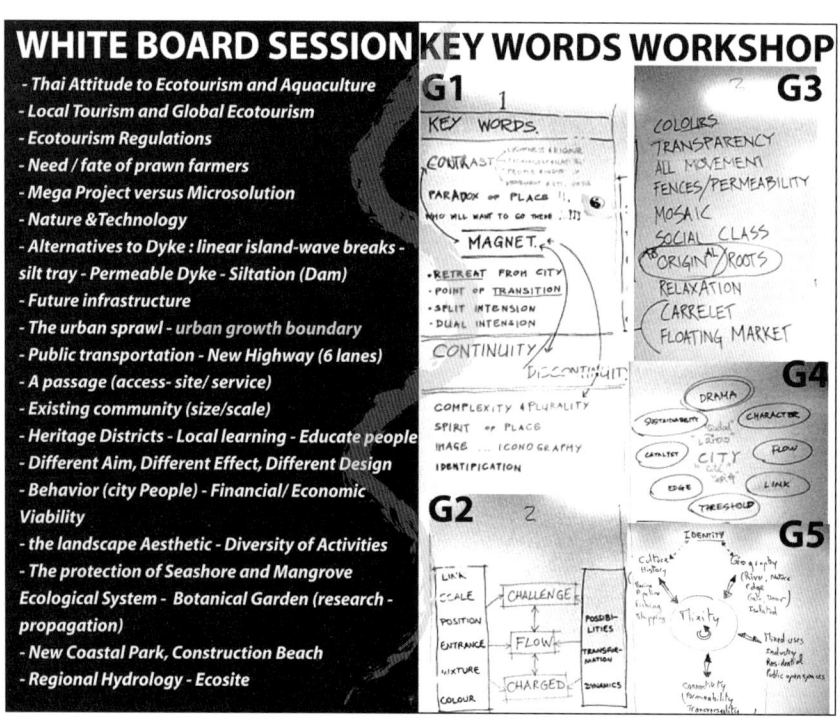

action by the leader and an immediate, meaningful reaction from the student or participant, followed by discussions that lead to a cycle of rapid action–reaction exchanges. These exchanges I nicknamed 'the ping-pong process': the leader serving the first 'ball' to her or his students with a particular spin, expecting an equally thoughtful 'return' and the feedback which enables the game to continue. In this regard, in Bangkok and Melbourne methods were quite similar, while the Bordeaux method differed slightly. The key difference was in the detail.

A comparison of workshop schedules shows that Bangkok and Melbourne started with the series of lectures providing the start-up 'tools' and empowering the participating students to begin. In Bangkok, the tools were more technically orientated and very site-specific (information about shrimp-farming techniques, mangrove planting and examples of concrete local sustainable development projects). In Melbourne, the tools were broader and varied from specific information about the Port Authority policies to the general introduction of design strategies employed by urban design and landscape architectural practices in Melbourne. The Bordeaux workshop started with an encounter with the sites. Lectures followed, focusing on the overall picture of urbanization and the current urban strategy there. The *problematique* of that workshop was identified by the Bordeaux teachers in advance, and five different situations were linked to five discrete sites. To varying degrees, all situations and sites demonstrated the interaction between the city, the Garonne, urbanization and use.

Another distinguishing characteristic was the way site visits were handled. In encounters between the site and the designer, the emphasis was on what the site 'tells us' – what does the place want to be? Although site visits were carefully organized for the whole group, individual perceptions were encouraged, even demanded. Every participant had to define their own position, based on their own cultural background, knowledge and feelings. After the site visits (which can be seen as the 'ping' action), the teachers reacted ('pong'). That process was organized as an intensive 'whiteboard session' in Bangkok, and as 'the key-words workshop' in Melbourne. This discussion about the power of words initiated at those sessions and the phase called the 'hints moment' of the project. In Bordeaux there was no such moment. Through the site visits and the series of lectures, the teachers had already identified the site and the problem, providing a short cut within the learning process. After the site visits, students' experiences of the site were not presented to the group as a whole, and those trips were followed only by internal discussion within each group.

In Bangkok and Melbourne, the sites were large, with various complex situations. Through the first experience with the site and development of initial feelings, together with knowledge based on preliminary information and lectures, students were asked to formulate phrases or words that best expressed their ideas, individually and as a group. That process helped to identify the key questions, their own points of interest, and it also guided selection of appropriate sites where both could be further explored. That exploration was facilitated through definition of the most significant key words as well as broader site analysis, the larger picture of the territory being established progressively. The selection of individual sites for further exploration by the students came later, when the *problematique* was clear and could be related to specific locations.

As the sites for design exercises were defined in advance in Bordeaux, the group organization focused more on answering questions of who to work with and that of most interest, helping students to frame their questions more quickly.

In Bangkok and Melbourne, after 'hints' were received, the 'ping-pong process' intensified. The task for students was to discuss and develop their own *problematique* (or questions) and they were asked to support their ideas and findings with a well-grounded urban analysis helped by the selected words. During this process, especially in Melbourne, the capacity to develop ideas differed significantly between groups. An important question was: to what extent was the cultural difference, and corresponding diverse meanings ('readings') associated with the key words, behind some obvious misunderstandings?

The ping-pong process continued throughout the workshop, within pin-up and tutorial sessions, until two days before the last presentation. The students were then left to finish, present and submit their proposals.

There was, however, no 'ping-pong' process in Bordeaux. The rhythm of interaction between the teachers and the students was slower than in the first two studios. Rather than immediately responding to the site visit as the first experience, students were given time to digest the impressions and to address them with the previously provided 'tools', i.e. knowledge gained from lectures and documents.

The pin-up and sub-jury sessions were important phases in all three workshops, moments when everyone gathered together to give and to listen to other participants. Students had to prepare what they would show, to revise their ideas and proposals; and everyone, teachers and students alike, was expected to discuss them. Such active, frequent and intense interactions fall within the definition of the 'ping-pong' action where everyone was learning and which provided students with the important opportunity to learn from each other.

Words as signs

The particular focus in the Bangkok and Melbourne workshops was on the process where key words were nominated, selected, interpreted and analysed. All nominated key words were listed on the whiteboard and discussed. During the discussion, the 'stronger' words stayed while the 'weaker' ones went through numerous modifications, or were eliminated. It was interesting to observe how the judgement of which words were 'stronger' was made and defended, and to compare the ways in which the teachers pushed the process forward, sometimes by giving a necessary push (the 'pong') or just encouragement. Both students and teachers were playing freely in the serious field of semiotics, the philosophy or the science of signs.

The word 'design' (with its roots and all the connotations that come from that origin) points to an activity that is centred on the sign. The word may mean 'from the sign', 'on account of the sign', 'concerning the sign', 'according to the sign' or 'through the medium of the sign' (Bouissac 1998). All understandings imply the semiotic nature of design activity.

Signs participate in a symbiotic relationship with language but are prior to language. Roughly stated, a sign is that entity which allows the interpretation of something that represents meaning in reference to something else. In other words, a sign evokes a process. Through signs we are able to represent and interpret and to develop knowledge and signification (Ockerse 1991).

In such a fashion, the students unconsciously sought those words or phrases that best represented the site and their own ideas about it. Those initial words only served as triggers of discussion, offering the raw material for teachers to start interpreting, to improvise upon ('what if') and to give advice about. They actively sought the signifiers, which represented the place, the site – as the signified.

In his discussion of the *genius loci* and the meaning of places, Christian Norberg Schultz mentions that 'a place is therefore a qualitative, "total" phenomenon, which we cannot reduce to any of its properties, such as spatial relationships, without losing its concrete nature out of sight' (Norberg Schultz 1980: 414). Places are designated by nouns. This implies that they are considered real 'things that exist', which is the original meaning of the word 'substantive'. 'Space, instead, as system of relation, is denoted by *prepositions*' (Norberg Schultz 1980: 17).

To explore this process I actively sought the meanings and multiple dimensions of the words (representing place or site) proposed, a process amplified by the coincidence that I was the only staff member who could speak the three languages of the participants – English, French and Thai. In such a situation I was expected, and also felt obliged, to facilitate complex tri-lateral, tri-lingual translation and interpretation (which was, in itself, a fascinating experience). Within that, my strategy was to put myself in the role of our students, to maximize the possible interpretations which any particular word could give, switching from one language to another

(English was the BMB working language). In each situation some specific local terms appeared. I purposefully then suspended my own judgment in order to leave those ideas to students to develop further, to question, accept or abandon.

The semiologist C. S. Pierce has said that 'we make meanings through our creation and interpretation of "signs"'. According to him, we even 'think *only* in signs' (Hartshorne *et al.* 1958: 302). Images, sounds, odours, flavours, acts or objects, even words, do not have any intrinsic meaning. Rather, they become signs only when we invest them with meaning. 'Nothing is a sign unless it is interpreted as a sign', declares Pierce (Hartshorne *et al.* 1958: 302). During the various site visits our students were 'reading' diverse signs of and within those places, and then expressing their own reactions through words, as signs for action.

Such meaning is never external nor is it universal, and there can be no meaning without mediation. We actively create meanings from the complex interplay of codes and conventions, of which we are normally unaware. Becoming aware of those codes is fascinating and intellectually empowering, as they contain our culture and express our commonalities and differences. That was an important aspect of the word games in the first two studios.

Roland Barthes (1964) has said that, logically, when a reader recognizes what a sign depicts, he then goes on to decipher the cultural, social or emotional meaning. Barthes accepted that while individual signs reduce the 'anarchic' tendency towards generation of endless meanings, the cultural diversity and constant change that make up the realm of connotative signification is global and diffuse. In the experiment, the cultural backgrounds of participants in these workshops were so diverse, a multiplicity of 'readings' was guaranteed.

Umberto Eco offered ten fundamental codes as instrumental in our shaping of images: codes of perception, codes of transmission, codes of recognition, tonal codes, iconic codes, iconographic codes, codes of taste and sensibility, rhetorical codes, stylistic codes and codes of the unconscious (Eco 1982). All were, one way or the other, proven relevant to the semiotic game.

The words, as signs for action on the whiteboard, summarized, to various degrees, the creative return, the 'pong', from the students. Each of the five groups formulated and expressed their ideas through a word-based system of signs – as single or linked words, as phrases or even as full sentences. During the process, a variety of words attached meaning to those aspects of place which left the strongest impression. Such impressions sometimes contained questions, or even hinted at possible early design solutions and it was at the moment when individual words hit the whiteboard that a rich and unpredictable semiotic game started.

The key words in the first two workshops did differ. In Bangkok the whiteboard session began early, at the very beginning. Any ideas were invited and there were no a priori rules, the name of the session itself suggesting a *tabula rasa*, a white space. In Melbourne, the session was actually called 'key words', assigning a priori significance to the words as 'keys' to future design solutions, a significant difference.

Comparative analysis of the words generated within the workshops shows that the words on the whiteboard in the Bangkok session (before working groups were selected) were much broader, often narrative and descriptive. In Melbourne, the key words were based on some analysis, and were structured on the basis of early in-group discussions. Such word games were not played in Bordeaux, although words were used within presentations.

The words generated at the Bangkok and Melbourne workshops related strongly to their sites. The Bangkok site was the more complex of the two, significantly different from the previous experience of visitors, who found the extent of water there dramatic. From everyone, but especially the visitors, Bang Khun Tien demanded particular concentration. It was difficult to react from previous experience, and to reach credible design solutions quickly. Here the selected words hinted at compromise, were softer and suggested longer-term solutions. The Melbourne site was more 'international' in terms of the issues and nature of questions it posed to the participants, both of which were more recognizable. Noticeably less complex, the Melbourne site hinted at more explorative, innovative and 'stronger' design ideas.

In the Melbourne workshop, only very few of the numerous key words presented persisted until the final presentation, including 'mixity', 'drama' and 'mosaic'. Were they stronger as words and signs than the other words from the original pool? Were they already concepts, or half-concepts, rather than reactions to the existing condition? Were they both?

At the completion of the key-words workshop in Melbourne, the 'pong' returned to the students by the teachers included both analysis and feelings, providing personalized expert comments. The word 'mixity', a neologism which does not exist in the English language, came from a loose translation of the French word *mixité* and, as such, was already a new 'sign' of, among other things, the workshop's cross-cultural mix. As a word to drive design it needed further elaboration. What, how, why mix? An analysis was needed to explain and support that single word. The second word, 'drama', is poetic and seemed to evoke a very personal response from everyone as a sign. To me, for instance, it evoked just one single but strong image from our boat trip along the Yarra River. It also had very strong conceptual potential and provoked many interpretations, even before the analysis started. The third word 'mosaic' related to the site as existing and hinted at its future potential.

In the Bangkok workshop, students proposed even more interesting key words, including 'sedimentation', 'flow and filter', 'water–land interface' and 'journey'. Those words eventually became part of the title of the project. To the group that suggested and argued for those key words 'sedimentation' and 'flow and filter' strongly aligned with the idea of belonging, alluding to the processes of transformation that take time. They also include elements of unpredictability, qualities usually associated with good urban design and offered a clear 'sign', an image of small particles floating in the water destined to slowly settle at the bottom of the river, or to get caught by the filter, or to go on, all the way through the estuary. While such words inspire, they also pose dilemmas because of their multiple meanings (expressed by repeating the word 'or' here). These dilemmas open space for imagination and action but also for analysis and interpretation.

Semiotic games were not used in Bordeaux, the French method having defined a priori a *problematique*. Five groups worked on five different sites, characterized by varying degrees of urbanization, and were guided towards comprehensive site analysis by predefined questions. The word, while treated as significant part of the teaching method in Bangkok and Melbourne, now appeared only as and within the communicative structure. Was this because the sites strongly reflected their long history and, thus, demanded deeper understanding through analysis? Bordeaux seems not to have the same pressures as Bangkok (environmental and cultural threats) or Melbourne (economic growth), suggesting that the rhythm of the city (Lefebvre 2004) and local culture shape the ways people not only perceive, but also conceive of, their city (Lefebvre 1996).

Conclusion

The three workshops provided opportunities to explore cross-culturally, both readings and interpretations of their sites. The experiences coming from those workshops have relevance not only for academic situations but can be generalized and applied within various situations of international practice.

Themes of place, words and history permeated all and were expressed by the three host cultures. In Bangkok, Melbourne and Bordeaux each site demanded specific ways of learning. Bang Khun Tien was about an expansive context, both natural and manufactured. The experience of being at the site was the key to its understanding and, it seems, its future. The Melbourne site can almost be considered a new land demanding more inspiration from its design response. That is when words became an appropriate tool for inspiration. Bordeaux is an old city whose established eighteenth-century glory can overwhelm the designer. Fascination with its past makes a deep understanding of its history, as well as its current situation, a precondition to planning its future. Such distinctions could oversimplify the differences, however, suggesting that rational analysis was used more in Bordeaux, whereas intuition and rationality, to varying degrees, were balanced in the Bangkok and Melbourne cases.

The workshop methods employed in Bangkok and Melbourne explored new ways to comprehend and imagine futures for their sites that provide valuable lessons for the workshop as a format for addressing sites with/of cultural difference. Along with the usual design tools and media, such as images, maps etc., words were needed to define, to signify and to generate visions of the future. The very choice of the words or other media has a potential to open up new dimensions of meaning that can then be used as guidelines for action and design.

To design is to create. But where does creativity come from? In urban design, especially, there is the tendency to see analysis as the main generator of ideas, but the duty of urban designers is also to create something new, to invent meanings for places, and that need renders classical analysis insufficient. Analysis needs to be combined with intuition. The capacity to manage both rational analysis and imagination is the gift of the good designer, but not everyone is equally gifted. The issue for educators that remains, is how to educate so that many can achieve better results.

Bibliography

Barthes R. (1964) *Elements of Semiology*, trans. Annette Lavers and Colin Smith, London: Jonathan Cape.

Boontharm D. (2005) 'Where Bangkok meets the sea: a reflection upon experiences from an international multidisciplinary urban design exercise: the BMB field study of Bang Khun Tien' in *Ranaeng*, Special edn for the tenth anniversary of the Faculty of Architecture, Kasetsart University, January 2006: 72–85.

—— and Radović R. (2004) 'Environments under strong development threats – on Bang Khun Tien and the possibility of a sustainable future' in *Planning Models and the Culture of Cities*, IPHS2004 (International Planning History Society) conference abstracts, Barcelona, Spain: U.P. Catalunya.

Bouissac P. (ed.) (1998) *The Encyclopedia of Semiotics*, New York and Oxford: Oxford University Press.

Buchanan, R. (1993) 'Semiotics and design', *Semiotica*, Vol. 97: 189–197.

Chandler, D. (2001) *Semiotics: The Basics*, London: Routledge.

Cobley, P. and Jansz, L. (1997) *Introducing Semiotics*, Cambridge: Icon books.

Eco U. (1982) 'Critique of the image' in V. Burgin (ed.) *Thinking Photography*, London: Macmillan.

—— (1984) *Semiotics and the Philosophy of Language*, Bloomington: Indiana University Press.

Gottdiener M. and Lagopoulos, A. (eds) (1986) *The City and the Sign: An Introduction to Urban Semiotics*, New York: Columbia University Press.

Hartshorne, C., Weiss, P. and Burks, A. W. (eds) (1958) Collected Writings of C. S. Pierce, Vol. 2, Cambridge, MA: Harvard University Press.

Hodge C. (2003) *Semiotics: A Primer for Designers*, www.boxesandarrows.com/view/semiotics_a_primer_for_designers (accessed October 2005).

www.aber.ac.uk/media/Documents/S4B/sem02.html (accessed October 2005).

php.indiana.edu/~ccolon/Semiotics/ (accessed October 2005).

carbon.cudenver.edu/~mryder/itc_data/semiotics.html date accessed October 2005.

www.code.uni-wuppertal.de/uk/computational_design/who/nadin/ publications/ date accessed October 2005.

Lawson B. (1990) *How Designers Think: The Design Process Demystified*, 2nd edition, London: Butterworth Architecture.

Lefebvre, H. (1996) *Writings on Cities*, Oxford: Blackwell.

—— (2004) *Rhythmanalysis*, London and New York: Continuum.

Nadin M. (1990) 'Design and semiotics' in W. A. Koch (ed.) *Semiotics in the Individual Sciences, Vol. II*, Bochum, Germany: Brockmeyer.

Norberg Schultz, C. (1980) *Genious Loci – Towards a Phenomenology of Architecture*, London: Academy Editions.

Ockerse T. (1991) *Semiotics: Principles in Action for the (Graphic) Designer*, reading material for lecture/workshop week at Arizona State University, 24–27 September. www.mkgraphic.com/semiotics.html

Riley, H. (1997) 'where do meanings come from?' in *The Social Semiotics of Design*, paper originally presented at 'Contextual Design – Design in Contexts', the 2nd European Academy of Design Conference, Stockholm, Sweden, April 1997.

Vihma, S. (ed.) 1995, *Semantic Visions in Design*, Helsinki: UIAH.

Chapter 21
Work and/or play?

Piyalada D. Thaveeprungsriporn

As a manifestation of globalization, design education in architecture tends towards standardization, both in its substantive and pedagogical domains. This chapter explores the pedagogical realm, looking at the mode of learning in the Thai tradition and suggesting its contribution as an alternative to current standard teaching and learning models. This, it is hoped, will reveal new possibilities for interweaving global modes of knowledge with the intricate threads of local ingenuity.

The incoming waves of Western modes of education impose Western concepts on traditional modes of understanding and learning, bringing with them paradigmatic clashes that manifest in both content and pedagogy. Western conceptions of content leave their traces in the curriculum, specifically the courses offered, as well as the underlying theoretical and analytical approaches.

Less obvious and therefore less explored in the Thai context, is the impact on pedagogy, particularly the attitude to learning. In the Thai tradition, the process of learning may not only involve the intellectual/rational capacity of the mind as is usually the case in the West. Rather, it is an essentially integrative process involving all the mental faculties, a holistic/integrative learning process which takes into account the 'humanized' nature of knowledge and learning, as opposed to the 'objective' or purely rational tendency of the mainstream Western model. Such respect for the human mind in the Thai context is manifest in the everyday words for various mental activities. For example, *tad sin jai* (literally, 'judging the heart') means to make a decision; and *khao jai* (literally, 'entering the heart') means to understand. In fact, the Thai word for mind/heart, *jai*, embraces all the mental faculties – whether emotional, cognitive, or imaginative. Such use indicates the integrative nature of the mental faculties in Thai, which are not isolated into distinct parts as they are in the mainstream Western way of thinking (Asawawirunkarn and Satha-anan 1995).

The integrative approach corresponds with Buddhist thinking on the process of learning, in which the human subject, the self, is neither something external to the intellectual system nor something to avoid or disregard so as to acquire an objective, or pure, state of learning. Rather, true learning can only occur when the information obtained through external factors has finally become internalized through the 'analytical reflection' process. The knowledge, so to speak, finally 'enters the heart'.[1]

This approach is evident in the Thai attitude to those essential (though, to the Western way of thinking, seemingly contrasting) activities in daily life, work and play. The Thai word for work, *ngaan*, means not only 'serious' activities which may entail monetary earnings such as a job but also festive gatherings such as *ngaan liang* (banquet), *ngaan tang-ngaan* (wedding party) or not-so-festive ones such as *ngaan sop* (funeral). In this sense, serious activities that usually imply principally intellectual engagement share the word along with activities that usually involve emotions – pleasurable or not.[2]

The Thai word for play, *len*, carries an even more intricate mix of meanings. In general, *len* means 'to do something for fun or pleasure, to be pleasurably engaged in or consumed by something, to speak or act casually'.[3] As such, it connotes the feelings of fun, playfulness and casualness. Yet according to P. Chalermphao

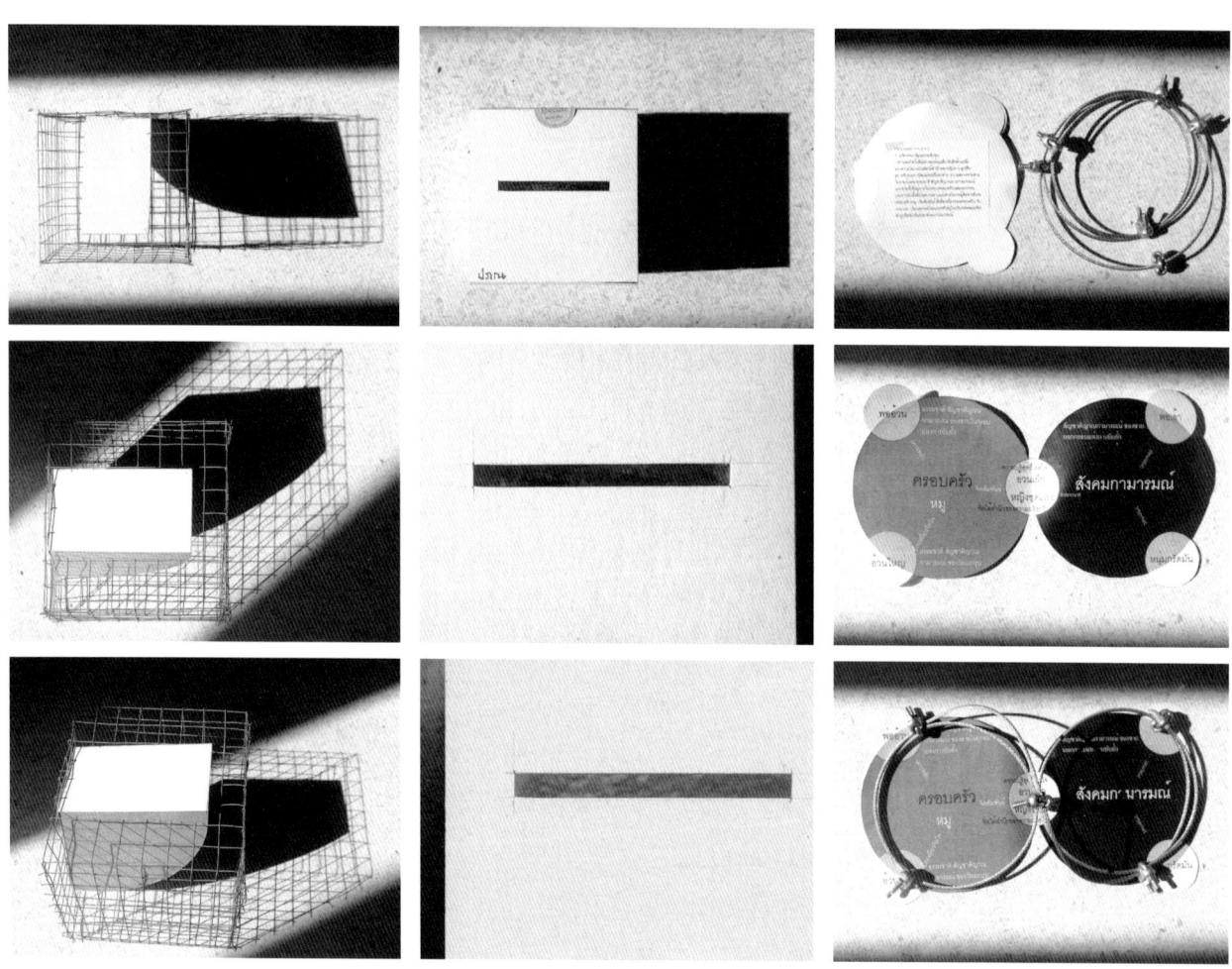

21.1
Three-dimensional objects, students' work from the 'think piece' exercise on their interpretation of the movie *Hollywood Hong Kong* (2001). From top: 'shifting urbanity' by Busakol Bowornchetnupong; 'the hidden structure' by Pongsakorn Tumpruksa and 'the closed world' by Papon Kasettratat.

Ko-anantakul (1995), the meanings of *len* can actually range from child's play (*len, kaan la len*), to games and sports (*len keela*), to gambling (*len kaan panan*), to theatrical and musical performances (*len lakorn, len dontree*), to collectibles and connoisseurship (*len khong-kao* – being an antique connoisseur), to 'serious stuff' such as politics (*len kaanmuang*) and even stock trading (*len hoon*). This implies that to the Thai these 'serious' activities, and even life, are viewed as being reliant on fate, almost like gambling. It is this attitude which helps the Thais cope with the instances of social instability they have had to face in their daily lives. What is more, it suggests a social mechanism that the Thais employ to avoid confrontation (Klausner 1997, 1987).

Some thinkers have discussed the elements of seriousness that exist in the concept of play in art, including Gadamer (1994), who proposes the concept of play as a model for understanding artistic/aesthetic experience.[4] In fact, the serious side of play is particularly evident in the sense of connoisseurship often associated with the word; to 'play' something in this sense (as in 'playing' antiques, 'playing' orchids, or 'playing' computers) would mean to be passionate about and perhaps becoming an expert in that area.

In traditional Thai agricultural society the line separating *ngaan*/work and *len*/play is even less distinct (Klausner 1987). To better understand what underlies this blurring of the line between *ngaan*/work and *len*/play, it is helpful to understand the social value imbued in the word *sanùk*, which may be translated as fun, or joyous pleasure.[5] Klausner explains the vital role of *sanùk* in Thai society as providing 'a respite, a release from the socially enforced constraints and demands imposed by the acceptance of one's place in the social hierarchy'. As such, it becomes an implicit 'mechanism for maintaining harmonious, non-threatening social relations'. (Klausner 1987: 290–291). In this light, it is more understandable that with *sanùk* as the underlying social value, *ngaan*/work is smoothed by elements of pleasure or levity, and *len*/play relieves dealing with serious, even hazardous, matters.

Such an understanding of the Thai attitude can inform design education by enabling a blurring of work and play in the learning experience. An example is an exercise given as part of a theory seminar. Called the 'think piece', the students are given freedom to playfully explore a cultural work as a case. The 'think piece' has, over the years of running this exercise, produced the students' best work, suggesting that it is the element of play in this exercise that allows the student's imagination and personality to come forth, even within the usually serious realm of theory.

What this 'play+learn' session has demonstrated, however, may actually go beyond the pedagogical dimension. It might even reveal the particular aptitude of students for what can be described as a 'bottom-up' theorization process. In the Western context, design theory in architecture and design usually evolves by reading built forms and then analysing and interpreting those forms in the light of pre-existing theoretical positions, a process which might be useful in some instances but may not be universally applicable to all cultural situations. By recognizing and incorporating local ways of thinking about work and play (the serious and the fun) the 'think piece' exercise encourages students to learn the process of theorizing by doing/playing. What can seem a complex and remote theoretical process is brought nearer to the students' everyday experience.

Such an experience suggests that the means to balance the local and the global in design education should include not only consideration of the content but also the pedagogy. The 'what' and 'how' are intertwined. Alternative approaches to teaching and learning based on knowledge of local culture may help redress the imbalance between local and global knowledge, encouraging architecture that celebrates cultural diversity as well as technological advancement and is more sustainable as a result.

Notes

1 Interestingly, this concept of understanding as an internalization process reminds me of a Heideggerian notion of understanding as a 'bringing near' of something. Cf. Herbert Dreyfus's chapter 'Space and spatiality' in Being-in-the-World: A Commentary on Heidegger's Being and Time, Division I (Cambridge: MIT Press, 1991).
2 The meanings of ngaan are discussed in more detail in Phongpan Maneerat (1995).
3 See Pojananukrom Chabab Rajabandittayasathaan 2525 (1983) [Dictionary of the Thai language], Royal Academy Edition, Bangkok: Rajabandittayasathaan: 732.
4 For Gadamer, play has a distinct relationship with seriousness. That is, while play is not and cannot be serious, its sole purpose is determined by seriousness; while it is somewhat mutually exclusive from seriousness as a quality in itself, yet, 'seriousness in playing' is what makes the play achieve its essence.
5 Klausner (1987) contested translating sanuk simply as 'fun' since he thinks this 'fails to capture the magic of this rather unique aspect of Thai culture'. As he points out in his essay of the same title, sanuk is not a mere feeling, but rather a social mechanism – 'an escape and safety-valve' – to avoid potential conflicts and confrontation.

Bibliography

Asawawirunkarn, P. and Satha-anan, S. (1995) 'Chid-Jai' in S. Satha-anan and N. Bunyanet (eds) *Kam: Rongroy Kwaamkid Kwaamchua Thai* [Words: Traces of Thai thoughts and beliefs] Bangkok: Chulalongkorn University Press.

Chalermphao Ko-anantakul, P. (1995) 'Len', in S. Satha-anan and N. Bunyanet (eds) *Kam: Rongroy Kwaamkid Kwaamchua Thai* [Words: Traces of Thai thoughts and beliefs] Bangkok: Chulalongkorn University Press.

Gadamer, H.-G. (1994) *Truth and Method*, trans. J. Weinsheimer and D.G. Marshall, 2nd edition, New York: Continuum.

Klausner, W. J. (1997) *Thai Culture in Transition*, Bangkok: The Siam Society.
—— (1987) *Reflections on Thai Culture*, Bangkok: The Siam Society.
Maneerat, P. (1995) 'Ngaan' in S. Satha-anan and N. Bunyanet (eds) *Kam: Rongroy Kwaamkid Kwaamchua Thai* [Words: traces of Thai thoughts and beliefs] Bangkok: Chulalongkorn University Press.

Chapter 22
Why use English?

Singh Intrachooto

Introduction

What benefit can students gain from learning in a language that is not native to them? Is their understanding of course materials compromised if they cannot fully understand all the relevant information? Such questions are fundamental to this discussion, which reports on a teaching experiment and seeks to understand effects of language on learning. With great effort and a large investment by various educational institutions in developing courses, workshops and lectures with international scholars, understanding such issues is increasingly important.

Although English is Thailand's official second language and the country's national economic development policy ranks English skill as a priority in education (Thailand Ministry of Education 2004), most students in the Faculty of Architecture at Kasetsart University face extreme difficulty when project information (teaching and research documents, books, lectures and desk crits by visiting scholars) is provided in English. With the growing number of international workshops, collaborations and exchanges carried out with foreign institutions in Europe, Australia and North America, the ability to relay information and communicate with multinational (and multi-lingual) colleagues is critical to the student learning experience.

The project

With the twin goals of addressing this language difficulty and enhancing learning through international co-operations, a third-year architectural design studio was conducted by-and-large in the English language. All presentations and assignments were given in English; guest reviewers at student presentations included architects, urban designers and planners from Australia, Canada and the United States; and, the most up-to-date publications, mostly available in English, were shared with students throughout the semester. To minimize the information gap, however, students were not required to speak English and an instructor who also served as a translator worked closely with them in the studio. In addition, a social scientist and a psychologist regularly observed and consulted with the students in class to ease their anxieties.

Students were evaluated three times during the 16-week-long semester: on the first day of studio; at mid-semester; and after final student presentations. The evaluations included language and stress tests, detailed questionnaires, in-depth interviews and focus groups conducted by a team consisting of a social scientist and a psychologist. Students also provided written comments about the effectiveness of this course and the use of foreign language. The contents of these three evaluation intervals were analysed, compared, discussed and summarized.

A number of specific developments were noted. It has long been acknowledged that a second language can be effectively learned when it is the medium of instruction, not the object (Campbell *et al.* 1985; Krashen 1982; Lambert and Tucker 1972). In addition to the improvement in the ability of students to understand lectures and discussions in English, which was the original intention, four specific developments beneficial to design practice were observed.

Committed attention and participation

Based on the prior observations of this student group, consistent attendance of studio sessions was not expected, let alone promptness. The attendance record during this studio, however, revealed that they rarely missed a class. It is widely recognized that most Thai students are only interested in their own projects and, as a result, group critiques are seldom successful; as soon as a student receives instructors' comments, they lose interest in the comments given to colleagues. During this experiment, however, students often stayed throughout the session and remained attentive to comments given to their peers.

Collaboration became the norm

In Thailand, architecture students typically prefer to work independently and group work is generally unenthusiastically received. Nonetheless, collaboration among groups of building professionals in practice is the norm and students need to develop this capacity. Although they were not asked to work in teams in this studio, students gathered regularly to discuss assignments and feedback. Students with poor English skills were keenest to engage in small group discussions with peers in their native language. They effectively became the drivers that sustained collaboration, and the sharing of ideas and information became routine. Collaboration, in fact, became a refuge, necessary for survival. 'We need to discuss our assignments together since none of us is completely sure if we fully understand the briefs,' stated one group of third-year students. Students learned to work together.

Students developed research skills

The ability to initiate independent research is not generally expected in undergraduate architectural training in Thailand. Information related to each studio project is usually provided for students and such information is searched out and collected by instructors. Student design processes are largely intuitive and results are based on the information provided. Because local websites are often limited in scale, deficient in information and out-of-date, and many students have not overcome the language barrier, the searching of local sites is uninspiring. This makes it difficult to rely on their own research. For example, the growing body of information about 'smart materials', such as *piezo* composite, cloud gel, electro-chromic glass and polyvalent wall, or the discourse on new urbanism, have not yet been published on local web sites. As a result, students rely more on information given them.

Although communicating in English during this studio raised their anxiety levels and proved a hurdle to comprehension during lectures and discussions, students unexpectedly initiated and conducted their own information searches, gathering information from various sources, including the world-wide web as well as local web sites. Student presentations, including digital presentations, gradually transformed into English (not without grammatical and spelling errors) and included information from diverse sources such as the Rocky Mountain Institute's Green Development, the University of Michigan's Smart Materials and Structure Design Lab (SMSDL), the MIT-based ArchNet and the National Aeronautics and Space Administration (NASA).

Reduced discontent

Many new graduates from the faculty at Kasetsart University have revisited their Alma Mater and shared their working experiences with students in the classes which follow. They describe a working environment characterized by uninspiring design routines, budget restrictions, low pay and long working hours. As a result, architecture students had begun to consider working in other industries upon graduation, including the related fields such as web-design, animation, product design, entertainment and marketing. After the completion of this experimental studio, student evaluations revealed that through their self-motivated investigation and peer group engagement, the enthusiasm for an architectural career was unexpectedly reignited.

Conclusion

Although several benefits were observed from this experimental studio teaching programme, there were also difficulties. Student anxiety levels were high and the time required for both students and instructors was excessive. The long-established schedule of a four-hour studio session became five to seven hours (to accommodate translation, clarification and elaboration). The team of instructors also needed to meet and prepare prior to each studio session. During the process, constant interaction with students was required and assignments needed to be especially detailed to prevent miscommunication. The objectives of each assignment, submission requirements, schedules, deadlines and a list of references had to be clearly stated to minimize confusion. References were particularly crucial since students reviewed them to pinpoint the intention of each assignment. Interestingly, students perceived such repetition of details and special effort as the devotion of instructors to their education and this, in turn, increased their commitment and perseverance in overcoming both language and intellectual hurdles.

Using the English language clearly added complexities to the conduct of this design studio. Was the additional effort worthwhile? It may be relevant to note here that renowned designers who practice in developing countries are few and far between (as are world-renowned urban planners). Those who have become known, such as Sri Lanka's Geoffrey Bawa, Mexico's Luis Barragan and India's Charles Correa, were educated in the United Kingdom, France and the United States respectively and were fluent with English as the principle language for architectural publications and research. On the other hand, the world's highly recognized urban planners and designers and scholars, such as the late Kevin Lynch of MIT, Christopher Alexander of the University of California Berkeley, Gary Hack of the University of Pennsylvania and Jane Jacobs (author of *The Death and Life of Great American Cities*) are actually native to the English language, which is used in international discourses on urban studies and planning.

The question arises as to whether language not only constrains understanding in design, but whether it actually restricts innovation. Does language have the dominating impact on learning behaviours that this experiment suggested? It is difficult to conclude from the data and results that language alone constrains the attitude to innovation and professionalism of students since there were other variables at play. Because of the use of English, for example, instructors devoted extended time to each student; each session was customized to ensure that both instructors and students understood one another. The studio pedagogy was, therefore, unavoidably student-centred and research-oriented, both of which are considered fundamental to integrating language into content instruction (Short 1991). Similar approaches resulted in highly motivated students in another design studio at Kasetsart University (Sangvachirapibal *et al.* 2003). References that helped students comprehend the assignments broadened their horizons and led them to further exploration. This self-initiated search appears to have become a personal quest and established a stronger sense of ownership of the learning process.

Nor should the sense of novelty be overlooked. Use of a different teaching method, also combining a student-centred and research-oriented approach but taught in their native language, might yield similar behavioural effects. The use of any non-native languages in educational settings may well yield similar results as students struggle to achieve sufficient understanding and communication, but it does seem that basic knowledge of and familiarity with that language are vital – to rouse their attention and encourage participation. In addition, students appear inspired by the opportunity to learn and use the language that is most widely employed in publications and research that is of most use to them, increasing their independence and capacity to choose a design direction.

International collaborations through workshops and student exchanges explicitly employ non-native language to achieve their goals despite the challenges this represents. In this experiment, the educational goals of the studio did not appear to be compromised, as many educators and students had feared, by the use of non-native language. The final design project outcomes were considered adept by their external reviewers who included visiting instructors and design professionals. Students found the studio challenging and were on the whole content. If, as this investigation suggests, the use of non-native languages, especially English, actually encourages learning, international collaborations and exchanges should be nurtured. While some may consider access to world-wide information as a threat to local identity because such access encourages globalization; equally, it can be argued that local identity can be strengthened and globalization avoided by better knowledge of broader political, economic and professional movements. This debate now underpins any debate about non-native language and learning, especially English.

Bibliography

Campbell R., Gray T., Rhodes N. and Snow M. (1985) 'Foreign language learning in the elementary schools: a comparison of three language programs', *The Modern Language Journal*, 69 (1): 44–54.

Krashen S., (1982) *Principles and Practice in Second Language Acquisition*, Oxford: Pergamon.

Lambert W. and Tucker G.R. (1972) *Bilingual Education of Children*, Rowley, MA: Newbury House.

Sangvachirapibal P., Suebsiri P., Intrachooto S. and Wirachpan S. (2003) 'Research-oriented design studio: a case of third year architecture students at Kasetsart University' in *The 6th Council of Deans of Architecture School Conference Proceedings* (The 1st Professional and Academic Collaborative Symposium, 30–31 May 2003, Bangkok, Thailand), Bangkok: Kasetsart University.

Short D.J. (1991) 'Integrating language and content instruction: strategies and techniques', *The National Clearinghouse for Bilingual Education (NCELA), NCELA Program Information Guide Series*, No. 7, Fall. www.ncela.gwu.edu/pubs/pigs/pig7.htm (accessed 20 February 2005).

Thailand Ministry of Education (2004) 'National Report 2004', 47th Session of the International Conference on Education, 8–11 September 2004, Geneva. www.ibe.unesco.org/International/ICE47/English/Natreps/reports/thailand.pdf (accessed 25 February 2005).

Chapter 23
Sustainability learnt from difference

Glenn Thomas

Introduction

This is a story about discovering how effective student-centred, multi-disciplinary team learning can be achieved in a cross-cultural setting. It began with a South African born former Dean[1] at the Queensland University of Technology (QUT), a direct descendent of the founder of the first mission in the village of Morija, in the tiny mountain country of Lesotho – the 'Kingdom in the Sky' – in the mid-nineteenth century. His ongoing family ties in South Africa, personal connection with Morija and a desire to establish closer ties between QUT and tertiary institutions in South Africa became the catalyst for student field trips to South Africa and Lesotho in 2002 and 2004.

The state of Lesotho, meaning the place, or home of the Basuto people, had been forged earlier in the nineteenth century by the great tribal ruler Moshoeshoe. In 1868, two years before his death, Lesotho became the British Protectorate of Basutholand until it once again became an independent state in 1966 (Ballard 1998: 763–766). Completely surrounded by South Africa, Lesotho is one of the world's poorest countries, suffering high unemployment and some of the worst soil erosion in the world. More recently it has joined much of Africa in the HIV-AIDS pandemic. The World Bank is arguably the most dominant external force operating in the country at this time through its involvement in the controversial Lesotho Highlands Water Project (Clarke 2002: 140; Go2africa 2004). South Africa's influence is also apparent. The South African rand has parity with the Lesotho maloti which cannot be exchanged outside the state borders, and the threat of the rand replacing the maloti and Lesotho losing sovereignty over its currency looms large.

The genesis of an experiment

The first field trip resulted from a visit to the village of Morija in June, 2002 by the dean and a former assistant dean.[2] After discussions with the local chief, village councillors, members of the church committee and members of the Lesotho government, the

23.1
South Africa and Lesotho: context.

assistant dean stayed on to work with the village community to develop a preliminary planning report. This report comprised an initial appraisal of the local setting, an audit of local assets or capital (social, environment and cultural), an analysis of potential local community projects and some assessment of ways in which these might be implemented. It was made available to the chief, members of the church committee and local villagers (Allison cited in Thomas 2003).

One of the recommendations was that students and staff visit the village in late 2002 to develop those projects of longer-term benefit to the community. A key objective was to involve local members of the community (especially young people) in working with the students, to the benefit both students and villagers, through a two-way exchange of knowledge and skills (Allison cited in Thomas, 2003). Planning for a three-week field trip began in August and, as I had been to South Africa as a visiting academic to the University of Pretoria in 2000, I was invited to join the staff later in the process. The final party comprised six academic staff embracing the disciplines of electronic and mechanical engineering, information technology, planning, architecture and landscape architecture and a guest historian from Macquarie University (also an expatriate South African and a personal friend of the dean). There were ten students of equal gender distribution from architecture, landscape architecture, engineering and interior design and, as is later discussed, the high staff to student ratio proved to be a significant factor in the outcomes of this venture.

The 2002 field trip had two phases. The first was an awareness-raising programme of nine days in South Africa. Formal lectures and site visits organized by the then Technikon in Pretoria (now a university) and the University of KwaZulu-Natal, Durban, gave insight into the cultural, economic and environmental context of post-apartheid South Africa. There were also visits to historical monuments, a long tour into the vast timber plantation regions of Mpumalanga, the Blyde River Canyon and Kruger National Park, Durban and Sentinel Peak National Park. South Africa's reputation as a high-risk environment limited accommodation to 'safe' areas and restricted movement to a cohesive group in two mini-buses. While there was restricted informal cross-cultural engagement, the country, its people and its history were formally interpreted by the expatriate staff.

The second phase was a two-week-long residency in Morija with accommodation and workspace provided on-site in a Mission Conference Centre. Lesotho was a complete contrast and surprise. Gone were the razor-wire-topped fences and threatening signs. The small urban capital, Maseru, was a small, rambling, ramshackle city with a core of bland buildings of modern design, but a city in which people freely moved about. The well-tended farms of South Africa were replaced by depauperate farmlands ravaged by more than a century of uncontrolled soil erosion (Rock 1994). Common to both countries was the poverty in the black townships and the small villages that dotted the open country.

Murray *et al.* (1998: 593) note that 'although traditional Basuto culture is breaking down through contact with the rest of the world and changes in society, much of the culture remains because it relates so strongly to the way people live'. The Basuto culture is clearly embedded in that of tribal Africa, but the influence of two centuries of Christianity begun by European missionaries is strong. The church occupies a central social and physical position. On both field trips members attended the Sunday church service the day after arriving. These resemble the joyous gospel hall model of Afro-America and the warmth and friendly openness of the people created an immediate and palpable cross-cultural engagement. We moved about freely, made acquaintances, used local transport to travel the 40 kilometres to Maseru and back, arranged 'sleep-overs' in the villages and engaged in conversation with many villagers who spoke good English learned in local schools.

This open and friendly environment seemed to assure the success of our projects. The reality, however, proved somewhat different, providing important lessons for the field studies programme to come in 2004. Formal communications with the community were orchestrated by academic staff. An unsuccessful early attempt to meet with the village chief resulted in a meeting with the chief's Urban Planning Council and an open public forum attended by community leaders, teachers and a number of younger people from the village. These meetings discussed the projects suggested in the planning report and sought to identify priorities and key issues. Project teams of staff and students were then organized and the work begun. However, this approach proved to be flawed in many ways.

Project 1 was an urban growth/economic development management plan. The project team comprised three academic staff, five students and a small number of villagers. One young villager, Refiloe Katu, an intelligent young man just graduated from high school, was a regular participant. Others spasmodically joined in. It was this project that taught us most about what not to do.

23.2
Public meeting to set agendas (2002 field trip).

23.3
Working together in a cross-disciplinary and cross-cultural environment (2004 field trip).

Project 2 explored the theme of appropriate technologies. The team included an academic, five students, the local high school science teacher and staff of an Appropriate Technology Workshop in the capital, Maseru, who scoured hardware stores for readily obtainable materials and constructed a working solar water heater. The heater, together with student-authored instructions and explanatory background text, was given to the school as an on-going teaching resource. This project gave us the critical insights we needed to devise future teaching strategies and achieve our objectives for cross-cultural learning.

Project 3 was the construction of a website for the country's museum and archives in Morija by two of the academic staff and a member of the museum staff. There were no students. The website remains a valued resource managed by museum staff.

Project 4 was the preparation of design concepts for extensions to the museum and archives by one staff member who had part-time assistance from an architecture student. Insufficient time was given to the functional brief and it has not progressed.

Project 5 was a long-term research project which I led, exploring appropriate techniques to rehabilitate eroded gullies, locally known as dongas. This project was more global than local in focus but the one that most influenced the trip in 2004.

Lessons from the first experiment (2002)

After the 2002 field trip, all of the visiting participants concluded that there was real potential for student learning in such cross-cultural and multi-disciplinary field trips. What we did not realize then, however, was that our host community in Morija was less enthusiastic. Further reflection on the first and second field trip experiences reveals that while students had the capacity for meaningful cross-cultural engagement, success depended on the students and the host community effectively working together as a team and developing mutual ownership of the outcomes.

Because academic staff dominated its development and its communication to the community, Project 1 was least successful as a learning activity. Students and local participants played a minor support role, preventing their development into a cohesive team. The project had, however, the most varied disciplines (across staff and students) and provided some insights into multi-disciplinary work. By contrast, while Project 2 evolved as a strong cross-cultural partnership with a shared sense of pride in its group accomplishments, all participants were from the same discipline.

On the negative side the informal nature of the field trip meant there was no formal assessment of student learning. This encouraged cross-cultural engagement through social activities rather than project-based activities, limiting realization of the potentials of learning objectives. Domination of the process by academic staff also limited the development of ownership of outcomes by students and villagers. Finally, the failure to meet with the chief himself at the outset inadvertently caused offense, creating the perception that his authority and scope of jurisdiction were not sufficiently taken into account (Gill 2004a). This last aspect threatened to derail the 2004 field studies just four weeks prior to departure, because his agreement to the projects was fundamental and there was the possibility that he would now be hostile.

The 'field studies in sustainable development' elective

A commitment was made to continue the southern Africa connections and to repeat the 2002 exercise in its broad structure in 2004, making it a formal elective available to all of the faculty's 19 disciplines. Preparatory work on the programme began early in 2004 but was immediately influenced by a major faculty restructure that aimed at increasing interdisciplinary contact within and between the three schools representing the breadth of professions currently operating within the field of urban development. This provided fertile ground for promoting multi-disciplinary opportunities for students to engage in 'exciting new combinations and applications of teaching and research' (Betts 2004). One identified research theme is 'sustainable living', which proposes that effective teamwork from a wide cross-section of disciplines is required to solve complex problems, and this new elective was embedded within that agenda and expanded to include the cross-cultural engagement objectives of the previous work.

Early in 2004 I accepted the task of leading the pedagogical development of this new elective unit in consultation with interested colleagues. The aim was to provide opportunities to deepen knowledge and experience of multi-disciplinary collaborations and their contribution to sustainable development, and to learn through direct immersion in a host community in a developing country. The programme would focus on sustainability issues outside core disciplinary knowledge; require engagement with different cultural beliefs and practices; and cross-disciplinary exploration of culturally appropriate technologies and development ideologies. Relevant theory and practice in the built environment and engineering fields would be explored, guided by the research and practice experience of staff and specialists.

The learning objectives were in two parts. The first dealt with learning outcomes, requiring students to develop: an understanding of people and cultures different from their own; sensitivity to their physical, cultural, economic and environmental contexts; an ability to work effectively in teams in a trans-disciplinary environment; their capacity to apply the knowledge and skills of their own discipline to multi-disciplinary problem solving; and their communication skills in a cross-cultural context. The first two of these seek to raise awareness of related but very different issues. First, sustainable development has many meanings influenced by prevailing socio-economic and environmental conditions, and particularly cultural contexts. Second, there was a need to increase respect for local identity within an increasingly global operating environment. The remaining learning objectives dealt with the less tangible goals for graduates, aiming to: develop higher-order understanding of socio-economic/environmental issues that influence human settlement and related communication skills; integrate higher-level applications of critical, creative and analytical thinking, problem identification and solving; integrate and implement advanced group collaboration skills to develop effective change outcomes; and actively contribute to social and ethical responsibility in the broadest sense.

The goal was a fully participatory learning experience, and the new elective expanded the 2002 model to include two half-days of discussions and workshops before the field work to cover issues such as cultural awareness, sustainability principles and the anticipated field studies environment, and prepare the students to quickly engage with the field studies programme. Discussions with those with South African experience were included, along with a workshop addressing techniques for building multi-disciplinary teamwork. Readings and web-based information were provided on sustainability, and the African context and its history, and an on-line learning and teaching site with integrated email linkage was established to facilitate exchange between staff and students.

To achieve learning and teaching goals, objectives and assessment instruments measuring student performance must be aligned. Here, the principle adopted for assessment was that credit should not be attached to the activity; it should be attached to the learning demonstrated. Since attendance, often the sole criterion in fieldwork, would not reflect this principle, an approach was taken that included team contribution, problem definition, critique and development of proposals in the assessed tasks. Participants were required to be reflective practitioners (Schon 1995) and keep a logbook recording those reflections. Assessment was based on active participation as recorded in the logbook and a 1,000-word report detailing experiences and perceptions.[3] A non-assessable seminar presentation of the field studies was required on the students' return as a means of dissemination. As it transpired, the students negotiated that the seminar presentation be replaced by an exhibition which, for a number of reasons, did not eventuate. This highlighted the reality that students become involved in other priorities if assessment is not at stake.

Preparation for the 2004 field studies

Within this framework, two important changes in the lead up to the 2004 field studies fundamentally influenced its final outcomes. The first was that the Technikon in Pretoria became too involved in its transition to university status to assist, and we relied on my links previously established at the University of Pretoria to fill the gap. The second was that, after staff changes, I became the person with the most African experience and, by default, leader of the field studies team in the final two months of preparation.

The team of staff was now reduced to three: myself (a landscape architect); a civil engineer and leader of the Faculty's research theme on sustainability; and a senior administrator whose inclusion proved to be a major contribution to the ultimate success of the project, as she was able to manage all finances and logistics including the itinerary. This left the academic staff to concentrate on academic matters without distraction.[4]

Without expatriate knowledge in the team, fine-tuning of the programme in South Africa was necessary, resulting in a multifaceted programme that involved: a specific two-day programme in and around Pretoria devised by my colleagues from the University of Pretoria, including visits with the South African Council for Scientific and Industrial Research (CSIR) and its Division of Sustainable Human Settlements and Low Cost Housing; inviting colleagues from Pretoria to join the party, resulting in one landscape architect joining us and contributing from Pretoria to Durban; and a one-day programme addressing diverse issues of sustainability including water and food security, housing, appropriate design, economic development and capacity building devised by colleagues in the School of Architecture and Housing at the University of KwaZulu-Natal in Durban. The remaining itinerary was adapted from 2002, modified by the availability of accommodation; logistical lessons previously learned; and the inclusion of relevant activities recommended by our South African contacts.

Establishing projects in Lesotho proved to be more problematic. Negotiation about potential projects, many building on the 2002 programme, had begun but had not achieved any conclusion, leaving a serious operating vacuum. The probability of a hostile reception by community leaders had now become clear. Stressing the 'new team' composition of the staff, we engaged in serious diplomacy and re-established a positive relationship. Just three days prior to departure a project finally emerged responding to my ongoing work on soil erosion and a draft paper that had been circulated to key agencies in Lesotho three months earlier. The government's Department of Forestry and Land Reclamation drew attention to Koapeng Stream, a century-old gully (or donga) bisecting Morija. It sought ways and means to rehabilitate this gully to a 'more attractive and stable system' (Gill 2004b). The chief added his blessing to this project and the stage was set. While some were concerned that this one project might not provide a sufficiently complex set of tasks to achieve the goals of cross-disciplinarity, we had little choice, and resolved to make the best of it.

Experiences in South Africa and Morija

The South Africa leg of the field studies proved to be an outstanding success in all but one aspect, the issue of meaningful cross-cultural engagement. Again, the need for safety requiring accommodation in 'safe' locations, and controlled movement in groups or in our mini-bus convoy, gave students a sanitized view of post-apartheid South Africa until we moved into the more rural parts of the country. Unanimously the students evaluated these as real limitations, raising the question of how much responsibility staff must accept when cross-cultural experience is the goal in places of known high risk. Both the 2002 and 2004 South African itineraries had limited contact time with locals in each location, exacerbated by long travel distances. Future offerings should allocate more time to increase the potential for developing deeper cross-cultural interaction and understanding; and risk assessment will require a clearly articulated agreement between staff and students for a shared responsibility in such places.

A full account of the community project outcomes is not possible here and this discussion concentrates on the learning activity. The academic staff to student ratio of 1:9 reduced the potential for staff to take dominant roles and students were deliberately encouraged to take charge of their own learning. Staff acted as mentors responding to needs as groups worked to identify and deal with problems. We also avoided the temptation to organize the students into task-oriented teams. Early discomfort quickly subsided as students themselves identified tasks and interest groups emerged. An initial perception that the project was oriented towards landscape architecture and civil engineering disappeared as a wider agenda of social benefit emerged. The students recognized the strategic location of Koapeng Stream and adopted objectives to maximize the benefits of its rehabilitation to the community, setting it up as an exemplar for wider efforts.

While our diplomatic efforts to secure the patronage of the chief included a request to meet with him soon after our arrival, parliamentary commitments prevented this, and we met with his executive assistants to establish our bona fides – a meeting conducted by two elected student representatives, with the rest of us as passive but respectful observers. These two students maintained on-going liaison with the chief's office and secured an invitation to address a village assembly that had been called to consider radical changes to local government in Lesotho. All of the party recognized the privilege this represented and were even more determined to succeed.

All but two of the 18 students quickly found a way to contribute meaningfully to the common goals. Our ritual of early morning walks through the donga developed familiarity with its physical condition and enabled staff to raise awareness of the processes of gully erosion and options for stabilizing and rehabilitating the system. Regular participation by interested villagers enhanced this exchange and widened our understanding of local capacities.

Community consultation

The students spent considerable time talking with a wide cross-section of the community before and during engagement with problem solving. The lack of a supply of affordable water and its impact on food security for poor villagers rapidly emerged as the major issue. Morija has a reticulated treated water supply sourced from a series of bores. Distribution to the wider village is via a series of locked public standpipes scattered through the village, but a number of villagers cannot afford the rental of a key to access this water. There is a daily ritual of women and children patiently filling containers of water from a small trickle, that is all that is left of once good supplies of spring water in a small valley above the village, and transporting it by wheelbarrow.

One impact of rampant gully erosion is the lowering of water tables leading to loss of stored moisture capacity of the soil (Rock 1994), and the drying up of a once plentiful supply of spring water from aquifers in the sandstone bedrock. The combination of these factors creates a national imperative to rehabilitate the remaining farmlands and maximize their sustainable production capacity. Knowing this, the students sought to add value to the rehabilitation, by proposing that the donga be used to harvest runoff water for villagers to irrigate home gardens, and contribute to restoring local water table levels.

Two other important factors that influenced the progress of the project emerged. First was the discovery that many villagers had skills, knowledge and experience to implement a range of potential technologies that might be applied to land rehabilitation. They were invited to participate in the project work and many quickly became essential members of the team. Two teachers from the local high school also became involved through their interest in practical skills development in their students. The second factor was, while there was wide recognition that land degradation was increasingly reducing food production potentials and quality of life, the struggle of day-to-day survival produced an all pervading attitude that nothing would be done to fix it unless the villagers were paid for their labour.

The co-operative engagement that became evident in the later field trip was in stark contrast to that in 2002. One of the most enthusiastic participants was Refiloe Katu, who had been consistently part of the 2002 work. On the eve of the presentation to the Village Assembly, Refiloe worked with students until 1AM to translate the text for the presentation drawings into the Sesotho language.

Learning from the locals

In parallel, to better understand potential technologies that respected the cultural context, we also investigated local examples of good land management practices, and successful rehabilitation of degraded ecosystems. This was informed by the lesson learned many years earlier in Australia's Landcare programme[5] that change in attitudes to land management is best achieved through peer leadership, the so-called bottom up approach. Earlier research by staff and information from our African contacts had identified sites of interest, and the students identified others during discussions with local villagers and aid agencies. One of the student initiatives was to invite our local helpers to accompany us on excursions to these exemplar sites. Poverty and lack of mobility meant that they had never seen these sites, even though the most remote was only 50 kilometres away and the nearest just across the valley. The locals got more actively involved through the incentive of seeing a possible alternative future first hand. In this one simple act, the success of the cross-cultural aspect of the field work was assured, with the programme providing learning for both the students and their village collaborators, in reaching a common understanding of what might be achieved in this physical and cultural context.

Following the students' presentation to the village assembly, the community resolved to adopt the broad strategy for rehabilitation of Koapeng Stream, and to seek the necessary aid funding to implement it. The community went so far as to promise that, if their guests were to return in two years, we would find the project substantially under way; an ambitious promise that showed how well the project had developed ownership of the outcomes among the host community. The fact that the students and their village helpers had delivered the package successfully confirmed the importance of learning about multi-disciplinarity and cross-cultural differences in addressing sustainability issues. The proud staff is confident that the lessons we have learned from 2002 and 2004 have established the capacity to design and deliver effective learning through such field study electives.

Student perspectives on their learning experience

Data from two sources confirmed our assessment of what had been achieved. The first was a simple student evaluation. The second was the students' reflective logbooks and summary reports that were academically assessed to confirm achievement of learning objectives. In their evaluations, the students were asked to identify the three aspects of the experience they most valued; the three aspects that they thought needed to be improved; and an open-ended question eliciting other suggestions for improvement.

Most valued by the majority of students were: the contributions of local knowledge by our colleague from the University of Pretoria who accompanied us for most of the South African leg; the emphasis on sustainability that helped them relate to the situation in Lesotho; opportunities for broadening perceptions of and consideration for those less fortunate; the experience of different disciplinary views and their thought processes; exposure to different socio-cultural, political and environmental contexts, and their concepts of sustainable development; and seeing different technical issues and solutions in place. They considered the programme would be improved by greater direct immersion into the encountered cultures; better preparatory emphasis on the history of the place; more discussion time to enable deeper engagement in the learning process; and stronger direction on how to deal with the projects and hosts.

The first of these comments related to the problem of cross-cultural engagement in South Africa has already been discussed. The second issue of history was intriguing since reading materials and web-based sources included references to history. There appears, however, to be a perception among students that reading history is boring and should be delivered directly. The third point is an important lesson for the future. Arguably both programmes in 2002 and 2004 were overcrowded with activities and travel, so that attempts to promote discussion at the end of the day usually found the students too exhausted or too ready to 'party' and were abandoned. A slower pace and specific programming to promote reflection is needed as students are always ready to party. While the evaluations were confidential, it is expected that the final comment came from the weaker students who typically prefer to be taught rather than take responsibility for their own learning. There was little in the way of additional insights offered by responses to the open-ended question except perhaps for a number of joking requests to be failed so that they could repeat the experience. The diary reflections did reveal the depth of appreciation and understanding many of the students had developed through the 2004 programme, although the lack of similar evidence from 2002 prevents any comparisons.

The 2004 evidence nevertheless suggests that we made significant progress and can confidently build on these collective experiences. Notwithstanding this, I believe there is a further change that should be considered: that of restricting cross-cultural engagement to developing countries, as is the case in the current elective framework. All manner of worthwhile learning experiences are achievable in the diverse cultures of the world and there is no need in my view for an implicit sense of philanthropy to be embedded in the field studies. I also suggest that there is a case for cross-disciplinary field studies within one's own cultural context, but that is a topic for another forum.

What did the locals gain?

While it is much more difficult to assess what the locals gained by the experience, there are some indicators. Their enthusiastic response to previously unseen local achievements of their neighbours will obviously contribute to their on-going discussions about the alternatives possible for Morija. The distribution of a comprehensive Project Report (Thomas 2005) to all community leaders and community participants will keep the strategy for rehabilitating Koapeng Stream tangible for them and the Lesotho government. Some of my research material on erosion control measures, also published in the report, is being used by the high school teachers to widen the skill base of future citizens.

Refiloe Katu has now completed a degree in tourism. His study was initiated by donations in 2003 from the former assistant dean and me. Others, recognizing his potential to contribute to a better future for his people, joined me in funding completion of his study. Refiloe and I have been corresponding since our first visit, and perhaps the most convincing evidence of local gains are these extracts from his email on discovering a news item I had written on the faculty web page about the 2004 field studies:

> I am so happy just now I was telling my friends about friends of mine from Au, we visited the site of QUT ... you guys wrote about projects you did in South Africa and Morija ... there was a photo of the presentation that you did to the community ... that photo brought me home a bit ... I told them I know every one ... I had to explain on how you we[re] carrying out the project and was my role and of my friends, it really nice ... imagine a boy from underdeveloped community talking to different people of different backgrounds, about this big guys from AU my interaction with them and every thing I did with them. It was really good I felt like a king.
>
> (Katu 2005)

An additional, and unexpected, response from the students was their donation of significant amount to a trust fund managed by the curator of the Morija Museum and Archive, to assist in the education and training of another two of our keenest local supporters. Such tangible investments in a better future suggest that those involved really did learn from difference.

23.4
Refiloe Katu with postgraduate planning student, Barry Clough.

Notes

1 The dean of the Faculty of Built Environment and Engineering, which embraces some 19 design, urban development and engineering systems disciplines involved in the built environment.
2 The assistant dean, a planner and urban economist, led the Faculty's Teaching and Learning portfolio.
3 Validity of the assessment instruments is confirmed by the fact that of the 18 students who participated, two were failed because their logbooks and reports did not demonstrate meaningful achievement of the learning objectives through recording, reflection and reporting.
4 This was so effective that I would not contemplate any future offering of such field studies without embedded administrative support.
5 Landcare (initiated in the late 1980s) is a uniquely Australian partnership between the community, government and business to 'do something practical' about protecting and repairing our environment. More than 4,000 volunteer community Landcare groups – including Bushcare and Urban landcare, Rivercare, Coastcare and sustainable agriculture groups – are tackling land degradation in every corner of Australia (http://www.landcareonline.com accessed 18/10/2006).

Bibliography

Betts, M. (2004) *White paper – the Founding Principles of the New Faculty*, Brisbane: Faculty of Built Environment and Engineering, Queensland University of Technology.
Ballard, S. (1998) *South Africa Handbook*, 3rd Edition, Bath, England: Footprint Handbooks.
Carruthers, V. (ed.) (2000) *The Wildlife of Southern Africa*, Capetown: Struik Publishers.
Clarke, J. (2002) *Coming Back to Earth: South Africa's Changing Environment*, Houghton, South Africa: Jacana (Pty) Ltd.
Gill, S. (2004a) Subject: QUT visit to Morija, email, 15 October.
—— (2004b) Subject: QUT visit to Morija, email, 18 November.
Go2africa at http://www.go2africa.com/lesotho/Lesotho/katse%2Ddam/ (accessed 24 April 2004).
Katu, R. (2000) Subject: Hi from Refiloe, email, 27 September.
Murray, J., Williams, J. and Everist, R. (1998) *South Africa, Lesotho and Swaziland*, 3rd edition, Melbourne: Lonely Planet Publications.
Rock, F. (1994) *The Mafeteng Development Project: Evaluation of Bund and Donga (Gully) Rehabilitation in the Matelile Region*, Lesotho: Lesotho Government, Morija, Morija Printing Works.
Schon, D.A. (1995) *The Reflective Practitioner: How Professionals Think in Action*, Aldershot: Arena.
Thomas, G. (ed.) (2003) *Final Report: Outcomes of QUT Community Projects in Morija, Lesotho, Summer 2002*, report to participants, Brisbane, Queensland University of Technology.
—— (2005) *Metsi a Sekhala (Fast Water) Metsi a Phallang Butle (Slow Water): Report on Community Project Outcomes, BNB301 Field Studies in Sustainable Development, Morija, Lesotho, Summer 2004*, report to participants, Brisbane, Queensland University of Technology.

Chapter 24
Experiencing cross-cultural practice

Catherin Bull

Introduction

What strategies increase the capacity of those in the disciplines designing the contemporary city to practise effectively across cultural and disciplinary domains? Much contemporary practice in urban design, including planning, landscape architecture and architecture, is cross-cultural in character. These disciplines work across national boundaries regularly – creating and adapting environments in locations and cultures where they have little direct experience, not only with professionals in their own fields but from other disciplines. Not only is such work carried out in unfamiliar surroundings, it is also carried out in the compressed time frames that now characterize the global work place (Savage 2005: 5).

In these conditions of global spatial and temporal compression, do practising professionals have the skills to respond to local cultural conditions and issues in a sensitive and timely way? Can they read these environments quickly and well? Can they work effectively with colleagues from other cultures and disciplines? Can they balance the demands of the global workplace with those of local environments? And, can these skills be developed?

The BMB experimental programme[1] of design workshops was established in the expectation that educational institutions should have such a role, in response to their commitment to international teaching and development of a global perspective among graduates and the imperatives of educational policies.[2] Specifically there was a commitment to develop the capacity to respond more responsibly in the global workplace, to help them become professional citizens, capable of responding sensitively to local particularities.

International educational programmes have become increasingly common over recent decades, including exchanges and study abroad. Students may spend one or more semesters of their degrees at institutions in other countries or may enrol in field studies and be taken to other environments as groups under direction. In the design disciplines, global studios, international studios and digital studios have enabled students to work beyond the traditional boundaries of space with students from other institutions, usually as paired partners. All result from the educational expectation that beyond theory, there is simply nothing like actual experience of place and people to produce the necessary sensitivities and skills – to put theory into practice (Knight 1999:14).

While such programmes have increased, there has been little, if any, rigorous analysis of their successes and failures to test the promotional rhetoric. Are they successful as educational tools to counter the negative impacts of globalization? Do students learn the kind of skills that the programmes set out to develop, whether generic or discipline-specific?

This workshop programme set out to create an environment where students could 'learn' cross-cultural and cross-disciplinary skills in a supervised learning environment as a pilot for their future professional lives. Based on the traditional design studio, it would be specialized in form, compressed in time and students would actually work with (rather than observe) a variety of cultures, backgrounds and disciplines. The project site would be 'exotic' to the majority of participants and need 'interpreting' by the host group who, in turn, would learn from the first impressions of their visitors. Their teachers, as guides from the three institutions, were experienced in the type of projects, in intensive workshop programmes and in working across cultures and disciplines.

The response of students participating in this programme over its three-year life is discussed here, along with the way that their feedback might inform such projects and the agenda to internationalize education in the future. Did they consider the educational goals had been met; and what had assisted or inhibited that?

24.1
Cross-cultural and cross-disciplinary workshop educational goals.

To provide disciplinary-based introduction to:	• Unfamiliar cultures, places and people • Alternative attitudes, models of decision-making, practices and techniques • The world of international practice
To provide guided field- and institution-based programmes that include:	• Working with unfamiliar student professionals in the discipline areas (as individuals and groups) • Working in unfamiliar physical and social environments • Observing the relationship between international disciplinary theory and local conditions
The purposes of these programmes are:	A. To support internationalization policies at an institutional and national level by relating these to disciplines within the built environment professions B. For individual students to develop: • Skills (and confidence) in understanding and navigating other cultures • Awareness of the ways in which other cultures (and their disciplines within those cultures) address environmental and social issues (thereby increasing the stock of models available to students) • Respect for other places, cultures and practices • Awareness of the value of 'culture shock' in stimulating creative thinking and problem solving • Awareness of the commonalities of many phenomena internationally (tourism, post-industrialization, post-colonialism and so on) as well as local particularities • Capacities in reflective and critical thinking, particularly in applying work practices and theory to unfamiliar environments and culture • Enriched personal and professional networks C. For staff to develop: • Reflective teaching practices, research and scholarship about teaching • Awareness of the variety of teaching methods available and their characteristics • Expertise in international teaching • Techniques for formal and informal benchmarking • Enriched personal and professional networks D. To use the programme to inform international teaching, professional practice and stakeholders, especially in the planning and design of sustainable cities

Programme goals and operations

Around the design theme of sustaining city, water, modernity and culture (each of the cities is on water and has issues relating to urban change) each participating institution was to host a workshop to which each would contribute an approximately equal number of students. Thirty students participated in each workshop, totalling 90 over the three years of BMB Workshop 1 Bangkok (2003), BMB Workshop 2 Melbourne (2004) and BMB Workshop 3 Bordeaux (2005). Staff meeting at the inception of the programme in 2002 jointly identified and agreed their goals and an operational protocol (part of which is illustrated).

The subject of this research is whether the students from each workshop considered that the workshop achieved these goals and to what degree; and, their assessment of the organizational characteristics which either assisted or inhibited that outcome.

The workshop processes and outcomes are described in more detail elsewhere but generally followed the format of: introduction to issue, site and process; lectures by specialist professionals and academics on technical, strategic or historical matters relating to the site and context; group formation and site visits; group work and presentation/feedback on initial 'ideas'/issues/words; group work and presentation/feedback on strategic proposition at urban landscape scale; group work and presentation/feedback on refined strategic proposition (at an urban landscape scale) and sample design application of that proposition (at site scale); final presentation.

The process

To elicit the students' views on their experience, each cohort was surveyed shortly after completion of their workshop. The programme goals relating to students and the organizational characteristics defined in the protocol formed the basis of a questionnaire along with a generic question as to whether the programme fulfilled their expectations. Students also had the opportunity to volunteer comments and suggestions of their own, in their own language – which many did. The questionnaire was translated into the first language of each group, acknowledging that even then, that might be a second language. Questionnaires were issued and collected electronically following the first two workshops and manually at the last session of the third, and the results transcribed and translated. Anonymity was ensured via the distribution, collection and data collation processes, from which the investigators were excluded. After review of the first results, an additional question was added seeking an evaluation as to the alignment of programme goals and student expectations.

24.2

Workshop student experience questionnaire.

A. Programme objectives: To what degree did the BMB (Workshop No.) experience help you, as a student to develop (on a 1 = least to 5 = best scale):	
A1	Skills (and confidence) in understanding and navigating other cultures?
A2	Awareness of the ways in which other cultures (and your disciplines within those cultures: urban design, landscape architecture and architecture) address environmental and social issues (i.e. thereby increasing the stock of 'models' or precedents available to you)?
A3	Respect for other places, cultures, people and practices?
A4	Awareness of the value of 'culture shock' in stimulating creative thinking and problem solving?
A5	Awareness of the commonalities of many phenomena globally (tourism, equity, post-industrialism, post-colonialism, relationship to water, etc.)?
A6	Awareness of local particularities?
A7	Capacities in reflective and critical thinking, particularly in applying work practice and theory to unfamiliar environments and cultures?
A8	Enriched personal and professional networks?
B. Contributing factors: To what degree do you think that the following factors inhibited or promoted achievement of the programme objectives and your expectations (1 = inhibited, 3 neither inhibited or promoted/neutral, 5 = promoted):	
B1	Language differences
B2	Different levels of study (under/post-graduate)
B3	BMB being part of an assessed subject for some students and not (i.e. an 'add-on' to normal studies) for others
B4	Sharing accommodation
B5	Different level of skills
B6	Different design methods
B7	Different disciplines
B8	Other (please nominate)
C. Your expectations: (1 = least to 5 = best scale)	
C1	To what degree did the BMB Workshop experience meet your expectations?
C2	To what degree did the outlined programme objectives match your personal objectives for the BMB Workshop?*

*Question C2 was introduced into the questionnaire for BMB Workshop #2 (Melbourne) 2004 and BMB Workshop #3 (Bordeaux), 2005.

The results of the first two workshops were reported progressively and comparatively (Bull 2004, 2005) and trends were identified, possibly: student interest in discipline-specific (rather than generic) goals; the negativity of a significant minority of students to the programme; the possibility that enthusiasm or negativity might run along cultural lines; the less positive response of host students; and the limitations or otherwise of using English as the language of instruction. These are discussed below.

Achievement of learning goals

Did students think the experience developed: generic skills; discipline-specific skills; and personal and professional networks? While the questionnaire specifically focused on cultural issues, responses also included comments on its cross-disciplinary aspects.

Generic skills in cross-cultural activities (questions A1 (skills and confidence in understanding and navigating other cultures) and A3 (respect for other places, cultures, people and practices)) were scored highly by students across all three programmes, although, perhaps predictably, the hosts tended to rate these less highly, not having the additional stimulation of experiencing a different place. The hosts benefited, however, from different views of that place through the comments of their colleagues and learnt to work with these fresh perspectives.

Analysis of the numeric results of the first workshop in Bangkok suggested that perhaps generic skills would not be valued as highly as the discipline-specific skills, but this was not borne out by subsequent surveys, which demonstrated no significant difference overall between the first three questions. The accompanying comments, however, particularly those expanding on the students' personal goals in undertaking the programme, demonstrated that interest in their disciplines underpinned their involvement.

The discipline-specific aspects of learning rated highly overall, with the desire to learn about how their disciplines operate elsewhere in design practice being as strongly identified in volunteered comments as the desire to learn generally about other cultures. Comments

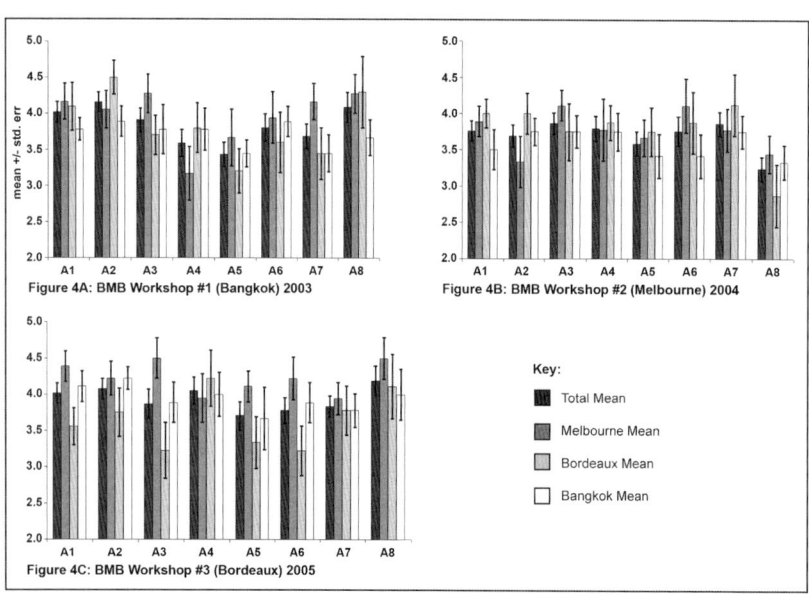

24.3
Responses to questions, Section A 'Programme Objectives'.

describing personal objectives included 'to learn about the way different cultures approach designs [sic]'; 'To engage in a multi-cultural team experience. To learn from other approaches to design problems'; 'To ... learn more about the design practices, cultures and interests of the respective countries'; '1. To get new perspectives in design as well as knowledge/skills in other related fields that could be practically applied in the future, 2. to learn about different cultures.'; 'The exchange of knowledge and thought processes about the city and environment'; 'Discovering and sharing different work methods'; 'To work in a multi-disciplinary, multi-cultural group. To experience a different place and culture'. Such comments support the conclusion that the disciplinary-specific aspects of such programmes are as important, if not more so, than the generic.

The goals and subsequent questions about discipline-specific skills (A2, 4, 5, 6) covered a wide range of design-related issues that teaching staff had wanted to explore, and the results demonstrate that while students considered the workshop experience achieved some of these, they were less clear about the achievement of others.

Notably with regard to developing knowledge of the commonalities of global phenomena, A5 had a mean of only around 3.5, despite students observing phenomena such as suburbanization, post-industrialization and depletion of natural resources resulting from poorly controlled land use, all of which they also studied in their home programmes and locations. By comparison, they always (even when local students were factored out) rated A6, awareness of local particularities, more highly. Perhaps, at this stage of their working lives, students simply lack the experience of many environments and the capacity to generalize that experience. Such programmes aim to develop awareness of these relationships but may merely act as an introduction despite this. It was also apparent to the teachers that the students, through their discussions and the resulting work, did apply solutions from their experience of similar situations elsewhere, a tangible indication that they were recognizing similarities. Their preoccupation with 'the site' and their project perhaps disguised their awareness of this more abstract aspect of their learning. An analysis of

24.4
Responses to questions, Section B 'Contributing Factors'.

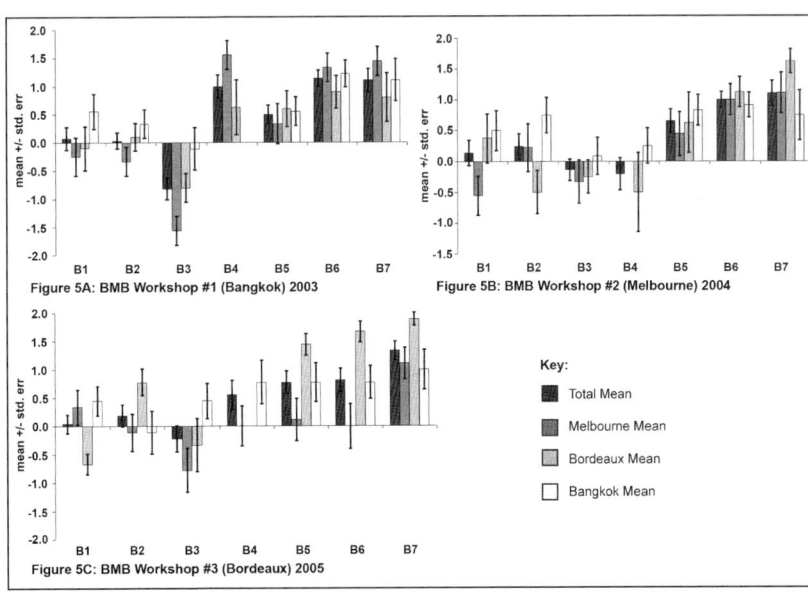

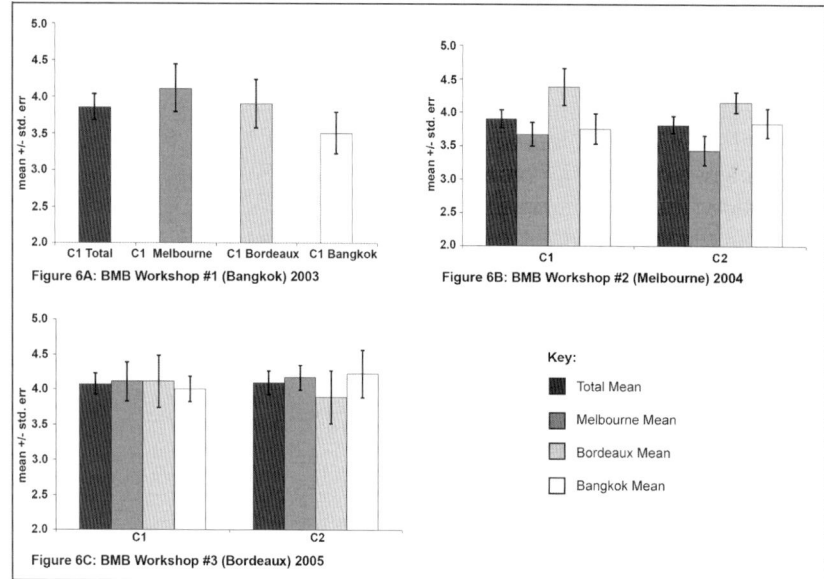

24.5
Responses to questions, Section C 'Expectations and Objectives'.

their comments about their goals reveals a preoccupation with learning about difference rather than similarity. Typically, phrases they use include the desire to learn about 'others with different thoughts and cultures'; how 'different cultures approach design'; and, 'to learn about different cultures'.

In responding to the question as to the value of 'culture shock' in stimulating creative thinking, students (whether hosts or guests) were remarkably consistent, with mean scores around 3.8 to 4 (with the exception of the Melbourne hosts for workshop 1). Ten students in workshop 3 valued this at 5 and another nine at 4 (all the visitors) and no significant change results from removing the hosts from the calculations. Again, a deeper analysis reveals that students found difference stimulating, a Bangkok student commenting after workshop 2 on his/her expectation that 'experience and certain phenomena creates new points of view and stimulates the urge to learn and work'.

Enthusiasm for the cross-disciplinary aspects of the programme is demonstrated by the comments of students following workshop 3: 'I also enjoyed working in a multidisciplinary context; to be able to ask an "expert" opinion about something and in turn do the same when it came to my area of specialization. This will be especially relevant going into professional work'; and from workshop 2, 'We should work collaboratively with other professions much more in a study environment – much more likely to generate professional understanding and respect.'

Finally, the assumption in much of the policy is that international programmes automatically generate more socially skilled students who gain networks of colleagues and personal contacts. In the light of these findings, this needs to be questioned.[3]

Two explanations can be suggested for this. First and most obviously in programme design terms, is the scheduled inclusion of social events in parallel with the work. With typical Thai hospitality, the Bangkok workshop had a number of parties throughout, from the first welcome, to the on-site lunch, to the last farewell. Likewise, consistent with French recognition of the value of the table, the Bordeaux workshop provided many opportunities for additional socializing (a welcome lunch, daily lunches for guests, evening functions and a farewell). The Melbourne Workshop took a more sober, work-oriented approach and while staff had plenty of opportunities to get together and students spent a lot of time together on site and in the studio, only two social events were co-ordinated, at the start and the finish. This may simply not be enough. Students themselves suggested that they need scheduled opportunities to break social and cultural barriers informally to enhance interaction, volunteering comments such as this Bangkok student after Melbourne, 'In the first day there should be a session that melts the behaviour to bring the participants closer to get use [sic] to each other and for better understanding'; 'I wish there was more ... time for socializing with those from other countries'; and 'the project should give knowledge while fun [sic] at the same time'. Even after the comparative sociability in Bangkok an Australian student suggested that 'More opportunities to relax and socialize with other students would have improved the group work dynamics' and went on to propose an additional two days together following the workshop proper.

Second, it may even be that where there were scheduled social activities, their effectiveness relies as much on individual social skills brought to the programme as those generated by it, irrespective of cultural background. The particular characteristics of the host student group in Melbourne may also have had an impact, as the majority of these students were new to Melbourne themselves, and being unfamiliar, were less prepared to act as knowledgeable (and sociable) hosts. In such cases however, scheduled social events hosted by the programmes may be even more important in generating co-operation.

Operational factors

The operational questions were included to gain an understanding of whether students considered that certain factors assisted or

24.6
Students participating in the first BMB workshop, held in Bangkok.

inhibited the learning experience, including differences in language, discipline, skill and educational level, design methods and accommodation. These are, it could be postulated, all common to cross-cultural and cross-disciplinary practice.

First, participants thrived on the differences inherent in the programme. As one Melbourne student put it after workshop 3, their personal goal had been about experimentation and that while they had thought the workshop would be about design, it 'ended up being about the process of working together, overcoming or managing difference'.

In particular, participants were positive about the different methods, ways of thinking and approaching problems that were made available to them, commenting typically: 'Our methods were turned upside down during the brainstorming sessions, but that was very stimulating!'; and from a French student, 'The exchanges with the Thais and Australians have been very instructive on work methods', 'From the BMB I can open my mind to different design theory'; 'Get the diversity of working methods which is interesting and can be adapted for use [sic]'.

Somewhat surprisingly, participants were neither distinctly negative nor positive about the matter of language, commenting on the extra time involved negotiating in what was a second language for the majority, but equally on the insights that came once common understanding was established – and the fact that sometimes taking longer actually made for better communication and work outcomes. After the second workshop, for example, a student said: 'The cultural differences and also different backgrounds bring us more ideas and opinions (while sometimes cause us a problem as well)', and another:

> The challenge of overcoming communication difficulties required a lot of patience and time – but when we had breakthroughs it was terrific (especially with the Thai students). The French and Melbourne students had a tendency to dominate with their arguing and so probably the Thais felt a little left out. Often though, they would be listening and start drawing out ideas and solutions to the issues we argued about – it was brilliant!

And from a French student:

> the reality is that communication problems sometimes made work slow and difficult … but the English communication was effective and therefore teamwork was productive. Sometimes the language differences can be a factor which contributes to teamwork because we need to be all the more thoughtful and open.

In contrast, a Thai student said after workshop 3:

some person in the group [foreigners] are interested to listen and are patient to let me speak or explain with drawings which is good because there is some exchange. But some person is not patient which makes me frustrated – the working style of the Westerners are through arguments which is sometimes boring and frustrating to listen to but when there is a consensus in ideas, the work becomes easier.

It was apparent from comments that students realized that certain techniques, particularly those of listening (one Thai student identified learning 'the willingness to listen to others'), are important to achieving communication and contributions when language proficiency is an issue, and that different cultures had different ways of dealing with this. The French and Australians typically resolved issues through argument, the Thais through observation and suggesting solutions to issues through design proposals to generate more comment. All were cognisant of the increased time involved, not necessarily seeing the short time-frame as negative. Some suggested the ways in which time could be increased to achieve outcomes, others saw the hothouse atmosphere (comparable to the international workplace) as being useful to force communications and outcomes.

After the second workshop, a Melbourne student commented: 'Such an amazing experience! Feel like I have learnt more about the design process in 5 days than in years!' Others commented: 'I think everyone learnt more in 8 days than one year of normal study …' and 'Really interesting to work on a limited time frame, it is necessary to go to the essentials'.

In summary, the factors that were identified negatively were insufficient time, differences in assessment and accommodation.

On time, comments after the second workshop ranged from the simple 'Too many lectures' to more complex explorations of the way that group communication could be better catered for with more time (which, many commented, would have also made the exercise less tiring). A Thai student suggested:

> Since there are differences in cultures and languages, there would be lots of effort to adapt to be able to work together. Before we can adapt and learn … to communicate, there is almost not time to brainstorm ideas. I think there should be a little more time for the adaptation process.

And others: 'Too little time because before we can adapt to language differences [or ways of communication] the time has run out. There should be some time allotted to living together for a certain time before work commences'; 'The time to learn the particular way of working is too compressed'; 'Should increase the time for workshop as it is very short'. One student even suggested a workshop length of a month!

The various approaches to assessment and the way that the workshops sat within each home programme had been seen by the initiators as matters for the contributing programme to determine. Approaches varied, with the Thais and French choosing the workshop as an optional addition to the student's programmes with participants selected for academic level, perceived capacity and personal qualities. In Melbourne, the same selection criteria applied, but because of the schedule and the fact that it could be taken for credit as an assessed component of an offered subject, the programme was integrated. Scheduling across three academic systems and annual timetables proved the major constraint, from the first meeting right through, as is evident from the comments, to student experience.

Juggling commitments to other subjects, scheduled preparation and examination periods, holidays etc., appeared almost insurmountable until the organizers explored how certain periods of the academic year might be more flexible than others. Even then, as the results show, this was not ideal. How the workshop lay within the broader academic programme and the issue of assessment affected both individual commitment to both the group and the project. The first workshop was scheduled in the period immediately after the Bangkok teaching year but before submission dates for their final project (but conveniently over the Easter break for the French and Australians). All students found this difficult because of the conflicting allegiances of the Thais, who predictably put most energy to assessable assignments. Likewise, the others found the Australians whose work was assessed, even over-committed, with one French participant describing them as 'frenzied'.

Concern about assessment was repeated after each workshop and proved the operational factor that most impeded achievement of the programme goals. Many comments were volunteered, including after the first workshop, those of a Melbourne student who said:

> The biggest challenge I faced in Bangkok was the varying levels of commitment among the student participants – the French and Thais had less at stake and so did not treat the experience as seriously as the Melbourne students ... otherwise a very valuable experience – in fact the highlight of my Melbourne University education

Other Melbourne students said, after the second workshop: 'The [workshop] should be better integrated into the design studio'; 'More credit should be given to students who participate.' And from Thais: 'The grading of the Australians makes the group work very stressful because the end product has to be useable for further development ... the workshop shouldn't be graded.' Later, even after the workshop had been more carefully integrated into the home programme, the comments persisted, albeit with a slightly different tone. One Australian commented: 'the imbalance set up with assessment of ONLY the Australian students creates an inequality of expectation in the group and potentially creates unnecessary tensions', and from another:

> The assessment factor caused problems in our group – lack of ownership for some, and lack of commitment to the team by my Melbourne counterparts. That being said, I was very impressed by the amount of dedication shown by the students who weren't being assessed.

While not anticipated as an issue, assessment proved one of the most significant variables, raising the possibility that they may be better delivered either with common assessment requirements, or without any.

Finally, the matter of accommodation stands out as a significant operational constraint. Guest participants were accommodated together at the school for the first workshop and in small hotels with limited self-catering for the third (costs were borne by the hosts). While guests were generally satisfied, comments included suggestions after the first workshop that all students, hosts and guests, should be accommodated together and mixed. Groups were then mixed for the second workshop, which was no more successful, students still resorting to their home groups to relax after hours. The results, excluding host responses, show that guests were generally neutral to positive about shared accommodation, with contrasting comments following the third workshop including 'aspects of our stay (hotel/room sharing/always out of home and with other designers) have positively influenced the experience' and the opposite 'sharing accommodation – no time out, and also at the mercy of other people's movements was exhausting and had a negative impact in terms of working to full potential'.

In summary, students perceived operational factors such as methodological and disciplinary difference and language positively despite negative expectations. By contrast, aspects that had not been anticipated to be significant (such as how the workshop was incorporated into the home programmes, assessment and accommodation), actually were negative.

Expectations

The final section of the questionnaire had aimed to establish whether participating students considered the programme fulfilled their expectations, rather than those of the educators. While the responses to the first workshop indicated that this was the case for most students, who scored it highly (medians of 4 with many scores of 5), there was a significant minority (one from each programme) who scored this section very low (rating it 2). This raised the question as to what their expectations had been and whether they even correlated with the programme goals. An additional question was posed to assess this in the following two questionnaires and the opportunity to list their goals.

A high mean level of satisfaction of expectations was revealed with mean scores of just below 4 for the first two and of over 4 for the third and a strong correlation between the expectations of its participants and the programme goals.

Notably however, for the second workshop, the correlation between the programme goals and the expectation of the hosts varied significantly, even though fulfilment of the guests' expectations remained high. The comments of the hosts reveal that a high proportion, although in their fifth year of study or higher, were (as has already been noted), new to Melbourne, Australia and the university, and these students were more interested in finding out about what was normal in this context, rather than different. Perhaps these were not the ideal host group, but at the time there was little opportunity to vary the composition given the need to fulfil other protocol requirements. Typical comments from these new host students were: 'Being the first design studio I am undertaking I wanted to get familiar with the teaching method, form an overall idea of what urban design is about and obtain some understanding of Melbourne'; and 'As an international student in first semester without study experience in Western countries, I expected to understand more about what urban design is and how students in relevant disciplines work'. Comments from those who had been at the university and in the city longer were more typical.

While the first workshop had not met the expectations of at least one student from each institution (i.e. 3 overall), this was never repeated – although there remained at least one at each of the following workshops who rated them at only 2 against their own expectations, suggesting that for such challenging programmes, extra care of some participants might be necessary.

Conclusions

With so much educational policy and resources now directed at international programmes, this research sought to throw light on whether and in what way participants considered the educational goals for an experimental programme like BMB were achieved. As Allen says: 'We can assure the students of the quality of our courses only if we listen to what they themselves need, be aware of where they are coming from' (Allen cited in Mason 1998: 40). The research also sought to gain greater insights into the impact that admittedly complex organizational factors might have, given that diversity on almost every dimension is the recognized hallmark of international programmes (Granger and Gulliver cited in Mason 1998: 40).

The responses reveal that experiences like these workshops, while complicated to run, achieve their goals to a high degree, even becoming the highlight of the entire study experience. It could even be said that the students surveyed here agreed with the goals of such programmes, that such experiences provide them with special knowledge and insights into work.

This is not, however, to say that all such educational experiences can expect such a positive response. These participants were motivated essentially by curiosity about differences within their own disciplines rather than by any interest in cultural differences for their own sake. They wanted to know more about how their disciplines worked in other places and wanted to experience that difference. From there, broader knowledge about other cultures was attained, rather than vice versa.

The earlier expectations of staff that there might be significant variations in motivation and modes of response between cultural groups did not materialize, with differences between hosts and guests being ultimately more pronounced. Participants learnt not only by being visitors, but by being hosts, observing at close quarters the response of their visitors to what they had seen as normal about their own conditions, and being questioned about assumptions and beliefs. As a hosting French student put it: 'I have been very happy to have a new vision of the terrain on which I live to remove the French blinkers.' Importantly, participants became aware of the fundamental skills necessary for cross-cultural and cross-disciplinary work and realized the need to develop skills, including listening, patience and respect for alternative views. They learnt that while these demanded additional time, the work outcomes might well be better in the long run because they reflected broader thinking. While these generic skills could, perhaps, be learnt in many ways, the intensity and group work of this programme structure highlighted their importance to participants.

Students also learnt not only that places are different but that ways of working also are – and they valued that. Thai students said after the Melbourne workshop: 'I am impressed by the foreigners' behaviour because it is different to what I expected'; and 'people there are very active in working which makes me realize that I waste a lot of time'; and from a French student, 'Contrary to the French who have a tendency to over-analyse, the Australian students are sometimes too aggressive and ... the Thais were not incisive enough'; 'The Australians wanted to apply their methods, to get more quickly to their results'; and 'The Australians forgot ... a level of study in their work: they went from the strategic level to the answer ... without asking questions before taking action ... they needed to produce a result, we just wanted to engage in reflection and debate'. Again, it was their work and the way it was approached that engaged their interest in difference, difference they learnt, through the experience, to accommodate.

Organizationally, such programmes cross temporal, cultural and institutional boundaries, are complex to mount and require difficult choices. Despite early concerns, students' considered differences in skill, level, work methods and disciplines proved neutral or even positive influences, even the use of English as the language of instruction, because of the extended negotiation it encouraged and the practice it provided for second language participants. The demands of such an intensive programme were challenging, but participants recognized that they learnt more because of that. As previously discussed, international work in practice is characterized by just this kind of activity and participants learnt its complexities, challenges, limitations and benefits.

In terms of student experience, the greatest challenges for the institutions involved revolved around the issues of assessment and scheduling. Both point to the issue of whether educational programmes that focus on preparation for cross-cultural and cross-disciplinary practice can or should be integrated in standard studies or are destined to remain optional extras.

International educational policy seeks to normalize such experiences, calling for their inclusion as a standard part of educational programmes (Knight 1999: 18). International education is, for example, seen as a response to globalization (de Wit and Knight 1999: 13) and a way to counter its negative effects. Such programmes are seen as essential for developing the skills for professional life (Gilbert cited in Mak *et al.* 1999: 76; English cited in Clyne and Rivsi 1998: 37). According to students, however, the issues that had most negative impact on the achievement of the programme goals were those that are integral, if not fundamental, to programme design – scheduling and assessment. These findings support the proposition by educational theorists such as Mason that 'assessment arrangements define the curriculum in the eyes of the learner' and to a lesser degree, Knight's conclusion that 'Grand aims without sophisticated assessment systems are virtually worthless' (Mason 1998: 40; Knight cited in Mason 1998: 42). It was clear that the BMB programme was far from worthless for its participants, achieving most of its goals and theirs. Students found, however, that the inequity of assessment and placement of the programme reactive to their enrolled course problematic. So should, then, as the literature suggests, such programmes be assessed, and should they, as policy suggests, be integrated?

As already discussed, this programme was both integrated and extra – integrated for Melbourne students and extra for the French and Thais. While the reasons for the inequity have been discussed, what became apparent as being of most concern was the inequity between groups – challenging future organizers to decide unilaterally and in advance, whether such programmes should be integrated or extra, and if integrated, how they should be assessed. Assuming that common assessment processes could and should be developed across participating programmes, the issue remains: should such programmes be integrated or be extra? This question goes to the centrality of such a programme to preparation for professional practice. The programme was, from the start, proposed as a joint experiment in cross-cultural and cross-disciplinary teaching, and this research shows that most students want and value such experiences, consider them relevant to their future working lives and are motivated primarily by the idea of learning about how their disciplines work in association and in other cultures. It also shows they learn important skills such as listening, patience, negotiation and reflective thinking. They expect to experience difference and value it. Importantly they see working with, rather than just learning about, other cultures and disciplines, as central.

Such outcomes suggest that, at the very least, students also expect such opportunities as part of their professional education. In that view they are in agreement with policy makers, the professions and educational theorists. What this experiment suggests is that the educational challenge is to maintain the richness (and difference) while ensuring that there is greater clarity – in their relationship to home programmes; in assessment; and, between participating groups. Initial working protocols may well need to include comparable assessment procedures, despite the difficulties of assessing outcomes for cultural skills.

A review of the original operational protocol suggests that while most of the issues it covered proved appropriate from the viewpoint of student experience, some factors did impact negatively on achievement of the programme goals. After assessment, scheduling was the threshold issue, accommodating three jurisdictions and two hemispheres. The very differences that made the programme so rich an experience, such as the three rather than two groups that forced participants to look beyond the simplest 'us and them' responses, made it much more organizationally complex and less than ideal. Given the students' equally strong support for the cross-disciplinary experiences, these might be more simply provided in their home programmes without the extra complexity brought by the cross-cultural agenda.

Other organizational matters impacting on the experience include accommodation, where the ideal appears to be for visitors to share with hosts, with opportunities for cross-group activity, individual retreat and in a location close to the work space, given the long working hours.

Of somewhat greater significance for achieving programme goals are opportunities for social interaction. While motivated by a desire to understand how their disciplines worked in other cultures, participants recognized that play (as well as work) helped them achieve the intercultural skills they sought. This survey suggests that development of the generic social skills (awareness, understanding and respect) that assist cross-cultural work (Unesco 2004: 16; IAU 2000: 1) and enhance professional and personal networks (awareness, understanding and respect) rely not only on scheduled work programmes. They also rely (as indeed is the case in the world of real life work and international practice) on social programmes, suggesting that these should be scheduled along with work – an outcome less surprising perhaps to some cultures than others.

The student experience research component of the BMB programme was carried out recognizing that as Unesco puts it, the development of international education needs to be accompanied by evaluation. It reveals that despite the difficulties and challenges in programme delivery such exercises present, students consider them valuable, even essential, in developing skills for their future working lives.

Notes

1 The BMB programme was initiated by three programmes from three institutions from three cities and cultures: the Faculty of Architecture at Kasetsart University, Bangkok; the Faculty of Architecture, Building and Planning at the University of Melbourne; and, École d'Architecture et Paysage de Bordeaux (EAPBx).
2 Such policies are in turn, manifestations at a programme level of national or regional commitments (Clyne and Rizvi 1998: 35, ERASMUS website). Responsible international practice is, after all, a stated goal of the international federations representing these disciplines (see UIA and IFLA websites).
3 While significant numbers of students do rate the experience highly in this aspect (a third rated this at 4 for workshop 2 and a half at 5 for workshop 3), at each workshop there were students from all programmes who rated this question very low (workshop 1, one each at 1 and 2; workshop 2, six rated this 2 and over half at 3 or less; workshop 3 two respondents rated this at 2). Notably, workshop 2 in Melbourne had by far the lowest mean overall for this question at 3.2 compared to 4.1 after Bangkok and 4.2 after Bordeaux.

Bibliography

Bull, C. (2004) 'Rhetoric and reality: the internationalization of education as experienced in the cross-cultural and cross-disciplinary studio', *Landscape Review*, 9 (2): 70–86.

—— (2005) 'The studio as a cross-cultural experience: lessons from the interdisciplinary BMB workshops', *Symposium BMB: Identity and Globalization: Design for the City*, proceedings of an International Symposium, Bordeaux, 7–9 April, Bangkok: Kasesart University.

Cannon, R. (1999) 'International education and a professional edge for Indonesian graduates: the third place' in J. Currie, R. de Angelis, H. de Boer, J. Huisman and C. Lacotte (2002) *Globalizing Practices and University Responses: European and Anglo-American differences*, Westport: Praeger.

Clyne, F. and Rivzi, F. (1998) 'Outcomes of student exchange' in D. Davis and A. Olsen (1999) *International Education: the Professional Edge*, a set of research papers presented at the 13th Australian Education Conference, Fremantle, Deakin, ACT: IDP Education.

Davis, D. and Olsen, A. (1999) *International Education: the Professional Edge*, a set of research papers presented at the 13th Australian Education Conference, Fremantle, Deakin, ACT: IDP Education Australia.

De Wit, H. and Knight, J. (eds) (1999) *Quality and Internationalization in Higher Education*, Paris, France: OECD.

ERASMUS program http://ec.europa.eu/education/programmes/llp/erasmus/erasmus_en.html (accessed 17 March 2007).

European Commission – Education and Training www.europa.eu.int/comm/education/policies/2010/et_2010_en.html

International Association of Universities (IAU) (1998) *IAU Statement on Internationalization*, report prepared for the Unesco World Conference in Higher Education 1998, formally adopted by the 11th IAU General Conference as part of the IAU Policy 2000, http://www.unesco.org/iau/p_statements/i_statement.html (accessed October 2004).

——, the Association of Universities and Colleges of Canada (AUCC), the American Council on Educations (ACE), Council for Higher Education Accreditation (CHEA) (2004) *Sharing Quality Higher Education across Borders: A Statement on Behalf of Higher Education Institutions Worldwide*, http://www.unesco.org/iau/p_statements/index.html (accessed February 2005).

International Federation of Landscape Architects (IFLA), www.ifla.org

International Union of Architects (UIA) http://www.uia-architectes.org

Knight, J. (1999) 'Internationalization of higher education' in H. De Wit and J. Knight (eds) *Quality and Internationalization in Higher Education*, Paris, France: OECD.

Mak, A., Barker, M., Logan, G. and Millman, L. (1999) 'Benefits of cultural diversity for international and local students: contributions from an experiential social learning Program (the EXCELL Program)' in D. Davis and A. Olsen, *International Education: the Professional Edge*, a set of research papers presented at the 13th Australian Education Conference, Fremantle, Deakin, ACT: IDP Education Australia.

Mason, R. (1998) *Globalizing Education. Trends and applications*, London: Routledge.

Savage, S. (2005) 'Urban design education: learning for life in practice', *Urban Design International*, 10: 3–10.

Unesco (2004) *Synthesis Report on Trends and Developments in Higher Education since the World Conference on Higher Education (1998–2003)*, http://portal.unesco.org/education/en/ev.php-URL_ID=31182&URL_DO=DO_TOPIC&URL_SECTION=201.html (accessed May 2004).

Chapter 25
Workshops as culture

Guy Tapie

The second international workshop in the BMB series was hosted in 2004 by the Faculty of Architecture, Building and Planning of the University of Melbourne, and in keeping with the agreed management of the programme that Faculty acted not only as host but was responsible for the teaching method and programme organization. While the design workshop is an internationally recognized working structure, observation revealed differences in methodological approach between institutions (and perhaps countries), in this instance Melbourne and Bordeaux or France and Australia.

While all students taking part, irrespective of native tongue, were required to use English as the language of communication, somewhat surprisingly this did not appear to pose major problems, despite their differing proficiencies. In the group work, however, superficial language skills might be expected to lead to superficial reasoning among participants, with group leadership automatically falling to those who have relative mastery of language, creating frustration among the others. Surprisingly perhaps, these minor problems seemed to be balanced by active discussion between groups and individuals from similar and different backgrounds about the meaning of the spatial problems at hand, demonstrating how the success of each group was dependent on personal involvement.

The introductory briefing by Melbourne's teaching staff explained the workshop structure, sequence and underlying reasoning. They emphasized, authoritatively, the quality of work outcomes expected and the intensity of the programme, which extended over two weeks and involved 30 students and about 12 teachers altogether. That authority was noticeable and contrasted with an expectation from some of a more interactive and relaxed process. The teaching philosophy and expectations were also outlined: to develop an initial point of view as the basis for reflection; to work with the context; to get involved; to communicate. To French sensibilities there was a striking emphasis on the programme sequence and a concern to adhere to it. Also noticeable was the purposeful relationship between various components of teaching, especially the familiar (lectures, group work, reporting sessions and discussions with stakeholders (or 'clients')) and the unfamiliar (teaching using 'key words').

The lectures conformed to some degree with universal pedagogical expectations, including presentations by an historian of the city, a designer of urban projects and a socio-economist. Visits to the site and its context were supplemented by discussions with urban managers and practitioners from the various areas of government involved. There were also, however, presentations of other projects that may have had relevance or provided models, including those valuing and incorporating nature in the urban setting (more apparent in Australia), and one given by an artist on the process of designing public space based on public art. These latter two were a subject of some discussion and surprise among the French because they seemed to have only an incidental relationship with the spatial problems, urban functions and flows and operational strategies that were specific to the site. They did, however, create a space for the development of ideas and encouraged reflection by students on the important historic, conceptual, artistic, socio-economic and professional domains of the site, and those they were expected to transcend in their projects. While not unfamiliar to the French, the lectures and presentations appeared to be organized so as to stress cognitive development based on a particular approach to educational theory.

The teaching sequence entitled 'key words' caused sharp reactions from the French teachers. While used as a familiar method to encourage creativity in schools of management, communication and marketing, this does not form a part of the French tradition of teaching urban design. From a pedagogical viewpoint, key words appear to be used as tools to help to transcend the fear of the blank white page, and to enable students to get beyond this to a design position within a very tight timetable. Their significance and function in the overall design process remains ambiguous however. Do they translate comprehension of the problems and site (economic, social)? Or are they a representation of a future solution? Key words might reflect similar experiences of, for instance, the use of the river (very different for an inhabitant of Bordeaux or of Bangkok) or the idea of difference. To the French teachers, initially, this approach did not appear to be based on an objective and thorough analysis of the characteristics of the site sufficient to identify key factors, these being urban history, function, morphology and use. They also felt it encouraged the students to enter too quickly into the solution phase, by-passing complex realities. With practice however, the groups transcended the potential superficiality of the key words by balancing them against 'the space of constraints' of the site realities in the field. This process was assisted, in particular, by a workshop session with professionals and operators. So, in fact, the heuristic device of using key words proved an effective way to enter quickly into the project.

Key words were also used as the focus of the first report back on progress by student groups, crystallizing their activities. The groups used key words both to represent their interpretation of the site and hint at their first concepts. Most importantly, using the strategy of key words appeared to encourage the formation of groups and helped established a working dynamic among participants. French students, however, wondered about the relevance of their reporting because they could not express the richness of their reflections. It became clear that even at this early stage, importance was not placed on 'the question', as the French teachers would expect, but on 'the answer' and efficiency in reaching it. The complexities of managing an international group of students who know the site only superficially, and are then obliged to discuss it in a foreign language and in a limited time period, seem to demand this. The second and the third reporting sessions even seemed repetitive with teachers not only judging proposals but also the vivacity of the groups and their capacity to transcend internal differences to produce projects ('They did the most important work. They went beyond the stage of initial ideas.'). While some groups achieved well with this method, some groups nevertheless appeared to remain trapped in a superficial initial phase, characterized by laborious internal discussions. Teachers used their understanding of the social psychology of each student group to explain their mistakes, their progress and to balance judgments.

Such workshops are promoted as valuable because they are undertaken in an unfamiliar context where participants are exposed to unfamiliar working methods. While this may be so, at a more basic level this example reveals two professional attitudes as well as teaching methods: the first being that of the formalists (the solution is in the project); the second, that of the analysts (the site provides the solution). The formalists, in this instance the Australian teachers, took a project-based approach to the work, with the designer anticipating and representing a future situation in form. Here, the facility to design and abstract from the data, and to communicate this, is highlighted. By contrast, the analysts (in this case the French), privileged analysis of the context and existing strategies, objectives and plans. Here, the facility to comprehend the structure and dynamics of the site provided the basis of the project as much as the concept. This universal difference crosses the domains of both teaching and the practice.

The French teachers conjectured that the dichotomy of the teaching methods might relate to underlying philosophies and approaches to teaching. Perhaps the more liberal system of education in Australia might lead to the project-based approach in the name of its effectiveness in formulating solutions? The recognized presence of 'urban designers' as a distinct profession in Melbourne supports such a vision, just as the design of the city appears to privilege the urban project and the negotiation between the private sector and various levels of government to achieve it. In this context, urban design seems to manifest some principles of Australian attitudes to space, nature and lifestyle (the relationship between the port, the city, the region and international territory). The training of professionals appears to be based on a system that directs the acquisition of competencies which is in turn based on theories relating design to project production. In contrast, the teaching of the French is based on the problematization of urban form, which emphasis theorization through analysis of the morphology of space and its meaning or representation. There seems to be less emphasis among them on the system of training, which remains secondary to the central goal.

In addition to demonstrating methodological difference, however, the Melbourne experience also showed that there are common ways to teach about urban projects and design and that there is a shared professional culture that transcends differences. The response of the Thai participants might expand even further the range of approaches to teaching methods, caught as they are between the realism exhibited by Australia and the more doctrinal French.

Conclusion
Urban design for a cross-cultural future

Catherin Bull, Darko Radović and Claire Parin

'Think globally, act locally',[1] the adage coined in the 1970s, expressed the importance of linking both global and local domains when making decisions about the environment. In reminding us that in practice, one affected the other, this catch-cry responded to an emerging global era and called for broader awareness from all those involved in the process of environmental change – architects, landscape architects, urban planners and urban designers included. The intervening decades have provided much to support 'global thinking', including broad access to digital and electronic communication, jet travel, the market economy, democratic values and concern about sustainability at the global scale. But what of the 'local action' and, perhaps, local thinking and global action implied by such a proposition? What are their characteristics? Just how do ideas of the global and local interact in practice in an era of unprecedented urbanization and environmental change, an era that has also witnessed unprecedented environmental degradation, immigration and population growth? And more importantly here, how do the professions practising urban planning and design position themselves and act responsibly in what appears as an ever-expanding and dynamic domain of international practice, a field of unprecedented complexity?

Such questions were raised and discussed in the introduction to this book where we suggested that one way – to approach, and even in some instances answer, the dilemmas presented to practice in a globalizing world – was to research urban design through an experiment.[2] That suggestion was based on an experiment structured as a complex series of activities over a three-year period. That experiment included cross-cultural symposia and workshops involving urban design practitioners from government, private practice and academia from many countries. Together with them, we wanted to scrutinize what urban design is in the international domain by observing, as put by Margaret Crawford, 'the way it is working in the world'.[3] Throughout that process, many methods of working with cultures different from their own were reflected upon, reported and discussed in a series of forums (symposia, workshops and meetings) by participants, contributors and authors. Initially our goal was to review activities that would reveal diverse aspects of contemporary urban design practice in the global and local domains in an environment characterized by open communication, continuing interrogation and debate among those involved. From these, observations could be made and conclusions drawn about what phenomena and experiences were emerging as common across an increasingly complex domain of international, cross-cultural urban design practice – whether global or local – and what methods were emerging as useful. From that basis of common experience, we expected, the operating environment and more effective practice within it could be described.

That experimental programme proved an unexpectedly rich source of data and information about how urban design as a field of endeavour acts in an increasing variety of domains. A window on that data and information is provided in the form of this book, which is structured to reflect the goal of its authors and editors, the co-ordinators of that experiment, to create what can be truly termed a greater dialogue[4] among many participants, from many places, from many forms of practice – a dialogue that manifests, we propose, the contemporary professional condition. That is why this volume includes so many voices and contributions. While neither exhaustive nor conclusive, the conclusions drawn from these contributions and reflections are, we suggest, an important first step in what we hope will be an evolving dialogue about what urban design is now and should be in the future.

The conclusions reflect the experimental process we undertook, enriched by the experience of numerous other urbanists. First, the conclusions present our approach to that process as a series of propositions, the value of which we consider is borne out by the multiplicity of voices articulating urban design experiences made available and accessible to that greater dialogue. These propositions both guided the experiment and structured our reflections on it. Second, the conclusions summarize a range of observations about practice, now and in the future, made possible by interrogation of the many experiences presented in this book, in all their variety and difference.

Both propositions and observations are the findings from our experiment, findings that should inform both day-to-day practice and thinking for urban design as cross-cultural practice. These findings arise not only from analysis in the academy but from the considered reflections of those in practice the world over, from contributors who have observed at first hand, the realities of practice as it has been in recent years, as it is today and suggest where it appears to be heading. They observe the many interactions between local specificities and global standards at various spatial scales, between local decision makers and global expectations, and between the ever increasing array of stakeholders in what each considers the urban design project. They observe the limitations of approaching urban design as an essentially technical practice and the increasing necessity for approaching it as cultural practice in response to increasing social complexities. It is observation of their experience across many cultural domains, as well as our own, that makes these conclusions possible and underpins our call for urban design as a cross-cultural practice in a globalizing world, a world where the local should never be considered too small or insignificant.

Facilitating cross-cultural dialogue and practice

Our approach to urban design as a cross-cultural practice roots it in the post-modern era, one characterized by spatial and temporal compression and global culture. Localized or place-based practice that welcomes local particularities and inputs on an equal footing is posited as a much-needed counterbalance to the dominating trends towards technical standardization, spatial homogenization and off-site decision making that provide the global context or 'frame', universal and modernizing. Further to Frampton's concept of what he calls 'Critical Regionalism' in architecture,[5] we conclude that not only should urban designers 'think globally, act locally' in such an environment, but think globally and locally, and act globally and locally. To do that we need to expand our knowledge of both the global and local domains and, just as importantly, to know more about how they interact in the contemporary world. While recognizing the Herculean dimension, and ultimately what may be the impossibility of such a task under current approaches, we believe that the solution lies in a new culture of urban design that shares and disseminates knowledge and experiences.

Our propositions for the establishment of just such a culture are broadly organized and discussed as topics dealing with the:

- Interactive formats that support collaborative cross-cultural projects;
- Dialectics that activate culturally complex discourse;
- Methods and skills that address the critical issue of cultural difference; and
- Complex outcomes from cross-cultural collaborations and endeavours.

Our experimental project provided a useful entry point into such discussions, because it was designed to be, simultaneously, a learning exercise, an exploration of real-life interactions between local and foreign urban cultures and, cross-disciplinary research. It was established to test both the methods for collaborative generation of ideas and the resulting design solutions in diverse situations, situations selected as environmentally unusual and culturally alien for the many participants. Common to the three threads of engagement within the experiment (symposia, workshops, research) was the willingness and the ability of the parties involved to: come together; reach across cultural differences; and commit to culturally and environmentally responsible design. Over the three years of its implementation, the project established itself as a self-learning system. Its workshops, symposia, briefings, debriefing sessions and heuristic games were conducted under the constant scrutiny of participants, who also reflected on and communicated with their collaborators, learning during the process. That process of learning reaches its climax in this book. The experiences captured in its pages suggest that collaborative cross-cultural endeavours in urban design practice are both experimental and educational by nature. Together they provide an exemplar of the cyclic process of reflective practice we propose should guide cross-cultural urban design in a dynamic and complex working environment where everyone is, irrespective of particular experience, a learner and a practitioner. The process we propose is iterative, one of 'learning–thinking–acting–reflecting–communicating' and, again 'learning'.[6]

The structure of the experimental project on which this book is based frames one of our most important suggestions: that culturally complex situations require (1) rapid accumulation and exchange of information and ideas; (2) a format where interaction enables partnerships to form and the unrestrained generation of ideas; (3) a rigorous reflective, parallel scrutiny of the process; and (4) timely and generous dissemination of findings to a broader audience of practitioners, stakeholders and decision makers.

Although such requirements may sound commonsensical, in practice they are far from common. They challenge normative practice, established boundaries between cultures (professional, operational and ethnic) and the deeply entrenched, counterproductive separation between professional practice and academia. They also challenge notions of competition between professional cultures and institutions, viewing them instead as complementary. All of these are separate efforts to understand and produce urban space. Design practice is seen, for example, as the production of knowledge through action and academic practice is understood as understanding, explaining and teaching. Both are, however, forms of practice focusing on the same territory. Our approach, therefore, considers cross-cultural urbanism and urban design holistically, balancing the permissive sensitivity and exploration attributed to design practice with the intellectual rigour expected of scientific research in academic practice. Such an approach to design combines two domains, objective knowledge as associated with science and the normative theory associated with the creative arts.[7]

Proposition 1: multiple formats for communication

In cross-cultural design environments, the quality and efficiency of communication among diverse contributors is of critical importance. At its best, it can establish an atmosphere that favours exchange of knowledge, the generation of ideas and which results in design outcomes that recognize both local specificities and international standards. At its worst, it can result in one-way communication, limited knowledge, standard approaches and solutions. The quality of communication can establish the kind of greater dialogue sought by Jencks and identified as a goal here, as the active agent of physical and cultural transformation,[8] at the local level of the project (both strategic and built) and at the international level of the profession.

Communicative Format 1: facilitating exchange – symposia

Practice within the context of accelerating globalization demands continual awareness of trends and developments across an ever widening spatial and cultural domain. It also requires expanded knowledge of professional methods and the efficacy of their application across diverse environments. While accelerated international publishing through the internet, books and journals provides a solid base for access to data, information, empirical research and theory, direct contact between practitioners (designers, researchers and professional specialists) remains critical to the process of advancing the application of ideas and knowledge, making the differences and particularities both of one's own culture, and that of others, tangible.

Symposia – as presentations, discussions and debates – that focus on issues of practice and thinking provide a forum for rapid face-to-face communication and live exchange among diverse actors in the field of urban design. They can operate at many scales – the global, the regional and the urban project itself. When framed to emphasize exploration of, and practice in, issues of acknowledged and immediate relevance (such as balancing global awareness and knowledge with local issues and sensibilities, an issue broadly recognized and experienced), the symposium topic provides the focus for open communication among professionals from all practice domains – planning and design practitioners from government and the private sector, educators and students.

Such rapid communication, as a form of reflective practice, goes against the accepted dogma originating in increasingly competitive academic circles, where quality of live exchange of ideas ranks lower than that promulgated through the peer reviewed and refereed journal system, often of limited circulation. It recognizes the rapid pace of our times and the realities of contemporary design practice, using the very unpredictability of face-to-face exchange to support creative advancement. Symposia, by definition, invite discussion, reflection and the cumulative development of ideas, the opposite of a research culture purposely characterized by postponed judgement and exclusivity.

Symposia allow the brainstorming of ideas as they are tabled, facilitate the exchange of experiences and expose the differences and similarities between urban design practices and products, without an excess of intrusive mediation. Such spontaneity is an essential constituent of cross-cultural encounters with the immediacy of communication adding to the critical mass of ideas generated around a topic. This was a technique employed in our experimental project and one that generated an unprecedented source of ideas for participants, whose experiences were made so easily accessible to a wider forum in an operating context now dominated by rapid and relatively universal access to relatively unmediated electronic information as well as the intensely mediated, less accessible information of the academic journal. They are recommended for all scales of cross-cultural endeavour.

If supportively structured, symposia can promote debate at the scale of the local project, the city or the globe. In our experiment they were used to provoke debate internationally about the whole field. Among the contributors here they were used at the scale of the urban project. They were most successful when participants were encouraged to contribute around broadly defined themes and where contributors were selected from the widest possible pool. Thematic definition structured contributions by providing an informal agenda for discussion. Encouraging the widest range of contributors enabled the widest possible range of issues and circumstances to be identified and similar phenomena to be observed across a great variety of individual territories. Standardizing forces and trends could be noted and their impacts compared across cultures and territories. Contributors were also able to locate themselves and their situations within the 'greater dialogue' as themes emerged, converged and even diverged at a global or local scale, rather than anticipate such themes a priori. The emergent themes, in turn, suggest topics for further research and investigation. Designers everywhere now appear to be hungry for knowledge about how, as Henri Lefebvre (1974) anticipated, the globalization process works and impacts on their projects. Such cross-cultural research activity, particularly where it engages practitioners and observers who are specialists in the urban field from so many different places, enables the systems that now underpin urban planning and design at the local level – whether economic, cultural or physical – to be decoded.

Nevertheless, we reiterate that there is no universal paradigm to explain the post-modern city (Dear 1999) and that global phenomena must be observed in the context of the particular situation, where meaning is engendered as perceptions and conceptions and where urban projects take place. Their change in response to global forces can be specifically measured as physical and social manifestations that can, in turn, be related to local decision-making processes. They can also be related to the methods and practices used by urban planners and designers, whether locally generated, or themselves manifestations (or adaptations) of international standards. Such complex processes of interaction, whereby global influences are mediated by various processes and practices, are the subject of many of the contributions we present and, in turn, the focus of our own discussions. As a collective artefact, a manifestation of both global and local culture and the site of urban design practice, the city seems an ideal place to observe that process as cross-cultural research.

Communicative Format 2: generating ideas – workshops and studios

Cross-cultural exchanges in the working environment not only demand recognition of difference but its appreciation. They are also supported by the formation of working partnerships among different contributors and stakeholders to achieve mutually beneficial ends. Many contributors to this book explore this theme, focusing on the way that diverse groups communicate, explore goals and reach agreement about means and ends. Their preferred format for interaction varied according to location and project, but as designers in the main they used the tradition of the workshop and studio, specifically adapted to achieve new communicative possibilities to accommodate cross-cultural practice. Workshops provided a robust framework for a number of activities among designers and non-designers, because they facilitate a choreographed but relatively open interaction among participants who for the duration of the process, are considered of equal standing. As a discrete domain with the goal of identifying, exploring and potentially solving problems, the workshop encourages the creative development of ideas and maximum participation.

Each of the workshops and studios (specializing in design alone) discussed here were a focus for investigation of cultural interaction as well as a means of producing solutions to urban problems. They were carefully framed and managed as processes to include and maintain: a high level of collegiality among the participants; an atmosphere of heightened cultural sensitivity; equity in communication; and an ethical approach to the particular urban situation. In summary, the structures employed had the goal of respectful interaction.

The workshop in its many guises (including the studio), and the processes employed to facilitate it described and discussed here, confirm its position as an important forum for successful cross-cultural communication and design. Diverse participants from different cultures (ethnic, professional, institutional and political) shared knowledge, debated meanings and intentions and worked together to create solutions to urban problems and, just as importantly, owned those solutions once they were defined. The structured informality of the workshop environment, as with the symposium, assisted the creation of a 'greater dialogue' among participants. Various semiotic games and choreographed cycles of interchange were employed and interrogated as techniques to advance interaction among contributors (see chapters by Radović, Thomas, Boontharm, Intrachooto, Bull and Thaveeprungsriporn).

It is notable that in their experiments with the workshop format, authors and contributors often rejected standard, 'expert' or 'top-down' approaches, where knowledge and solutions to problems were handed down from urban experts (often visiting) to other participants and urban communities. They adapted workshops to find more inclusive approaches. This reflected a trend apparent in many of the cases towards finding and establishing, through communicative techniques, more collegial relationships among diverse groups – be those groups dialogic, tri-logic or even, multi-logic in character. In the examples they describe, contributors revealed a highly experimental aspect of urban design practice for cross-cultural situations – the creative adaptation of the workshop as a method for generating an expanded field of knowledge, creative exploration and decision making – a field characterized again, by learning among all participants, choreographers and neophytes alike.

For example, cross-cultural workshops are revealed as sharing several characteristics, irrespective of location. They provide a shared site for territorial analysis, with each contributor objectivizing his or her interpretation of place graphically and verbally. Such ethnocentric subjectivity is immediately counterbalanced by alternative interpretations from other cultural viewpoints and is thereby decoded, a process that parallels the deconstruction of literature and philosophy recommended by Derrida (1978). This is the stage where the normative character of many perceptions can be revealed and confronted prior to the process of design. With such perceptions exposed, the designer can organize space to accommodate diverse viewpoints and spatial practices.

This being said, they recognized the additional time such cross-cultural modes of communication and interaction demand, compared with standard practice based on more rapid and standard consultation and decision-making processes.

Communicative Format 3: from reflective practice to research

In the introduction to this book, the idea of reflective practice as originally proposed by Schon (1995) was discussed as a fundamental source of inspiration. The cross-cultural domain of urban design was proposed in that introduction as an expanded field for reflective activity, responding to the essentially expanded and international domain that now characterize practice. Indeed reflection is proposed here as the essential partner to action in practice, one that is often ignored in an era where spatial and temporal compression create a working context of unprecedented complexity – both technically and culturally – and again, as with the communicative formats already described above, a perceived shortage of time.

Despite the forces against it, reflection on that complexity seems to us and many contributors to this book, to be fundamental to the successful future of urban design as cross-cultural practice. But, it can be asked, what form should such reflection take? Purposely, the authors have sought contributions to this book from a diverse group of actors and thinkers in all forms of practice, rather than from the more traditional domain of academics alone. The key to effective, reflective practice is, in their view, that it applies to all practitioners of cross-cultural urban design, irrespective of their working domain – government employees, consultants, academics alike. While their ways of acting differ; their ways of thinking and reflecting differ; and their ways of communicating differ, all are valuable since, as a whole, they define what the field actually is.

What the authors observed, and what was confirmed by the symposia, workshops and papers, was that many in urban design already work in cross-cultural environments, whether in other places or at home. Confronted by change and difference on a daily basis, they are seeking not only to reflect on and expose their experiences to others but to learn from others as well. They recognize that, mature professionals as they may be, they practice in a world where they need to learn continually. The learning they need is driven by change, not only in urban structure and phenomena but in social relations, in influences and expectations and in the very processes of decision making and delivery. Through reflection, communication and exchange about the nature of practice now, they learn, relearn and become better prepared.

Our first proposition argues for more and diverse channels of communication about cross-cultural urban design. The previous sections present the case for the face-to-face, rapid communication through symposia and workshops. Here, in contrast, we argue for greater rigour in the process of reflection. The very complexity of each of the two component domains of cross-cultural urban design – the urban and the cultural – along with the complexity of the contemporary context of international practice and rapid change, suggests that reflective practice and rapid communication alone will be insufficient to inform its future. They need to be paralleled by comprehensive and thematic research projects that facilitate rigorous comparative studies of phenomena and methods. Such projects would theorize and clarify what processes are occurring and what methods appear useful and successful in particular (local) and general (global) circumstances. Such, indeed, is the aim of this book, which presents a series of cases in urban design thinking and practice, related, but also distinguished, by theme and territory. It presents and explores experiences and ideas about the intersection of the global and the local in urban design as a means to focus on the cross-cultural working domain. It summarizes a sequence of related activities and collected experiences from diverse sources around that focus. Emerging themes are identified – themes that can form the basis for more specific theoretical interrogation. As a result it suggests ways forward for professionals in design practice and the academy around that topic.

In doing so, the book critically interrogates the assumptions and analytical practices that inform professional action, the methods applied to particular projects and of the way that we learn to interact in the cross-cultural world of urban design. A number of assumptions about how cultures interact in urban development are challenged, including assumptions about the hegemony of the modern and indeed 'the West' (see chapters by Sintusingha, De Wandeler and Bradbury). The changing influence and roles of decision makers are analysed, revealing the potential of some institutions (such as Unesco at a global level and royal families and government at a local level) to resist or redirect standard forms of development driven by global flows of capital, usually manifest as large scale commercial and tourist infrastructure projects and what many contributors observe as the more insidious process of mass suburbanization (see chapters by Anukulyudhaton, Feveile et al., Ben Mahmoud, Tournier).

The increasing capacity of local interest groups to protect the character and form of local settlements in the process of change is also revealed, especially where there are urban design experts in place with the capacity to harness their energy and knowledge and work across both local and global domains at the project level (see chapters by Margueritte, Bergeron and Godier, Latouche). This supports the views of Czerniak that what he calls 'pre-design' – representation, advocacy, communication, consensus-building – are extremely important components of the field and that public participation is a key to urban design, if orchestrated as strategic input and feedback by the designer (Czerniak 2006: 23).

This view is exemplified in some countries where such activities are considered by contributors as fundamental mediators of, and links to, the development process. Framed as urban projects, they create a dialogue between decision makers (often economic or social elites) and traditional or local communities who have difficulty shaping their environments in the face of externally driven change. Such dialogues are usually technically based, even if they are framed to operate in the cultural or political sphere. The cross-cultural approach appears to support such activity because of its emphasis on the interaction between the local context and global phenomena and its reflection on and questioning of diverse values and objectives.

What is also revealed by the contributions is the relevance and value of research carried out at an intensely intimate and local level, about the way urban settlements everywhere change in the face of standardizing trends. At its most revealing, that research uses methods available internationally, applying and usually adapting them locally to show those familiar with the formal language of the urban – at the scale of city and settlement – how this process is occurring in both the international and local domains. The objective scrutiny of the researcher, often from elsewhere, combined with the local knowledge they access through careful cross-cultural interaction, brings the best of international practice to light and demonstrates the power that can be sourced by harnessing both domains. The chapters by Sutthitharm, Limthongsakul, Panin and Anukulyudhaton in Thailand and Tournier in North Africa are cases in point, contributing new ways of thinking about the urban domain to the debate as well as knowledge generated from the cases themselves. The broader contribution of such new ways of thinking is discussed further in the following section.

Many contributions compare experiments that deal with similar themes and topics such as the cross-cultural workshop and the role of various interactive techniques and language (typically English as discussed by Intrachooto and Bull). These reveal the power of techniques such as semiotic games (see chapters by Radović, Boontharm and Thaveeprungsriporn) and the power of the third to enhance communication (Radović) by creating a greater dialogue among diverse groups and contributors. Trilateral, rather than bilateral, interaction is seen as creating unusually rich opportunities for objective analysis. One of our conclusions and recommendations for cross-cultural practice is to, as the norm, introduce a third party to any process of exchange. The very introduction of the third brings about, in the experience of our experiment and as supported by the theory, a greater possibility of rigour to design and research processes (see Radović). Diverse formats for interaction, enhanced by the inclusion of the third, not only enable the dangerously dualistic them-and-us relationship common to interactive environments to be transcended, but also assist the distance necessary for rigor and greater objectivity in research.

Without the in-depth analyses, critiques and comparisons that are enabled by such comparative studies, urban design remains trapped between two extremes – the universal and unavoidable generalizations about global phenomena and standard approaches, and the detail particularities of each site and situation. That condition is challenged by propositions that suggest that not only is more rapid exchange required to reveal and communicate experience in the field as it evolves, but systematic and rigorous scrutiny of emergent themes is also required to investigate and open areas for further and more detailed analysis and debate. Such scrutiny characterizes more traditional research – with its accompanying investigative agendas, protocols, experimental programmes and independently assessed reporting. Cross-cultural urban design will benefit from establishing sequences of integrated and related investigative projects. Such projects enhance learning and create opportunities for broader synthesis, testing and, ultimately, if widely disseminated, confidence in practice (Armstrong 1999).

Communicative Format 4: disseminating experience and findings

Effective and reflective practice of cross-cultural urban design needs various kinds of interaction: first, exposure to the latest information, experience and thinking in the field of practice internationally through fast and efficient face-to-face exchange (e.g. local, regional or international symposia), especially among practitioners and decision makers; second, exploration of and creative debate about possibilities and decisions through project-specific interaction (e.g. workshops and studios), especially among stakeholders; and, third, rigorous scrutiny of experimental approaches to practice through integrated and comparative investigative programmes that enable approaches, methods and findings to be formalized as research – for broader dissemination.

Various communication media are needed as support for the three forms of 'working' interactions, for immediate dissemination and for research. For symposia, precirculated short papers that incorporate written and graphic (spatial diagrams and photos) content suited to rapid exchange and communication provide the agenda for, support debate on, and act as record of interaction. For workshops and design studios, graphic and written materials generated in situ act as working records of ideological and spatial explorations, analyses, propositions and group decision making. For programmes of reflection and research on methods of cross-cultural interaction, all of the foregoing provide the basic data for systematic assembly and rigorous analysis.

We propose that the very process of interaction, whether exploratory and/or practice-based, is of value. It provides the basic data for the generation of knowledge useful to reflective cross-cultural practice in urban design. Urban planners and designers, as cross-cultural practitioners with the skills to observe the processes that transform urban space, can contribute to research processes by collecting and disseminating that data – as action-research.

This position contrasts with contemporary assumptions about how knowledge is generated, where the more rigorous forms of knowledge remain isolated from and largely inaccessible to the world of practice. Such action-research forms the basis for analysis of what constitutes effective practice and of the evolution of the urban domain itself. It grounds emerging theories of both. Treating the outcomes of cross-cultural interactions as data and analysing and disseminating them recognizes that all urban designers are learners in the cross-cultural context by linking their various worlds of practice: in government, in commercial consulting and in academia, across professional and ethnic cultural traditions.

Proposition 2: conceptual open-mindedness and cross-cultural inclusivity

Cross-cultural practice in any field is predicated on inclusivity in the face of recognized difference. As a field of design, urban design should aspire to openness to new alternatives, creative thinking about what is and about what methods will best achieve its goals in its working domain. By acknowledging and valuing difference, cross-cultural urban design adds a further dimension to an already complex creative realm, demanding that we

> unmake many of our methodological habits, including the desire for certainty; the expectation that we can usually arrive at more or less stable conclusions about the way things really are; the belief that ... we have special insights that allow us to see further than others into certain parts of social reality; and the expectations of generality that are wrapped up in what is often called 'universalism'.
>
> (Low 2004: 9)

Such sentiments are echoed by many of our contributors, who have consciously sought to adapt standard methods of analysis, design and decision making to what they see as specific and different situations and have reported on these methods and their findings. Their willingness to draw conclusions and to practise in an environment of 'uncertainty' underpins our expectation that it may yet be possible to maintain the specificity and essential difference of the local in the face of standardizing global forces.

An important aspect of what is reported in this book is the inclusion of what the authors and editors see as a 'third' domain, the Asian. Our initiating tri-logue included two parties from the West: the old world or world order, represented by France (and via the symposia, Europe); and, the new world represented by Australia, (and again via the symposia, North America and New Zealand). An initial third party, Thailand, represented the East and was also expanded to include other Asian countries as the interactions evolved. In time, through the symposia, parties also went on to include Africa. Difference was maximized as parties and contributors multiplied, forcing participants to reconsider what their assumed cultural positions actually were and exposing not only difference but convergence. As is typical in our globalizing environment, those from one domain may have been educated in or practising with colleagues from another.[9] They confirmed or adapted their 'different' philosophies and practices as these were challenged in the process of interaction as a result. The complexity exposed the key challenges to cross-cultural interaction and the way that a professional position of inclusive openness supports learning about other cultures and other environments and about urban design methods that effectively support cross-cultural difference. Just how can we communicate and work together in the cross-cultural domain?

Contributions were selected specifically to explore these issues by editors who have themselves been challenged through the process of scrutinizing papers and workshop materials by different professional methods and forms of discourse. Sutthitharm, Thaveeprungsriporn and Amougou Mballa provide particular cases where so-called Western models of thinking, working and learning are challenged in practice and reported upon. Thomas also discusses how presumptions about effective interaction in the cross-cultural workshop environment (led from outside experts) were challenged on-the-ground in Africa, requiring quite specific adaptations of technique to be effective. Whitford discusses how we are all challenged to rethink our positions, even relearn, in the face of globalized expectations, in his case suggesting a 'third' way for the future.

It was in this notion of 'the third' that our initial experiment was particularly active, because of the systematic analysis of interactions and outcomes among experimenters. The roots of what is generally considered Eastern and Asian thought lie in classical Chinese thinking, which sees the world differently from standard Western ways. In the place of the logic which underpins the dominating modernist, positivist worldviews, in classical Chinese thought we find a type of dialectic which is

> not quite the same as the Hegelian dialectic in which thesis is followed by antithesis, which is resolved by synthesis, and which is aggressive in the sense that the ultimate goal of reasoning is to resolve contradiction. The Chinese dialectic instead uses contradiction to understand relations among objects or events, to transcend or integrate apparent oppositions, or even to embrace clashing but instructive viewpoints.
>
> (Nisbett 2005: 27)

Through the experiment, we have discovered that acceptance of the contextualism implied in such thinking is of particular importance to cross-cultural practice, since it sees things and events as, at a fundamental level, inseparable from their contexts.

> Events do not occur in isolation from other events, but are always embedded in a meaningful whole in which the elements are constantly changing and rearranging themselves. To think about an object or event in isolation and apply abstract rules to it is to invite extreme and mistaken conclusions. It is the Middle Way and that is the goal of reasoning.
>
> (Nisbett 2005: 27)

In that sense, cross-cultural interactions in urban design practice, including symposia, workshops and research programmes, including dissemination of these, need to be inclusive environments that embrace difference, even outright contradiction, 'accepting it or transcending it or using it to understand some state of affairs better' (Nisbett 2005: 176). It is this that creates the much sought after 'greater dialogue' that reflective cross-cultural practice in a globalizing domain seeks, accepting contradiction (not to be confused with consensus) as an accepted, even welcomed and necessary part of the cross-cultural working process.

A specific reference to such thinking is made in Chapter 16 by that most pragmatic practitioner, the contributor Margueritte who says

> On the one hand, the urban planning and design process must now aim to go beyond sectoral interests and demands of individual stakeholders and project champions. On the other hand, it must accept the uncertainty of their influence. Urban professionals must also keep control of the process, adjusting it repeatedly and progressively to achieve overall project goals. Needing access to more than the few previously accepted methods, urban professionals are now required to respond in a great variety of ways to the inherent reality of the contemporary city, which can be seen as a site subject to slow sedimentation and accretion where each urban project, however complex, becomes just another part of an evolving work-in-progress.
>
> This complex reality must be confronted and worked with. The focus must be on involving and guiding stakeholders and project champions and on harnessing their power and influence via robust decision-making systems. The management (or governance) of all this at the level of the project must in turn operate within the systems of governance operating at the level of the city, suggesting that greater knowledge of urban management is now necessary. In order to be effective, urban

professionals also need advanced knowledge of project management processes to involve and gain commitment from all stakeholders, be they ultimate decision makers or local residents. The techniques that guide planning and delivery processes must be readable, accessible and motivating. They must focus on issues and outcomes that are widely recognized as important so as to capitalize on local experience and knowledge, to build a shared sense of what is achievable in the communal imagination.

In such discussions, the determination of practitioners to rethink their positions and practices in the face of contemporary challenges is palpable and supports our argument for inclusivity and open-mindedness in a global context where everyone is learning.

Proposition 3: culturally responsive methodologies

As a specialist in issues related to the processes of thinking, Nisbett reports the disturbing loss of local cultures and concludes that

> if social practices, values, beliefs, and scientific themes are to converge, then we can expect that differences in thought processes would also begin to evaporate. There is in fact evidence that changes in social practices, and even changes in temporary states of social orientation, can change the way people perceive and think.
>
> (2005: 226)

As already discussed, such flattening also accompanies much global practice of urban design in contemporary conditions, where the ready-made, standardized approaches are offered as readily available 'solutions' to problems and opportunities in places characterized by profound cultural, as well as physical, difference (Kreiger 2006: 35).

The dialectic between the general (or global) and the circumstantial (or local), the centre and the periphery, is at the core of all cross-cultural projects. From scrutiny of these contributions, we do not see globalization in itself as a villain since it underpins the whole field of international practice, interaction and learning and makes projects such as this book possible. It can be, however, a very dangerous process, because of its power and its tendency towards standardization. In the field of the urban, whether at the scale of the city or the village, standardization includes ideas, ideologies, aspirations and thinking as well as products. It can take the form of whole typologies of development, as in commercialization, suburbanization and mass tourism. Panin and Tournier discuss such cases in Asia and North Africa. It can take the form of the standard design and development methods, processes and technologies that are applied to design and development processes, typically those dominated by outside experts and standards at the expense of local communities and spatial particularities as described by Latouche.

As cross-cultural practice, urban design can be positioned to resist the standardization that accompanies global forces, or by contrast, to actively harness and direct those forces to support locally focused and supportive projects. Examples of such approaches are discussed in contributions by Mahmoud, Bergeron and Godier, Gotlieb, Latouche, and even Feveile et al. in Montenegro. When global standards and forces are considered as one contributing factor among the many that need to be co-ordinated to advance a project, their power can be harnessed along with that of other contributors and participants. Contributors and participants include not only development agencies (commercial or governmental) but local communities, who can articulate the value of their historic places and practices as tangible manifestations of local culture, in a collaborative (if complex) process of development orchestrated by the urban designer.

In assigning such a choreographic role, the score for urban design practice includes not only those planning strategies generated at a city-wide level, usually by governments and institutions but the tactics that emerge more spontaneously from individuals and groups at a smaller scale. As suggested by Michel de Certeau (1984), while adding a less predictable dynamic to the process, such tactics initiate interactions and dialogues among local stakeholders. These in turn expose issues and can be used by urban designers to strengthen the resilience of local space in the face of change.

Such collaborations, however, assume the need for power sharing and cross-cultural interpretation at a level that is rarely recognized and, even more rarely, understood.[10] In this book, De Wandeler and Sintusingha describe, through detailed analysis, previously unrecognized processes where local communities have themselves creatively harnessed imported development models to their own ends. As professionals working with communities and development agencies, in diverse situations across the globe, Anukulyudhaton, Sutthitharm, Bradbury, Thomas and Feveile et al. all describe attempts by urban designers to do that.

In all these situations, the key is to recognize that professional urban analysis and design methods need to be culturally responsive and to recognize the value of local conditions and methods. Only then will they become responsible. Sutthitharm in particular challenges those in and from the West. She challenges them to consider methods that differ significantly from those common to their (and our) thinking and proposes that methodologies must respect the ethical and philosophical traditions of people as well as the places they serve. Such approaches support the proposition put by Sorkin (2006: 15) that practice today is configured by a 'matrix of traditionalism, environmentalism, Modernism, and self-help', where all must be considered. In such a view, which he describes as 'Everyday Urbanism', equity and social justice are key measures of achievement and the creative focus in urban design is not only on the formal outcome but on methods, processes and social outcomes.

In their experiments with methods of cross-cultural interaction, many contributors (Thomas, Radović, Intrachooto and Thaveeprungsriporn) explored the role of format and language in the workshop as a means of encouraging a greater dialogue among participants. Their goal was to move towards partnerships, with experts (whether hosts or guests) encouraging greater involvement and contribution by stakeholders. In some situations, as it was with our own experiment, the local team provided leadership, including methodological guidance with the goal of revealing indigenous, culture-specific nuances, opening these methods to scrutiny from those who brought standard methods or simply radically different views from outside. Such processes led to creative cross-fertilization between the local and the foreign, often challenging expert views and standard approaches to what methods were most effective (whether initiated locally or not) while encouraging greater ownership of outcomes at a local level. The reflections on such processes suggest that they provide a steep learning curve for everyone involved in the experiment and, most importantly, demand awareness among participants that methods in cross-cultural urban design not only can but should be diverse and contextual. While they may even, in some instances, be incompatible with the globally accepted, standard practices, in some instances the reverse might apply. In a number of instances discussed and analysed here, for example, those from outside may bring new ways of seeing everyday realities, revealing the invisible ubiquitous to those most familiar with it (Thomas, Bull, Feveile *et al.*). This process in itself stimulated positive change.

With regard to language, a logical starting compromise is often to accept English as the *lingua franca* of the working environment. In these examples, however, compared to normal practice, what was important was the awareness by experimenters and participants that language is never culture-neutral (Radović 2003). In cross-cultural communication, how words and nuances of terminology are used demands careful scrutiny by all participants (Boontharm, Thaveeprungsriporn, Bull and Singh). The language used in cross-cultural practice provides not only a medium for communication it becomes a tool, too, to expose zones of interaction and separation between participating cultures. It may be a vehicle of precision and accuracy or it may be the opposite – a space of uncertainty. Indian writers such as Rao, Achebe and Rushdie accept English as a world language but warn that, with involvement of the other, it will be used in increasingly new ways (Watson 2000: 706), as is apparent both in the contributions to this book and in the cases they discuss. In this project it has been fascinating to observe the emergence of new words, phrases and ephemeral neologisms in communications as working interactions and products evolved, including the flourishing of numerous hybrid words as tools and accents. In such an inclusive working environment, these hybrid words and phrases, because they were valued, added a positive dimension to comprehension and creativity instead of impeding mutual understanding. The evolution of language provided a tangible example of how, in acknowledging the importance of reflexivity and reflective practice in cross-cultural urban design, we will always need to ask 'whether we are able and willing to recognize that our methods also craft realities' (Low 2004: 153) and be flexible about those methods. We will also need to support such methodologies with the additional time they demand (Bull).

Proposition 4: accepting non-standard outcomes

One of the emerging themes in cross-cultural urban design is that of multiplicity – multiplicity of ideas, multiplicity of communication channels, multiplicity of ways of working. As John Low observes, when it comes to the complexity of social fabric,

> if we focus on practice then we are led to multiplicity since there are many practices crafting many realities. Truth is no longer the only arbiter and reality is no longer destiny. There are (to put it too simply) choices to be made between the desirability of different realities.
>
> (Low 2004: 152)

The propositions already discussed focus on the approaches, processes and methods in urban design that might be described as cross-cultural. This proposition focuses on products. Many contributors to this book describe and analyse what they call 'the urban design project', a broad definition that can apply to everything from strategies to guide conservation and development at the metropolitan scale, to infrastructure provision, to neighbourhood or precinct plans and work programmes, even to works at the scale of the individual site. The urban design project appears in all its varieties as the working focus and product of the field and its form is as varied as the situations where that work occurs. Urban designers, it would seem, create projects as a means of harnessing otherwise disparate energy and activity towards specific goals, and that very act of creation can be as important a test of their success as the formal outcomes on the ground.

Some contributors, as independent observers of other cultures, turned the very act of critical analysis of otherwise unobserved phenomena or places into projects (Guillot, Amougou Mballa, Sintusingha, Limthongsakul, Whitford, Sutthitharm, Panin, Gotlieb and Tournier). These insights provide useful information on cross-cultural urbanism or are methodological exemplars for others practising in similar circumstances. Others, as visiting experts working with local communities, interrogated the processes of urbanization and the social and physical degradation that accompanied it, created projects that intervened (Thomas, Anukulyudhaton, Pinijvarasin and Sunakorn, Feveile *et al.*, Bradbury). Some, working within their own communities, who recognize the cross-cultural ambit of their diverse stakeholders and the complex interactions necessary to achieve outcomes on the ground and in the community, created projects to channel and focus their energy towards agreed outcomes (Margueritte). Yet others, recognizing that the cross-cultural in their environment manifests as an interface between global or international standards and local expectations, created or observed projects that orchestrated that relationship (Bergeron and Godier, Latouche).

Such activities support the proposition put by Crawford, and already reported above, that the urban design project is an agent of transformation – of people, thinking and organizations or institutions as well as places – and that what Czerniak calls 'pre-design – representation, advocacy, communication, consensus-building' is an extremely important aspect for urban design everywhere. Such concepts challenge us to redefine what an outcome in urban design is and by extension what an outcome is in cross-cultural practice. They suggest variety in scale and format with equal emphases on social interactions, processes and physical form.[11] In summary, cross-cultural urban design projects address and generate multiple realities and celebrate difference. They seem, at an essential level, to struggle against homogenization and standardization, the hallmarks of globalization. They suggest that valid and acceptable outcomes may be diverse and to some even ambiguous by providing space for multiple voices to be heard and respected in the process of decision making. They may manifest as form, but they may also have other manifestations that are or may be of equal value.

In achieving such outcomes, urban designers must be able to: invite questions; generate a living ecology of interactions; and to ensure decisions are made locally as well as globally (or at a distance), even where that approach challenges the accepted determinism of cultural hegemony and domination. In such a working domain, urban designers are seen as the directors and choreographers of a complex drama where many players interact and dance, and where the audience is participatory rather than passive. The scripts they write for such interactions have many acts, many scenes and many parts, all of which – large or small – are important contributors to the process and the outcome.

Strategies and tactics for urban design in a cross-cultural context

Finally, and in summary, a number of characteristics of contemporary urban design practice and its context can be identified from analysis of the material in this book. These include trends towards practice at an increasing range of territorial scales (from the neighbourhood to the regional) in an increasing variety of cultures and geographies. The context for that work is characterized by: increasingly complex relationships between global phenomena (tourism, sub-urbanization, commercialization and post-industrialization) and local conditions; increasing degradation of landscapes and urban areas (recognizing the increasing importance of functioning natural systems within the urban matrix); and increasingly complex and rapid decision making, delivery and urban management processes.

Urban design teams operating in culturally sensitive environments need, as a result, to develop working capacities that detect and respond to such issues. They must learn and apply in their practice a greater range of methodological models and precedents to address the increasing range of project types and settings, recognizing that adaptation of those methods will be inevitable and regular scrutiny and dissemination of results necessary, as previously discussed. Their skills will need to include cultural as well as technical capacities including, in sum: sustained and greater ingenuity/innovation at all project scales; sustained commitment to retro-fit sites and reverse landscape and urban degradation; and, a greater capacity to engage in complex work, contributing to and orchestrating debates and decisions, cross-disciplinary, cross-cultural or a combination of both. The ethics of their professional positions need to recognize these demands, embodying them in their professional work as philosophical positions as well as fundamental skills.

Despite the increasing complexity of urban design work and its context, the authors and contributors to this book see a positive future for urban design as cross-cultural practice and the professions who contribute to it, including landscape architects, architects, planners, urbanists. The characteristics they need for such a future demand however, that in summary, they learn to be:

1   reflective in their practice;
2   accepting of and able to work respectfully with 'difference' and 'the other';
3   cultural, and cross-cultural, practitioners as well as technical experts;

4   effective communicators able to develop 'greater dialogues' across diverse groups;
5   able to access, analyse and learn from an emerging and increasingly diverse range of international experiences in urban design;
6   able to understand and model the many processes that manifest as physical and social phenomena in both global and local cultures;
7   knowledgeable about the range of methodological models available to effect change; and
8   able to imagine, script and choreograph complex processes of interaction to effect physical and social change.

Such professional characteristics can be developed from exposure to and command of certain domains of knowledge as skills. Consideration of the many contributions and analyses presented in this book, that broadly map the emerging territory of urban design as it operates internationally, reveals the need for fluency and an ability to act as professionals in the following broad domains that constitute the field of urban design in a globalizing world:

- the ecology and dynamics of natural and urban systems at a global, regional and local scale;
- the technologies of conservation, management and construction in the urban, suburban and natural domains (including 'sustainable technologies' as they evolve);
- the history and theory of practice, including the failures and successes of various projects in conserving, managing and constructing natural and urban areas;
- spatial analysis of the processes of change that are manifest as urban areas and landscapes – globally, regionally and locally; past and present;
- conceptualizing the form and function of future, alternative territories at all scales;
- converting concepts into realizable urban projects, whether at the strategic or site scale;
- communicating as cultural and cross-cultural practitioners across a wide range of territories; and
- the organization, legal framework and ethics of practice, globally and locally.

From such an analysis it can be seen that urban design, to be practiced responsibly in the cross-cultural global domain, requires a range of skills greater than those expected at present. Such a requirement has direct consequences for the professions and how they encourage existing and incoming practitioners to learn and prepare. To harness and balance the standardizing forces that accompany globalization, the technical skills to prevent and redress environmental degradation and create urban environments that support social interaction need to be paralleled with greater capacities to navigate more diverse places and cultures and access a greater range of methodological and formal models. With such capacities urban designers will be more equal to the task of turning global forces to their advantage, rather than, as they often seem to be at present, be at their calling.

All practitioners need greater access to theory, in particular about what global culture and globalization actually are, and how these forces influence their disciplines. They need to know how to observe and generalize the elements of place and the processes of change that occur, whether ubiquitous (and 'every-day' and invisible) or the beguiling exotic (and 'different') at all scales. They need more methods, more examples of application and greater skills in adapting those methods to the expanding variety of cultural and physical situations that will confront them. Finally, they need to gain real experience in reflective (analytical) practice and learn its value as a skill fundamental to practise at any scale (Schon 1995). Overall, learning in specialist educational environments and in practice needs to prepare urban designers for future challenges as cross-cultural professionals who can act expertly and ethically in an increasingly complex global domain to improve its potential not only for cultural and physical survival but for improvement. Such an approach shifts emphasis from the pragmatics of learning skills to a broader vision of knowledge.

It may be that, as put by Alex Krieger, 'there has to be time to overcome the shock of the new ... We've not yet come to terms with things ... and therefore we resort to traditional urban models. We need to move beyond this shock.' (Kreiger 2006: 35).[12] That is what this project and this book set out to do. We trust that not only we, but our readers, will continue to contribute to the evolution of cross-cultural urban design – even when crossing cultures means no more than simply understanding and accepting the otherness inherent in their own culture and place. In this we challenge the proposition put by Michael Sorkin and others that urban design 'has reached a dead end' (Sorkin 2006: 5)[13] and call on all those practising urban design in its many guises the world over, to transcend stultifying standards and orthodoxies and prepare themselves, enthusiastically and passionately, to be cross-cultural practitioners, who not only think globally and act locally, but think globally and locally and act globally and locally, effecting real change.

Notes

1 'This phrase was originated by Rene Dubos as an advisor to the United Nations Conference on the Human Environment in 1972. In 1979, Dubos suggested that ecological consciousness should begin at home. He believed that there needed to be a creation of a World Order in which "natural and social units recapture their identity, yet interplay

with each other through a rich system of communications". In the 1980s, Dubos held to his thoughts on acting locally, and felt that issues involving the environment must be dealt with in their "unique physical, climatic, and cultural contexts".' (Eblen and Eblen 1994: 702) downloaded from http://capita.wustl.edu/ME567_Informatics/concepts/global.html (accessed 12/05/06).

2 Edward W. Soja in his essay 'Designing the postmetropolis' (2006: 43–49) discusses how 'The theory and practice of urban design need not explore the full complexity of this evolving multi-scalar spatial configuration, but at the very least it should not close itself off from it, especially at a time when cities all over the world are experiencing an extraordinary re-configuration arising in part from extra-urban forces such as globalization.' In an earlier volume Peter Rowe suggests the need in what he calls 'shifting, urban circumstances' for 'new and different frameworks and technical skills' (Rowe 2006: 55).

3 Margaret Crawford, Professor of Urban Design and Planning Theory, Graduate School of Design, Harvard University, quoted as saying 'I think its really important to talk about actual urban circumstances and redefine urban design based on the way it's working in the world' in a discussion on 'Urban design now', (2006: 19).

4 What Charles Jencks describes as necessary for communication in what he terms 'hetero-architecture', where he calls for acceptance of the many 'different voices that create a city, and make from their interaction some kind of greater dialogue' (Jencks 1993: 75).

5 In his essay (and subsequently) 'Towards a critical regionalism. Six points for an architecture of resistance', Kenneth Frampton discusses Critical Regionalism as a design strategy that 'is to mediate the impact of universal civilization with elements derived indirectly from the peculiarities of a particular place.'. To support such a strategy he promotes first, the 'deconstruction' of the 'overall spectrum of world culture', then design that is a 'manifest critique of universal civilization' (Frampton 1983: 23).

6 The cycle we propose develops the hermeneutic cycle of action, reflection, interpretation, action etc, as discussed by Helen Armstrong (1999: 5–23). She particularly refers to the work of James Corner (1991) and Kvale (1983).

7 As Jon Lang suggested the very dialogical character of the design process encourages this (Lang 1987).

8 In the same discussion as reported above, Margaret Crawford describes the *IBA Emscher Park* in the Ruhr District of Germany, an overall strategy, part of which was the *Landscape Park Duisberg Nord*, designed by Peter Latz as seminal because it 'redefined urban design, using it as an agent of economic, regional, landscape and urban transformation' (Crawford 2006).

9 The initial Thai team were educated in Thailand, France, Australia and the United Kingdom; the Australian team in Australia, the USA and Yugoslavia; the French in France, the USA and Argentina.

10 In his essay on contemporary urban design, Peter Rowe calls for 'reflective realignment with and sometimes against prevailing socio-political attitudes and ways of doing things' because of the 'relative deployment of international practices' and the need for what he calls 'Critical cultural interpretation' (2006: 58).

11 This approach directly challenges that by Cuthbert (2006: 223–233) who bases his exploration of what urban design is fairly and squarely on its impact on the spatial realm and challenges those who base their analysis of its future as a profession primarily on what it does. He claims that the over-emphasis on analysing what urban designers do

and a lack of theoretical underpinning prevents its development as a true profession.
12 Given that Frampton (1983) called, as is discussed above, for the capacity of designers, not only to know the cultural and spatial specifics of the places where they work but also to be able to deconstruct world culture before they create an appropriate design response, this claim suggests, as we do here, that the design professions have done less than they should in recent years to develop the means to analyse world, or global culture in a useful or responsive way.
13 Cuthbert also makes a similar claim in his essay where, bemoaning the lack of theoretical underpinnings for urban design as a profession, he claims that 'While there are clues as to future directions ... the spatial and physical consequences remain largely in the realm of speculation.' (2006: 225).

Bibliography

Armstrong, H. (1999) 'Design studios as research: an emerging paradigm for landscape architecture', *Landscape Review*, 1999 5(2): 5–23.

Certeau, M. de (1984) *The Practice of Everyday Life*, trans. S. Randall (1988), Berkeley, Los Angeles and London: University of California Press.

Corner, J. (1991) 'A discourse on theory II: three tyrannies of contemporary theory and the alternative of hermeneutics', *Landscape Journal* 10(2): 115–134.

Crawford, M. (2006) 'Urban design now. A discussion', *Harvard Design Magazine*, Fall 2006/Winter 2007: 19–35.

Cuthbert, A.R. (2005) 'A debate from down-under: spatial political economy and urban design', *Urban Design International*, Vol. 10, September/December: 223–234.

Czerniak, J. (2006) in 'Urban design now. A discussion' in *Harvard Design Magazine*, Fall 2006/Winter 2007: 19–35.

Dear, M. (1999) *The Postmodern Urban Condition*, Oxford and Malden: Blackwell Publishers.

Derrida, J. (1978) *Writing and Difference*, trans. Alan Bass, Chicago: University of Chicago Press.

Frampton, K. (1983) 'Towards a critical regionalism. Six points for an architecture of resistance' in H. Foster (1998) *The Anti-Aesthetic: Essays on Postmodern Culture*, New York: The New Press.

Jameson, F. (1994) *The Seeds of Time*, New York: Columbia University Press.

Jencks, C. (1993) *Heteropolis. Los Angeles, the Riots and the Strange Beauty of Hetero-Architecture*, London and Sohn KG, Berlin: Academy Editions and Ernst.

Kreiger, A. (2006a) in 'Urban design now. A discussion', *Harvard Design Magazine*, Fall 2006/Winter 2007: 19–35.

—— (2006b) 'Where and how does urban design happen?' *Harvard Design Magazine*, Spring/Summer 2006: 64–71.

Kvale, S. (1983) 'The qualitative research interview: a phenomenological and a hermeneutic mode of understanding', *Journal of Phenomenological Psychology* 14(2): 171–196.

Lang, J. (1987) *Creating Architectural Theory*, New York: Van Nostrand Reinhold.

Lefebvre, H. (1974) *The Production of Space*, trans. Donald Nicholson-Smith (1991) Oxford, UK and Cambridge MA: Blackwell.

Low, J. (2004) *After Method. Mess in Social Science Research*, Abingdon, New York: Routledge.

Marshall, R. (2006) 'The elusiveness of urban design. The perpetual problems of definition and role', *Harvard Design Magazine*, Spring/Summer 2006: 21–32.

Nisbett, R.E. (2005) *The Geography of Thought*, London and Boston: Nicholas Brealey Publishing.

Radović, D. (2003) 'Celebrating the difference – design, research and education for cultural sustainability' in R. King, O. Panin and C. Parin *Modernity, Tradition, Culture, Water*, Bangkok: Kasetsart University Press.

Rowe, P. (2006) 'Unforeseen urban worlds. Post 1956-phenomena', *Harvard Design Magazine*, Spring/Summer 2006: 52–58.

Schon, D.A. (1995) *The Reflective Practitioner: How Professionals Think in Action*. Aldershot, England: Arena. First published (1983) New York: Basic Books.

Soja, E.W. (2006) 'Designing the postmetropolis', *Harvard Design Magazine*, Fall 2007/Winter 2007: 43–59.

Sorkin, M. (2006) 'The end(s) of urban design', *Harvard Design Magazine*, Fall 2007/Winter 2007: 5–18.

Watson, Peter. (2000) *A Terrible Beauty. A History of the People and Ideas that Shaped the Modern Mind*, London: Wiedenfeld & Nicolson.

Index

Aasen, C.T. 30
accommodation, BMB experimental programme 197
action programmes 121
action-in-practice 77–87
adaptation 113–14
adaptive approach 66–7
Aga Khan Awards for Architecture 97
Agdal 49–50, 51, 54n5
agriculture 89–90
Alexander, Christopher 171
Amougou Mballa, Emmanuel 8, 21, 46–8, 221, 227
analysis 150–61
analysts 206
Ang Khang 119–22
L'Angélus de Gaia (Dali) 138, 147, 148
Anukulyudhathon, Eggarin 83, 89–93, 217, 218, 224–5, 227
Appadurai, A. 37, 61
Appleyard, D. 96
Appropriate Technology Workshop, Maseru 177
architecture of becoming 41–4
Armstrong, H. 13n6, 219, 231n6
Art of Painting (Van Delft) 138, 148
Asawawirunkarm, P. 163
Ashcroft, B. 141, 147
Ashihara, Y. 146
Asian domain 220–1
'Asianization' 34–7
assessment, approaches to 196–7; field studies, South Africa 179; issues of 200
Association de Sauvegarde de la Medina de Tunis (ASM) 95–6
Atelier (Van Delft) 138, 148
Atlas Mountains 49, 53
Augé, M. 47, 139
Australian teaching system 206–7
Awareness-raising programmes 175

balance, search for 104–5
Ballard, S. 174
Ban Sol Sukhon 57–63
Bang Khun Tien 151, 152, 153–6, 160
Bangkok: business districts 71–5; *soi* 57–63; workshop in 193
Bangkok–Melbourne–Bordeaux (BMB) experimental workshops 135–48; international workshops 187–202; 150–6; second international workshop 204–7
Barcelona 78, 81–2, 110–11
Barker, M. 200
Barragan, Luis 171
Barthes, Roland 158
Basso, K. 62
Bawa, Geoffrey 171
Benjasiri Park 30, 31
Bergeron, Michel 124–7, 217, 224, 227
Betts, M. 178
Biochemical Oxygen Demand (BOF) 90, 91
Bo-Bae 71–5
Boontharm, Davisi 129–34, 142, 144, 150–61, 215, 225
Bordeaux: making the city 124–7; projects in 78, 81–3, 151–61; urban development 115–18; workshop in 192–3
'bottom-up' theorization process 165–6
Bouissac, P.157
Bourdieu, P. 47
Boutinet, Jean-Pierre 46
Bowornchetnupong, Busakol 164
Bradbury, Matthew 85, 99–102, 217, 224–5, 227
Brecht, Bertold 135
Buddha/Buddhism 30, 31, 69
Buell, F. 5, 9, 12n1, 13n4
Bull, Catherin 1–12, 13n1, 32n1, 129–34, 215, 218, 225

bungalows 34–6, 37n3
Burks, A.W. 158
business districts 71–5

Canada 112–14
Carthage 95
casts 135–48
Certeau, M. de 3, 62, 63n5, 224
Chalermphao Koanantakul, P. 164–5
change: as driver for learning 216; need for 80–1
chaos, desirable 145–6
China, garden urbanism 99–102
Chinese Association 73
Chinese thought 221
Chuturachinda 32n5
City of the Captive Globe project 41
Clarke, J. 174
'clash of civilizations' 135–6
clustered settlement pattern 25–6
Clyne, F. 200
Cohen, E. 58, 62
collaboration 224, design studio 169–70
collegial relationships 215
colonial buildings 34–6
colonization 50–2
committed attention, design studio 169
common language 130
communal projects 46–8
communication, multiple formats for 212–20
communities, expectations of 83–4
community consultation 182–3
comparative studies 217–19
complexity 216–17
concept 150–61
conceptual open-mindedness 220–3
condominiums 34–7
contemporary cities 99–100; as work-in-progress 116–18
context-driven/context-gathering environments 60–2
contextualism 222
continuity 125–6
Corner, James 231n6
Correa, Charles 171
Crawford, Margaret 227, 231n3, 231n8
creative thinking, stimulating 192
'critical regionalism' 29–30, 210–11
cross-cultural interactions 129–34
cross-cultural practice, experiencing 187–202

cross-disciplinary endeavour 85–7
cross-disciplinary interactions 129–34
cruciform buildings 114
cultural groups, motivational differences 199
cultural heritage 46–8
'cultural landscapes' 29–30
cultural otherness 138–9
culturally responsive methodologies 223–6
culture: Besotho 176; of (non)debating 144–5; workshops as 204–7
'culture shock', value of 192
Cuthbert, A.T. 231–2n11, 13
Czerniak, J. 227

Dali, Salvatore 138, 147–8
de Silva, L. 68–9
de Wandeler, Koen 8, 19, 57–63, 217
Dear, M. 2, 10, 213
debate, role of 144–5
Deleuze, G. 39–40, 41
Department of Fisheries, Thailand 90–1
Department of Forestry and Land Reclamation, Lesotho 180–1
Derrida, J. 39, 140, 215
'de-sign' 150–1
design, meaning of 157
design studio 168–80
Diagonal Avenue, Barcelona 110
dialogue, facilitation of 210–11
Dick, H.W. 34
difference: complexities of 133–4; dimensions of 131; learning to read 17–19; new ways to read 15–23; power of 130; sustainability learnt from 174–85; teaching to see 132–3; workshop programme 194
directive approach 67
discipline-specific aspects of learning 190–1
disciplines 84–7
discontent, reduction of 170
disintegrated globalization 39–44
dispersed settlement pattern 25–6
dissemination, experience/findings 219–20
dissolved identity 39–44
Dissolved Oxygen (DO) 90
diversity 103–4
Douars 53, 56n18
Drapeau, J. 112–13

Dreyfus, Herbert 166n1
Dubos, Rene 230–1n1
Durand-Lasserve, A. 63n3
dynamics, urban design project 77–87

Eco, U. 158
eco-cultural planning 68–9
economic approach 67
economic development management plan, Lesotho 176, 177
eco-planning 65–9
Eisenstein, Z. 138
El Hafsia, Tunis 94–8
'end of history' 135–6
English, use of 168–72, 204, 225–6
environmental damage 89–93
environments, manipulation of 84–5
E-Sarn 73
Europe, urban transformation 124–5
European Capital of Culture 109
European models 108–11
European Union 111n1
evaluation, medina restructuring 97–8
Everist, R. 176
exchange, facilitation of 212–14
expectations, BMB experimental programme 197–8
experience, dissemination of 219–20
experimentation, cross-cultural practice 1–12

facilitation: cross-cultural dialogue and practice 210–11; of exchange 212–14
Faculty of Architecture, Building and Planning, University of Melbourne 204–7
Feld, S. 62
Feveile, Laurence 103–6, 217, 224, 224–5, 227
'field studies, Lesotho/South Africa: community consultation 182–3; experiences of 181–2; learning from locals 183; locals gains from 185; preparation for 180–1; student perspectives on learning experience 183–5; in sustainable development elective 178–9
findings, dissemination of 219–20
fisheries 90
Forest Research Office, Thailand 89
Forestier, Jean-Claude 51, 52, 53, 55n9, 55n13, 55n14

formal traditions, convergence of 29–32
formalists 206
fragmentation 103–4
Frampton, K. 13n7, 18, 29, 30, 210, 231n5, 232n12
French teaching system 206
Fukuyama, Francis 135–6

Gadamer, H.-G. 165, 166n4
games 130–1; in othering 142–7
garden urbanism 99–102
gardens 50–1, 54n4, 55n15, 55n16
Garonne River 151, 153–6
Gateway Center, Pittsburgh 112
generic skills 190
Genoa 78, 81–3, 108–10, 111
Gibbs, P. 25, 26
Gill, S. 178, 180
global–local confrontation, places of 19–20
global mediation 57–63, 112–14
global phenomena 213–14; knowledge on commonalities of 191–2
'global thinking' 208–11
globalization: dilemmas to practice 208–9; resistance to 29–32; and traditional landscapes 49–54
Go2africa 174
Goad, P. 32n6
Godier, Patrice 124–7, 217, 224, 227
Goldblum, C. 36
golf courses 53, 55–6n17
Goodman, D.S.G. 34
Gornja Lastva 103–6
Gotlieb, Carlos 108–11, 224, 227
Graafland, A. 43
green buffer zones 91–3
Griffiths, G. 141, 147
Group of 8 (G8) 108–9
Guangzhou 100–2
Gueliz 51–2, 55n12
Guillot, Xavier 18, 19, 34–7, 227

Hafsia quarter, Tunis 94–8
harbour, Genoa 108–10, 111
Hartshorne, C. 158
'HDB housing block' 36–7, 38n6
hierarchy 145
Highlands Water Project, Lesotho 174–85
high-rise living 36–7
Hillis Miller, J. 140
hill-tribe villages 119–22
Hollywood Hong Kong (2001) 164

Hough, M. 32n2
housing, Singapore 34–7
housing compounds 26
Housing Development Board, Singapore 36–7
Huntington, Samuel 135–6
hydrological systems 49–54

ideas, generation of 214–15
identifying referents 34–5
identity of place 25–7
Illinois Institute of Technology, Chicago 41–4
Immeuble Menaçant Ruine (IMR) operations 95, 98n1
inclusivity 220–3
inequity 200–1
Inquiry into the Good (Nishida) 147
integrative approach to learning 163–4
interactions 129–34
interactive techniques 218
International Association of Universities (IAU) 202
international institutions 82
International Meeting of Contemporary Art of the Biennial of Cetinie 105–6
interrogation of local identity 80–2
Intrachooto, Singh 168–72, 215, 218, 225
introductory briefing, BMB workshop 204

Jacobs, Jane 171
Jameson, F. 3
Japanese urbanism 145–6
Jemma-el-fna 50, 53, 54–5n7
Jencks, Charles 2, 10, 231n4

Karahasan, D. 137, 138
Kasetsart University, Bangkok 119, 168
Kasettratat, Papon 164
Katu, Refiloe 176, 183, 185
Kerk University 120
key words, BMB experimental workshop 205–6
khettaras 49–50, 52, 54n1, 54n3
Khob Dong village 120
Khon Kaen 68
King, A.D. 6, 36, 37
Klausner, W.J. 165, 166n5
Knight, J. 188, 200
Koepeng Stream, Morija 180–1
Koolhaas, R. 34, 41–4
Kopytoff, I. 63n7

Korten, D.C. 68
Kotor Bay, Montenegro 103–6
Koutoubia, minaret of 50, 54n6
Kreiger, A. 223, 230
Krishnamurty, S. 32n5
Kvale, S. 231n6

Landcare 186n5
landscape architectural practice 100–2
landscape elements 26
Lang, Jon 231n7
language: English as *lingua franca* 204, 225–6; interactive techniques of 218; issue of 143–4; learning of 168–72; students reaction to 194–5
Lastva, Gornja 103–6
lateral expansion 58
Latouche, Daniel 112–14, 217, 224, 227
Latz, Peter 231n8
learning: change driven 216; discipline-specific aspects of 190–1; from locals 183; language 168–72; modes 163–6; student perspectives 183–5
learning goals, BMB experimental programme 190–3; field studies, South Africa 178–9
lectures, BMB experimental programme 205
Lee, K.L. 37n3
Lefebvre, H. 140, 141, 213
Lesotho 174–85
Levi-Strauss, Claude 18
Limthongsakul, Sani 17, 25–7, 218, 227
listen, willingness to 195
local, mediators of 57–63
local action 208–11
local antecedents 34–5
local authorities 84
local cultures, loss of 223
local identity: a shared interrogation 80–2; subjective value 15–17
local interest groups, contributions of 217–18
local landscapes 25–7
local leaders 116–17
local mediation 112–14
local qualities 79–80
local research, value of 218
local urban projects 78
locals, learning from 183
Logan, G. 200
Long, S. 34

Low, J. 143, 147, 220, 226
Lyautey, Hubert 51, 52, 53, 55n15
Lynch, K. 96
Lyotard, J.-F. 43

McCormick Tribune Campus Centre 41–4
Macquarie University 175
Mahmoud, Wassim Ben 94–8, 217, 224
main roads 57–8
Mak, A. 200
Malaysia 25–7
Mandarin Oriental Dhara Dehvi 31–2
Maneerat, Phongpan 166n2
Margueritte, Jean-Claude 86, 115–18, 217, 222–3, 227
Marrakech 49–54
Maseru 175–6
Mason, R. 198–9, 200
mediation, local and global 112–14
medina, Tunis 84, 94–8
Melbourne 137, 151–6, 159, 161; workshop in 192–3, 204–7
Menara 50, 51, 54n5
methodologies, culturally responsive 223–6
metropolitan regions 78
metropolitanization 125–6
Mhok Jham Royal Project 121
Millman, L. 200
Mingui, Julien 105
mobilization 82–4
Mon settlements 65–6
Montenegro 79, 84, 103–6
Montlibert, C. de 47
Montreal 78, 81–3, 112–14
Morija, Lesotho 174–85
Morocco 49–54
motivation, differences in 199
Muchielli, A. 35, 37n2
multiplicity 226–8
Murray, J. 176
Muslim communities 27
Myer, J.R. 96

Napredak 104–5, 106n3–4
Na-Talang, E. 26
nature: luxury and leisure in 35–6; saving 90–1
negotiation 82–4
neo-Moorish architecture 51
'new cosmopolitanism' 34–7
New York 41
New Zealand, garden urbanism 99–102

Nhong Han Basin 89–93
Nikolic, Marija 103–6
Niljang, S. 25, 26
Nisbitt, R.E. 29, 137, 144–5, 146, 221, 222, 223
Nishida, Kitaro 147, 148
Njegosh, Nicolas Petrovitch 103–6
non-native language 172
non-standard outcomes, acceptance of 226–8
Norberg Schultz, C. 157
novelty 172

observations, experimental project 209–10
'occupation zones' 101
Ockerse, T. 150, 157
O'Hare, D. 29–30
Olympic Stadium, Montreal 114
open-mindedness 220–3
operational factors, BMB experimental programme 193–7, 201
othering 139–42; game in 142–7
otherness, scripts of 135–48

palmeraie 49–52, 53
Panin, Ornsiri 19, 71–5, 218, 223–4, 227
Parin, Claire 1–12, 15–23
participation, design studio 169
pedagogic outreach 105–6
Peleggi, M. 29
personal(ized) theory 136–8
Phimal 68
Pierce, C.S. 158
Pieterse, J.N. 37
pilot projects 105–6
'ping-pong process' 156, 158, 159
Pinijvarasin, Wandee 119–22, 227
place, imagining/encountering 142–3
Place Ville Marie (PVM) 114–16
places: concatenation of 59–60; meaning of 157
play, learning as 163–6
political action 126
Porphyrios, D. 43
port, Barcelona 110–11
Port de la Lune, Bordeaux 153–6
Port of Melbourne 151–6
positions 84–7
post-colonial housing, legacy of 36–7
post-modern era 210–11, 213–14
practice, facilitation of 210–11
precious other 147–8

process, BMB experimental programme 188–9
professionals 84–7; role of 126
programme goals/operations, BMB experimental programme 188–9
progress reports, BMB experimental programme 205–6
progressive agendas 39–44
project champions 116–17
project production 82–4
propositions, experimental project 209–10, 212–28
Prost, Henri 51–2, 55n8
Protectorate treaty, Morocco 50–2

quayside, Bordeaux 124
Queensland University of Technology (QUT) 174

Radenahmad, J. 25
Radio-Canada Tower, Montreal 114
Radović, Darko 11, 77–87, 129, 131, 133, 135–48, 215, 218, 225
Rajabandittayasathaan, P.C. 166n3
Rajchman, J. 42
Rattanajorrana, K. 25
Rattanakosin Island 72–4
reflective practice 212–13, 216–19
Regent Chiang Mai 30, 31
research 216–19
research skills, development of 170
restructuring, Tunis 94–8
'reverse drainage' 49–50
revitalization, Montenegrin villages 103–6
ribbon settlement pattern 25–6
Riegl, Alois 15–16
Rimmer, P.J. 34
Rivzi, F. 200
Robertson, Roland 13n4
Robinson, R. 34
Rock, F. 176, 182
Rockefeller Center, New York 113
Rohan, Koda 146
Rohe, Miles van der 42
roles 135–48
Rowe, Peter 231n10
Royal Bank of Canada 114
Royal support 84
rural village settlements 25–7

Sakon Nakhon 89–93
Saleh, E. 25
Salobol, S. 120–1
Sangvachirapibal, P. 172
Sartre, J.-P. 140
Satha-anan, S. 163

Sattha, C. 32
Saul, J.R. 135
Savage S. 187
Schiller, H. 13n5
Schon, D.A. 12n2, 16, 179, 230
School of Architecture Paris-Val de Seine 105–6
Schulz, Evelyn 146
self-sufficiency 36–7
semiotic games 130–1, 215, 218
settlement patterns 25–6
Shamsul, A.B. 25
Short, D.J. 172
Siam Paragon 74
Siam Square, Bangkok 73
side streets 57
signs 150–1; words as 156–60
Singapore 34–7
Singer, P. 39, 40, 44
Singh Intrachooto 11, 129, 132, 133–4, 225
Sintusingha, Sidh 17–18, 29–32, 217, 227
skills 134
social interaction 201–2
social spaces 27
socially skilled students 192–3
Société Nationale Immobilière of Tunisia (SNIT) 96, 98n3
soi, Bangkok 57–63
soil erosion 174–85
Soja, Edward 140, 141–2, 231n2
solidarity, actors/participants 126
Sorkin, M. 225, 230
Souk el Hout, Tunis 95, 97
South Africa 174–85
South African Council for Scientific and Industrial Research (CSIR) 180
spiritual, power of 66–8
spontaneity 213
Srakampangyai 67
Srikoraphum 67
stakeholders 116–17
standard analysis methods, adaptation of 220
standardizing trends 218, 223–4
Strategic Plan (1999), Genoa 109
strategies: implementing at territorial scale 22–3; to support urban identity 108–11; for urban design 228–30
structure, experimental project 211
student expectations, BMB experimental programme 197–8
student perspectives of learning experience 183–5

student-centred multi-disciplinary learning 174–85
studios 214–15
Suebsiri, P. 172
Sukhon family 60–1
Sunakorn, Pasinee 119–22, 227
sustainability learnt from difference 174–85
sustainable development, field studies 178–9; transparency in 89–90
Sustainable Development Plan (SDP), Thailand 90–1
sustainable tourism 119–22
Sutthitham, Thada 9, 22–3, 65–9, 218, 221, 224–5, 227
symbolic approach 66
symposia 212–14

Tabtiang, P.W. 32n5
tactics for urban design 228–30
Tai 65–6
Tapie, Guy 11, 77–87, 129, 133, 204–7
teaching sequence, BMB experimental workshop 205
Teknikon, Pretoria 175, 180
territorial analysis, shared sites for 215
territorial scale, implementing strategies at 22–3
Thailand: Bang Khun Tien 151–4; Bangkok business districts 71–5; Bangkok *soi* 57–63; convergence of formal traditions 29–32; culture 131; eco-planning for development 65–9; eco-tourism 79; hill-tribe villages 119–22; learning tradition 163–6; Nhong Han Basin 89–93
Thailand Ministry of Education 168
Thaveeprungsriporn, Piyalada D. 163–6, 129, 131, 163–6, 215, 221, 225
thematic definition 213
'thematic narrative' 131
thematic research projects 217
'think piece' 165–6
'third' way 220–1
'thirding as othering' 139–42
Thomas, Glenn 129, 132–4, 174–85, 215, 224–5, 227
Tiffin, H. 141, 147
time issues 131–2
tourism 29–30, 52–3; new models of 105–6; sustainable 119–22

tourist operators, expectations of 83–4
Tournier, Jean-Noël 8–9, 22–3, 49–54, 217, 218, 223–4, 227
Towards Culturally Responsive and Responsible Teaching of Urban Design (Radovic) 147
tradition, honouring of 82
traditional landscapes 49–54
tram systems 115–18, 124–5
transparency, sustainable development 89–90
transparency method 91–3
trilateral interaction 218, 220–1
Tumpruksa, Pongsakorn 164
Tunisia 79, 82, 84, 94–8

UNESCO 53, 54–5n7, 84, 95, 98n2, 103, 106n2, 202
Universal Forum of Cultures (2004), Barcelona 110
universalism 220
University of KwaZulu-Natal, Durban 175, 180
University of Melbourne 204–7
University of Pretoria 180, 184
urban agglomeration 125
urban crisis 52–4
urban development: new practices 115–18; strategies 68–9
urban edge 57–63
urban form 66–8
urban growth plan, Lesotho 176, 177
urban identity, supporting strategies 108–11
urban pioneers 110–11
urban professionals: defining role of 20–1; new practices of 115–18
urban rehabilitation approach 97–8
urban transformation 124–7
US 41–4

values, reinforcement of 46–8
Victor Emmanuelle gallery, Milan 113
village land-use 26
village revitalization 103–6
village settlements 25–7

Warnier, Jean-Pierre 35, 37n1
Wat Baromnivas 74
Wat Lai Hin 32
water pollution 90–2
Watson, P. 139, 143, 226
website construction project, Lesotho 177

Weiss, P. 158
Western: model of learning 163–6; models of thinking 221
Western cities 84
Whitford, Steven 8, 20–1, 39–44, 227
whole cities 80
Williams, J. 176
Wilson, P. 25, 26
Wirachpan, S. 172
words, value of 150–61
work, learning as 163–6
working styles 199–200

workshops 154–60, 214–15; as culture 204–7
World Bank 97, 174
World Tourism Organization (WTO) 120
world views 135–6

Yap, K.S. 58
Yarra River 151, 152–3
Yinyeod, S. 63n1
Yuan, Lim Jee 25, 26

Zoning Law (1916), US 41